Alternative Narratives ...
Early Childhood

Challenging dominant discourses in the field of early childhood education, this book provides an accessible introduction to some of the alternative narratives and diverse perspectives that are increasingly to be heard in this field, as well as discussing the importance of paradigm, politics and ethics.

Peter Moss draws on material published in the groundbreaking *Contesting Early Childhood* series to introduce readers to thinking that questions the mainstream approach to early childhood education and to offer rich examples to illustrate how this thinking is being put to work in practice. Key topics addressed include:

- dominant discourses in today's early childhood education – and what is meant by 'dominant discourse'
- why politics and ethics are the starting points for early childhood education
- Reggio Emilia as an example of an alternative narrative
- the relevance to early childhood education of thinkers such as Michel Foucault and Gilles Deleuze and of theoretical positions such as posthumanism.

An enlightening read for students and practitioners, as well as policymakers, academics and parents, this book is intended for anyone who wants to think more about early childhood education and delve deeper into new perspectives and debates in this field.

Peter Moss is Emeritus Professor of Early Childhood Provision at the Thomas Coram Research Unit, UCL Institute of Education, University College London, UK.

Contesting Early Childhood

Series Editors: Liselott Mariett Olsson and Michel Vandenbroeck

This groundbreaking series questions the current dominant discourses surrounding early childhood and offers instead alternative narratives of an area that is now made up of a multitude of perspectives and debates.

The series examines the possibilities and risks arising from the accelerated development of early childhood services and policies and illustrates how it has become increasingly steeped in regulation and control. Insightfully, this collection of books shows how early childhood services can in fact contribute to ethical and democratic practices. The authors explore new ideas taken from alternative working practices in both the western and developing world, and from other academic disciplines such as developmental psychology. Current theories and best practice are placed in relation to the major processes of political, social, economic, cultural and technological change occurring in the world today.

Titles in the *Contesting Early Childhood* series include:

The Posthuman Child
Educational Transformation Through Philosophy with Picturebooks
Murris

Constructions of Neuroscience in Early Childhood Education
Vandenbroeck, De Vos, Fias, Mariett Olsson, Penn, Wastell and White

Alternative Narratives in Early Childhood
An Introduction for Students and Practitioners
Moss

Be Realistic, Demand the Impossible
Penn

For more information about this series, please visit: www.routledge.com/ Contesting-Early-Childhood/book-series/SE0623

Alternative Narratives in Early Childhood

An Introduction for Students and Practitioners

Peter Moss

Routledge
Taylor & Francis Group

LONDON AND NEW YORK

First published 2019
by Routledge
2 Park Square, Milton Park, Abingdon, Oxon OX14 4RN

and by Routledge
711 Third Avenue, New York, NY 10017

Routledge is an imprint of the Taylor & Francis Group, an informa business

© 2019 Peter Moss

The right of Peter Moss to be identified as author of this work
has been asserted by him in accordance with sections 77 and 78
of the Copyright, Designs and Patents Act 1988.

British Library Cataloguing-in-Publication Data
A catalogue record for this book is available from the British
Library

Library of Congress Cataloging-in-Publication Data
A catalog record for this book has been requested

ISBN: 978-1-138-29154-6 (hbk)
ISBN: 978-1-138-29155-3 (pbk)
ISBN: 978-1-315-26524-7 (ebk)

Typeset in Garamond
by Apex CoVantage, LLC

Contents

Acknowledgements

In writing this book, I have been informed and inspired by the authors who have contributed to the *Contesting Early Childhood* book series and whose work I refer to throughout. I would also like to thank a number of colleagues in the early childhood field, far more experienced than myself in working with students and practitioners, and who read and commented on earlier drafts; they include Alison Clark, Jeanne Iorio, Liz Jones, Karin Murris, Will Parnell and Guy Roberts-Holmes. Their comments and suggestions were always thought provoking and to the point. However, I take full responsibility for the final text as it appears here.

Chapter 1

Dominant discourses, alternative narratives and resistance movements

This groundbreaking new series questions the current dominant discourses surrounding early childhood and offers instead alternative narratives of an area that is now made up of a multitude of perspectives and debates.

Some years ago, I was invited to edit a new book series, along with my Swedish colleague, Gunilla Dahlberg. The book series was called *Contesting Early Childhood*, and we co-edited it for ten years before handing it over to the new editors, Michel Vandenbroeck from Belgium and Liselott Mariett Olsson from Sweden. At the time of writing, *Contesting Early Childhood* includes 17 titles (you can find a list of these at https://www.routledge.com/Contesting-Early-Childhood/book-series/SE0623). I have started this book with the stated aim of the series because my purpose is to explain this aim, to argue for its importance and to illustrate what it means in practice. I will introduce you to the 'current dominant discourses' and how and why they are questioned, as well as to a few of the 'alternative narratives' and some of the 'multitude of perspectives and debates' currently on offer in early childhood education.

Put another way, this book is an introduction to critical thinking about early childhood, and in particular early childhood education. Critical thinking, as understood here, has two sides to it. There is the process of identifying, questioning and challenging those views and opinions that forget they are just one of many possible ways of thinking and talking about a subject – say, early childhood education, and instead insist that they are the one and only way: we can call these 'dominant discourses', of which more in a moment The other side to critical thinking is to construct, present and explore alternatives, to demonstrate there are other ways of thinking and talking about a subject. So, critical thinking and this book are about both deconstruction and reconstruction, about scepticism and hope.

The book, then, is a beginner's guide to contesting early childhood education. It is intended to serve as a bridge that leads readers away from more familiar ground to encounter new ways of thinking about and doing early childhood education. I hope it will encourage some to travel further into an exciting and provocative world 'made up of a multitude of perspectives and debates'. But I recognise that the world of alternative perspectives and debates, exciting and provocative as it may be once encountered, can also seem on occasion rather forbidding and unwelcoming, shrouded sometimes in the mists of puzzling jargon and abstract writing, a place where it can be hard to make out what is going on. I've felt that way myself. My intention, therefore, is to disperse these mists as far as possible by plain writing and frequent examples of how people are actually putting new thinking, alternative perspectives and debates to work in early childhood education – not just theorising but doing. I will also tackle some of the questions that come up when dominant discourses are questioned and alternatives proposed, one of which is 'What to do next?'

Who is this book for? The intention is to reach out and appeal to a wide readership: students and practitioners; but I also hope to engage with some policymakers, academics and parents – in fact, anyone who wants to think more about and delve deeper into early childhood education. Some readers may just be curious, wanting to find out what is going on in parts of early childhood education outside the mainstream and so broaden their understanding of the field. Others may be driven by disquiet with that mainstream, harbouring a sense of unease or distaste about the way things are going that makes them seek out critiques and alternatives that can help them to better understand and articulate their disenchantment.

Some may already have turned away from the mainstream and be heading towards what Stephen Ball, a British sociologist of education and critical voice in the world of education, calls a 'politics of refusal'. This requires self-questioning, asking 'What kind of self, what kind of subject have we become, and how might we be otherwise?' (Ball, 2016, p. 5). This is a questioning of personal identity that involves the care of the self: 'a continuous process of introspection, which is at the same time attuned to a critique of the world outside. . . . [This is] the art of voluntary inservitude, of reflective indocility' (ibid., p. 8). For all those struggling with such questions of identity in relation to early childhood education, all those asking themselves (like Alice in Wonderland) 'Who am I then?', all those who want to become less accepting and more questioning – I hope this book will help in formulating some answers and casting off lingering feelings of servitude or docility.

But it is important to establish from the start that being critical – to be someone who chooses 'reflective indocility' as an integral part of their professional identity, an answer to the 'Who am I then?' question – is a choice and not a necessity. It's been my choice as an academic, for reasons that will become evident as the book progresses. However, it was not always so; I only made the turn to a critical identity well into middle age. But you may not agree with such a choice of professional identity. You may prefer instead to choose another identity, to be, for example, a proficient manager or skilled technician of early childhood education, someone who is very competent at applying established best practice. You may choose the mainstream rather than alternative perspectives.

I also want to make something very clear from the start. It is not the intention of this book to condemn such a chosen identity, this 'kind of self', or to rubbish anyone who decides that the story she or he likes best about early childhood education is the 'dominant discourse', the mainstream narrative that I will introduce shortly. What matters is not so much the choice itself but realising that a choice exists and must be made: a choice about identity, 'what kind of subject' you become, constructing an identity that feels right to you and that you can justify, both to yourself and others – and accompanying this, a choice too about which narratives you choose to assist you in making meaning of early childhood education, a choice made in the full knowledge that other narratives exist, that there are alternatives. So I can accept and respect those who have made a choice of the position they take and the identity they assume, acknowledging that it has been a choice carefully made from among alternatives; what I find harder to accept is the taking of a position and the assuming of an identity as if this involved no choice, as if both position and identity are self-evident, as if there are no alternatives.

I hope this book will leave you with a clearer idea of *some* of the 'alternative narratives' and 'multitude of perspectives' in early childhood education today, of the different ways of thinking, talking and doing early childhood education that are out there; 'some', note, not 'all', as I do not claim to know, understand and therefore cover the whole rich diversity of narratives and perspectives that are out there. I hope, too, that this book will leave you feeling unsettled and uncertain, questioning things you had previously taken for granted; more ready and able to be critical; but also excited, optimistic and more ready and able to explore new perspectives on early childhood education. Last but not least, I hope this book will encourage you to read further into the rich literature of books and articles that contest early childhood education and offer alternative narratives.

In the following chapters I will introduce you to two broad issues that are basic to contesting early childhood education: the importance of paradigm and the importance of politics and ethics. I will then look in some detail at four examples that very much question the current dominant discourses in early childhood education: first, the municipal schools in Reggio Emilia, which practice a very distinctive early childhood education far removed from the mainstream dominant discourse, offering a prime example of an alternative narrative; then some theoretical perspectives that though not specifically addressing early childhood education are being put to work in innovative and productive ways by researchers and practitioners in the field – just a sample of the 'multitude of perspectives' available to enrich early childhood education and that can help to create alternative narratives. In the final chapter, I look to the future, both for readers of this introductory book and for early childhood education.

But first things first. I want to start by unpicking some of the ideas under-pinning the stated aim of the *Contesting Early Childhood* series, with which I started this chapter. I need to explain what that statement of intent is about and why it uses the language that it does – and one of the recurrent themes of this book is the importance of language, how it shapes the way we construct understandings of life.

Narratives, dominant discourses and alternatives

The stated aim of the *Contesting Early Childhood* series connects three impor-tant ideas: the importance of narratives or stories (I use the two terms inter-changeably); the power of certain narratives – or dominant discourses; and the existence of other narratives, alternatives that resist or contest dominant discourses. I will attempt to explain these ideas more clearly.

First, the ***importance of narratives***, that is the stories we hear and tell, for how we interpret or make meaning – of ourselves and our lives, of our fami-lies and other relationships, and about what goes on in the world around us. As a species, mankind has an innate tendency to communicate and to make sense of existence through stories (Bruner, 1990). Stories are, in short, the way in which we make meaning of our world and our place in it, rendering our existence meaningful. This idea is captured by the Dark Mountain Pro-ject, an American environmental group of writers, artists and thinkers, who write that they 'believe that the roots of [the converging crises of our times] lie in the stories we have been telling ourselves. . . . We will reassert the role of story-telling as more than mere entertainment. It is through stories that we weave reality' (Dark Mountain Project, 2009a).

Stories, then, construct or weave reality for us and, as such, have conse-quences, sometimes bad ones, for example justifying the destructive rela-tionship that mankind has developed with the environment (and other exploitative relationships). Confronting this, the Dark Mountain Project has

> stopped believing the stories our civilization tells itself . . . [as the world enters] an age of ecological collapse, material contraction and social and political unravelling. . . . [Stories that] tell us that humanity is separate from all other life and destined to control it; that the ecological and eco-nomic crises we face are mere technical glitches; that anything which can-not be measured cannot matter. But these stories are losing their power. We see them falling apart before our eyes.
>
> (Dark Mountain Project, 2009b)

Stories, then, are ubiquitous. They are how all of us 'weave reality'; they help us explain and justify what we think and do. Depending on your perspec-tive or viewpoint, stories can be good or bad, enchanting or disenchanting, can have beneficial or harmful consequences, can trap us in dysfunctional positions or help us to move on. But whatever their consequence, they are stories which we tell ourselves and others. Perhaps the biggest danger of all is when we forget that our stories are just that – stories – and come to believe instead that they are some revelatory and fundamental truth.

The importance of storytelling has been extended to the realm of policy making. Australian educator Allan Luke puts this idea eloquently when he says that 'policies – successful and unsuccessful – are ultimately epic poems or stories, with problems to be solved, heroic agents, participants, false starts and dead ends, and with endings, at times happy and at times tragic' (Luke, 2011, p. 17). Rather than policy making being a process of dispassionate technocrats carefully weighing up evidence to arrive at the best course of action, this view sees policy making as a contest between conflicting stories, different ways of weaving or viewing reality, with storytellers trying to persuade others of the virtues of their narratives.

This leads me to a second idea: the existence of ***dominant discourses***. We live in a world of stories, or discourses, ways of thinking and talking about things: when I use the term 'discursive' later on, I refer to the way we make meaning of life through stories or discourses. But within the multitude of stories or discourses, certain ones can become particularly influential. For the Dark Mountain Project, as crises multiply and worsen, stories of human separation from and mastery over the environment become increasingly incredible and lose their power to convince. But they have been and still (at least in some quarters) remain potent – they have wielded great influence, shaping economies, societies and how many people think and act, in short weaving reality. They have become, in the words of Michel Foucault (a French philosopher who will figure prominently in this book), 'dominant discourses', a term you will recall that appears in the aim of the *Contesting Early Childhood* book series as something to be questioned.

'Dominant discourses' are stories that have a decisive influence on a particular subject, for example early childhood education, by insisting that they are the only way to think, talk and behave, that they are the only reality. They seek to impose, in Foucault's words, a 'regime of truth' through exercising power over our thoughts and actions, directing or governing what we see as 'the truth' and how we construct the world or weave reality. Typical of dominant discourses is how they make 'assumptions and values invisible, turn subjective perspectives and understandings into apparently objective truths, and determine that some things are self-evident and realistic while others are dubious and impractical' (Dahlberg and Moss, 2005, p. 17). In dominant discourses, fictional stories claim to be non-fictional statements, presenting themselves as natural, unquestionable and inevitable. This is simply how things are, the dominant discourse asserts: no need to add any qualifications, to say 'in my opinion' or 'it seems to me' or 'from my perspective'.

By behaving in this way, by insisting they are the one and only truth, dominant discourses also stifle alternative discourses or stories. They exclude, or attempt to, other ways of understanding and interpreting the world, of weaving reality, marginalising or drowning out other stories. A person putting forward an alternative view or story is treated as out of touch with reality, to be living in the past, to not know what they are taking about, or some other put down that insists their position is irrelevant or absurd. Put another way, and this time using the powerful image offered by the Brazilian philosopher Roberto Unger (2005a), dominant discourses seek to impose a 'dictatorship of no alternative' – there is no alternative, they assert or imply, this is the only reality there can possibly be.

Shortly I will introduce what I think is the most dominant discourse in today's early childhood education, but for the moment let me offer a simple and very different example, the story of 'The Emperor's New Clothes', told by Hans Christian Andersen, a 19th century Danish writer best remembered for his fairy tales. This is a story about how two dishonest weavers attempt to weave reality – in this case by weaving a reality about weaving! They promise an arrogant and foolish emperor that, for a large sum of money, they will make him a wonderful new suit of clothes; these clothes, they say, will be invisible to those who are unfit for their positions, stupid or incompetent. The king is persuaded, telling himself that 'if I wore them I would be able to discover which men in my empire are unfit for their posts. And I could tell the wise men from the fools'. In actual fact, the two weavers do nothing, pocket the money and proffer the Emperor a non-existent set of clothes. When the Emperor parades before his subjects in his 'new clothes', which are of course non-existent and leave him stark naked, no one dares say that they don't see any clothes on him for fear they will be decried as unfit, stupid or incompetent. It is left to a child to challenge this charade and to cry out in the crowd, 'But he hasn't got anything on!'

It would be wrong to claim that this story is a perfect example of a dominant discourse. Those who subscribe to and tell such discourses or stories are not in general foolish, deluded or dishonest and may well believe what they say and that what they say is for the common good. But Andersen's tale does capture the idea of how a dominant discourse, by determining what can and can't be said, closes down other views or perspectives, other stories. Those with doubts about the dominant discourse are often reluctant or unable either to voice their doubts or to suggest alternatives, afraid of the reaction, while others have no doubts but simply accept the story as true.

Andersen also illustrates how a dominant discourse is closely bound up with power. Such a story finds favour for some reason among those in power, who help ensure its dominance by endorsing it; having first been told the story, they constantly re-tell it through privileged channels of communication, increasing its reach and impact. And because the powerful – the Emperor in Andersen's story or, in early childhood education today, those who make policies and disperse funding – adopt the story, those dependent on them do so also. In this way, through such mutual reinforcement, *a* story gathers momentum and influence, becoming *the* story on everyone's lips.

Which brings me to the third idea: ***the existence of other narratives resisting or contesting dominant discourses***. A discourse may be dominant, yet it never manages totally to silence other discourses or stories. Some, like the small boy, will always speak out and contest the dominant discourse, for, as Foucault contends, 'where there is power, there is resistance' (Foucault, 1978, p. 95). Put another way, if there was to be no resistance, the relationship would no longer be one of power but simply of slavery, and we are not reduced to that relationship, certainly not in education. Developing this theme, Stephen Ball adds that '[l]ike power itself, resistance is manifold and operates at a multiplicity of points in different forms, in many small acts and passing moments' (Ball, 2013, p. 32).

Resistance, therefore, is to be found in many shapes and sizes. It finds expression in many alternative stories that give voice to the 'multitude of perspectives and debates' to which the stated aim of the *Contesting Early Childhood* book series refers. These stories may be unheard by power and consigned to the margins, for the time being at least, but they are out there to be heard by those who choose to listen. One of them is told in a later chapter. But for the moment, I will suggest that we can speak of a resistance movement, diverse and global, contesting the dominant discourses in early childhood and exploring alternatives; I will return later in the chapter to discuss this resistance movement in more detail.

These three ideas – the importance of narratives or stories, the dominance of some and the possibility of resistance to such dominance – explain the title for the book series, *Contesting Early Childhood*. The basic premise of the series is simple. Early childhood education can be viewed from many different perspectives: there is no one objectively true viewpoint; rather, there are many ways of thinking about, talking about and doing early childhood (or any) education. Therefore, there are many stories to be told, each one of which deserves listening to and each one of which can be questioned or contested – and in particular those that become dominant discourses.

Some may find this an unsettling prospect, a source of anxiety and uncertainty. From my perspective, the 'alternative narratives' and the 'multitude of perspectives and debates' from which they are derived are not only inevitable but something to be welcomed, reflecting a world rich in diversity; it is invigorating, since encounters with difference can provoke experimentation, movement and new thinking. It is, moreover, a necessary condition for a democratic politics of education, since democracy requires the creation, articulation and valuing of alternatives and confrontation and contestation between them. In healthy and vibrant democracies, 'contesting early childhood', meaning confrontation and debate between 'a multitude of perspectives', should be an everyday and everywhere occurrence, whether in services themselves, in their surrounding communities, in the academy, or among policymakers and politicians. It is both sad and worrying that this is not happening today, or not nearly enough, leaving a democratic politics of education that is in the same moribund state as democracy in general.[1] Rather than vibrant and exciting debates about diverse contemporary projects and different visions for the future, education like so much else has come to be dominated by one or two stories and how best to manage things to ensure their enactment – a stultifying dictatorship of no alternative.

Two dominant discourses in early childhood education

I have talked a lot about 'dominant discourses' and even offered an example of 'The Emperor's New Clothes', though one that has nothing to do with early childhood education. I turn now to give more relevant examples. But before I do so, I want to reiterate an earlier point. I am very critical of today's dominant discourses in early childhood education; as I shall explain, I neither believe nor like them and prefer other stories. However, just because they don't appeal to me does not mean you too must find them unappealing. It's your choice, but recognise you have a choice and have made a choice. If you do so, that's fine and I respect your decision.

The story of markets

Some 'dominant discourses' have a more local sphere of influence, in other words they dominate in some places, but not in others. For instance, one that is commonly heard in my own country, England, and also in other English-speaking countries, though perhaps less elsewhere (for the moment anyway), is 'the story of markets'. This is a narrative about how early childhood education should be provided by businesses competing within a marketplace for the custom of parent-consumers. This, the story goes, is the best way to deliver early childhood education because a marketized system based on incessant competition between service providers guarantees the most efficiency, the most innovation and the most quality at the lowest price and enables each individual consumer (i.e., parent) to choose the service provider (e.g. a nursery, kindergarten or school) best suited to their preferences and pocket. 'Parent choice' is a recurring theme in this story, considered a pre-eminent value. In fact, the story mostly speaks of 'childcare' rather than 'early childhood education', with the main aim of the market being to provide parents with safe minding for their young children while they are out at work. In this scenario, 'childcare' is a commodity, a product, for parent-consumers to choose and pay for from service providers competing in the childcare marketplace.

Here are some excerpts from the story which give an idea of the storyline and of just how unquestioningly the story is told in a country like England.

In a 2013 report titled 'More Great Childcare: raising quality and giving parents more choice', the English government speaks about wanting 'to give parents more choice of early education. . . . We will achieve this by making it easier for new providers to enter the market and for existing providers to expand' (Department for Education (England) (2013, p. 13). Two years later, the same government department commissioned Deloitte, a US-based multinational corporation and one of the 'Big Four' global accountancy firms, to undertake 'An economic assessment of the early education and childcare market' in England. Deloitte's report has a section setting out 'current market strengths and weaknesses', which concludes that 'close examination of "typical" business practices suggest [sic] considerable potential for efficiency across the market as a whole' (Department for Education (England), 2015, p. 9).

Meanwhile, a business that describes itself as 'the UK's leading healthcare market intelligence company' produces a 'UK nursery market report', the 13th edition of which was published in 2014. This offers (for those able to pay the report's price of more than £1,000) 'unique data on UK market values, covering capacity, occupancy, nursery fees and market spending, staffing pay rates, and corporate penetration', 'insight on nursery market prosperity now as the economy has turned a corner', and the identification of 'new strategic developments and key business and structural activity trends in the nursery marketplace'. The report, its publishers assure us, is 'essential business reading for all organisations involved in the provision of children's daycare services in the UK, including nursery businesses, investors, local authorities and childcare policymakers/planners, regulators, trade associations and market valuers' (LaingBuisson, 2014).

This is not the only business services company profiting from a burgeoning childcare market in England. Another describes itself as 'the leading specialist advisor for buying and selling businesses' in a variety of sectors, including childcare. In an item posted on the website for the Childcare Expo, held in Manchester in June 2017 ('Where early years means business'), this company assures readers that

> [f]or Christie & Co's Childcare and Education team the first quarter of 2017 has seen a hive of activity from both sellers and new entrants to the market. As a company we are now seeing worldwide interest in the UK childcare market from smaller asset owners to the larger groups which have already or are in the process of being transacted.
>
> There has been increased interest from Far East investors who look to the British education sector as the 'gold standard' and this is creating ample opportunities for UK operators to either expand their day nurseries in Asia, or to work closely with Chinese developers to create nursery settings. With the fall in the pound on the back of Brexit there are also plenty of opportunities for foreign investors who can take advantage of

the monetary gains to move into the British market, and with the opening up of entrepreneurial visas there is more scope for these investors.
(www.childcareexpo.co.uk/the-state-of-the-
uk-childcare-market-by-christie-co/)

I could continue with other examples of how early childhood education, or
rather 'childcare', in England today is matter-of-factly treated as a marketized
business, with the owners of these services viewed as entrepreneurs and the
services themselves as investment opportunities, and all without any apparent
awareness that this narrative is contestable and might need to be justified. But
I hope the point is made. The story of markets in early childhood education is
a dominant discourse in England, widely treated as self-evident and inevitable, as if (in the hubristic words of a senior civil servant) it was 'the only show
in town' (Archer, 2008).

There are indeed some critical voices around, arguing not only against the
principle of early childhood education as a marketized business but showing how the story of markets is not convincing even in its own terms; I will
come back to these voices shortly. But these voices are not easily heard and
find no place in the torrent of documents that pour out not only from government but from think tanks, academic researchers, businesses and others
who make a living from furthering this dominant discourse. To mix my
metaphors somewhat, a dominant discourse is also like a band wagon on
to which many people jump for fear of missing out or being accused of
irrelevance.

The story of quality and high returns

I turn now to what I consider to be the most dominant of dominant discourses in early childhood education today. This claim is based on the volume
at which it is broadcast and its extensive reach, being told insistently and
assertively not only in individual countries but amplified through the regional
and global reach of influential international organisations, bodies such as
the World Bank, the United Nations Educational, Scientific and Cultural
Organization (UNESCO), the Organisation for Economic Cooperation and
Development (OECD) and the European Union. I refer to what I call 'the
story of quality and high returns'.

There are many examples of this story being told, both by academic
researchers and in policy documents from governments and by those who
seek to influence them. You are probably familiar with a number of them.
Here is just one example, a short pamphlet titled 'Investing in high-quality
early childhood education and care', published online by the OECD, a very
influential international organisation.

Looking at ECEC [early childhood education and care] as an *investment*
makes sense because the costs today generate many benefits in the future.

> And the benefits are not only economic: benefits can be in the form of social well-being for individuals and society as a whole. *Economists* such as Nobel prize-winner, James Heckman have shown how early learning is a good *investment* because it provides the foundation for later learning. The big insight from these economists is that a dollar, euro or yen spent on preschool programmes generates a *higher return on investment* than the same spending on schooling. . . . [But] early childhood education and care needs to be of sufficient *quality* to achieve beneficial child-outcomes and yield longer term social and economic gains. . . . The OECD is now developing an Online Policy Toolbox for identifying how to improve quality. . . . The toolbox will include checklists, self-assessment sheets, research briefs, lists of strategy options etc.
>
> (OECD, 2011a, pp. 1, 7, 8; emphasis added)

This is an apparently simple story with a clear beginning, middle and end. The beginning is a world full of problems, including national survival in a fiercely competitive, dog-eats-dog global marketplace and a host of economic and social troubles, including a current failure to fully realise the nation's 'human capital'. The middle is the application of the correct mix of 'human technologies' to young children (I will say more about 'human capital' and 'human technologies' shortly, but for the moment we can equate them, respectively, with realising individuals' economic potential and the idea of 'quality'), while the end is the promise of large returns on the investment made in early intervention, many pounds, euros or dollars flowing back for every one initially committed. The moral of the story is that if only early intervention is done right, with 'quality', education and employment outcomes will improve, social problems will diminish, and survival in the 'global race', that vortex of ever increasing competition in the global marketplace, will be assured.

The range of problems solved in the story can be quite awesome, as exemplified by this excerpt from another OECD document, which lays out the 'Quality Toolbox' promised in the earlier report.

> A growing body of research recognises that early childhood education and care (ECEC) brings a wide range of benefits, for example, better child well-being and learning outcomes as a foundation for lifelong learning; more equitable child outcomes and reduction of poverty; increased intergenerational social mobility; more female labour market participation; increased fertility rates; and better social and economic development for the society at large.
>
> (OECD, 2012, p. 9)

Equally awesome are the claimed rates of financial return. A UK report, for instance, concludes that '[t]he consensus among. . . . American approaches and reviews, including even the most cautious and circumspect in its recommendations, have suggested returns on investment on well-designed early years interventions [that] significantly exceed both their costs and stock market returns', with rates of return for every dollar invested ranging from $1.26 to $17.92 (Wave Trust, 2013, p. 38). An appealing prospect encapsulated in the title of a 2011 report for the English government: 'Early Intervention: Smart Investment, Massive Savings', and whose cover design that is full of gold ingots adds more allure to the message (Allen, 2011). What's not to like in this story! Intervene early and add the special ingredient 'quality', and, in the story, everyone lives happily ever after.

A major plot line in the story of quality and high returns is **human capital theory** (HCT), which provides an explanation for the relationship between early intervention with correct 'human technologies' and some of the most profitable later returns. HCT 'has developed into one of the most powerful theories in modern economics . . . [and] lays considerable stress on the education of individuals as the key means by which both the individual accrues material advantage and by which the economy as a whole progresses' (Gillies, 2011, pp. 224–225). Formally introduced in the 1950s and developed mainly by economists in the Chicago School of Economics, HCT is based on certain assumptions about human behaviour:

> Individuals are assumed to seek to maximise their own economic interests . . . [through for example investing] in education and training in the hope of getting a higher income in the future. . . . This approach is closely associated with *methodological individualism* . . . the doctrine that the roots of all social phenomena could be found in the individual's behaviour.
>
> (Tan, 2014, pp. 1, 2)

Working with these assumptions, HCT argues that education and training increase human capital through the acquisition of knowledge and skills, which increases productivity, brings about higher earnings and is the key to competitive success in a global marketplace. Leading HCT academics, such as James Heckman from the University of Chicago (one of the characters in the OECD story quoted earlier), contend that the early years offer the best time to invest in education – but since young children can hardly be expected to think and act as rational, economic decision-makers and make calculated investment choices for themselves, government and parents must necessarily do this for them by funding early childhood education, with children and society reaping later rewards from the subsequent realisation of enhanced human capital. The young child, in this scenario, is viewed as a unit of economic potential, a potential to be realised only through the application of correct technical practice-or 'human technologies'-at a young age.

Let me further digress to explain this term *'human technologies'*. When hearing the term 'technology', it is understandable to think of machines and gadgets; but the concept of technology can be extended to processes and methods of working applied by people to people with the aim of better controlling or governing them. In the words of the English sociologist Nikolas Rose, human technologies are 'technologies of government . . . imbued with aspirations for the shaping of conduct in the hope of producing certain desired effects and averting certain undesired events'. Their purpose is to understand and act upon human capacities so as 'to achieve certain forms of outcome on the part of the governed'. They cover numerous and varied technical means, some quite mundane, others more sophisticated, such as 'forms of practical knowledge, with modes of perception, practices of calculation, vocabularies, types of authority, forms of judgement, architectural forms, human capacities, non-human objects and devices' (Rose, 1999, p. 52).

What does that look like in practice? Think a moment about today's early childhood education and examples of such technologies come readily to mind: child development knowledge, including concepts and vocabularies that we use to discuss what children should be like; developmental and learning goals, which set targets to be achieved; early years curricula, especially those that are tightly defined and specify what children and adults should be doing; pedagogical and other programmes, such as developmentally appropriate practice, which lay down how education should be done; the authority of various expert groups, who define targets, curricula and programmes; child observation techniques and normative assessment methods, which measure the performance of children against the demands of programmes and goals; regulatory and inspection regimes, which rate the performance of adults and institutions; payment of workers by results, which reward that same performance; and some kinds of research, often of the 'What works?' variety, which provide ways of refining and improving technologies.

One of the more recent and most powerful 'human technologies' to emerge in early childhood education is what has been termed 'datafication' or 'dataveillance', the collection and analysis of data on children based on standardised assessments, so as to monitor and manage children and staff in ever greater detail – in short, data to ensure compliance to prescribed standards and targets. In a study of three English early childhood settings, Guy Roberts-Holmes and Alice Bradbury report on this latest technology, with the teachers describing

> how they were increasingly subjected to the demands of data production. . . . For the early years teachers in this study, the focus of assessment data was the concept of constant progress through the Early Years Foundation Stage [the early years curriculum in England]; everyone must be tracked to ensure they are moving forwards. This requires ever more detailed data, to show the incremental progress of the children. . . . [As the head of a nursery school said]:
>
> > Where do you stop with it because there is so much of it! Health data, education data, family support data and well-being data and to be

> perfectly honest I just can't cope with that much data all the time! So I have put people in place who can manage that data.
>
> (Roberts-Holmes and Bradbury, 2016, p. 605)

Collecting escalating quantities of data leads to a next step: putting the data to work by contracting data-processing and analysis to private businesses, which return the processed data in standardised formats (e.g. tables) to the centres and schools paying for this technical service (for a detailed account of the growing dominance of data and data analysis in early childhood and primary education in England, see Bradbury and Robert-Holmes, 2017). How long before further development leads to technologies and algorithms that handle all stages of performance assessment – not only the processing and analysis of data, but its collection direct from the children, so making assessment and surveillance of children, adults and schools possible without any direct human intervention?

Human technologies in early childhood education have mainly operated at local and national levels. But we are now seeing the development of international technologies, with the OECD leading the charge. The OECD is an international organisation that exercises increasing influence over education in its 35 member states and beyond, for example through its huge cross-national PISA (Programme for International Student Assessment) project. First performed in 2000, this three-yearly assessment of samples of 15-year-olds covering science, mathematics and reading extends today to half a million students in 72 countries and economies.

Now, the OECD has started on a cross-national assessment of children's 'early learning outcomes', the so-called International Early Learning and Child Well-being Study (IELS), already mentioned in note 1 of this chapter as an example of the feeble state of democracy in early childhood education. This new project, the first round of which takes place between 2017 and 2020, will measure the performance of samples of 5-year-olds in participating countries, using common and standardised instruments to assess a number of 'domains' that, in the words of the OECD, 'represent a balance of both cognitive and social and emotional skills that, as a package, will provide coherent and reliable insights into children's early learning' and that are 'malleable in the early years' (OECD, 2015, p. 18). As with PISA, the results from IELS will doubtless be placed into league tables (if not by OECD, then by others) that compare the performance of children in participating countries, with recommendations offered by OECD to countries on how to improve their children's performance and hence their league table rankings. Here is a major new addition to the repertoire of technologies for governing children and adults alike, a technology that will lead to growing uniformity of curricula, outcomes and therefore education across countries. Instead of comparative work acting as a provocation to critical thinking, this technical approach will make such work a tool for regulation.[2]

I wondered, above, how long it will be before technology enables assessment data to be captured direct from children. IELS provides the answer. For OECD proposes that the '[c]hildren will complete the [standardised] assessment on tablets', albeit 'within the presence of a trained Study administrator' (OECD, 2017, p. 17), having already introduced this method of data collection to their larger PISA study. So, data will flow seamlessly (or so OECD hope) from entries made by young children on tablets to some centralised processing and analysis centre, from which it will be reduced to numbers that will form tables and charts. And over time, so OECD must further hope, those tables and charts will come to shape the conduct of countless early childhood policymakers and workers, as each government strives to improve its national performance relative to other countries using the results from the IELS as an indicator of that performance.

A final point on human technologies: none of the mentioned technologies may be particularly effective in isolation. But link them together into an assemblage of technologies – or, as the OECD has put it so graphically, create a '[p]olicy toolbox [that] will include checklists, self-assessment sheets, research briefs, lists of strategy options etc.' – and you have a very powerful array. It is important, therefore, to understand how separate technologies connect up and reinforce each other, becoming far more than the sum of their parts, and how collectively they form an important part of the dominant discourse of quality and high returns.

Neoliberalism – the big story

Dominant discourses do not become dominant just by chance. They don't emerge out of the blue, and they don't become dominant because of any intrinsic merit. There is always a reason why certain stories, with their distinctive ways of thinking, talking and acting and of making meaning of the world, become so widespread and dominant; why they get taken up by the powers that be; why they get amplified and broadcast far and wide; and why, for example, we find people and organisations everywhere using words like 'quality', 'outcomes', 'programmes', 'evidence based' and 'human capital'.

What might account for the dominant position that the story of quality and high returns has gained today? Let us consider the story in more detail. It is clearly very instrumental and calculative, about how to ensure certain predetermined outcomes, including financial returns, can be achieved with as much certainty as possible.

There is a focus on the technologies that this end requires – technical practice applied to human beings lies at its heart. It is a story, therefore, about management and control. Last but not least, it is couched in economistic terms, using the language of investment, returns and capital.

Bearing these features in mind, my conclusion is that the story of quality and high returns (as well as the story of markets I referred to earlier) has gained such a powerful hold because of wider economic and political forces at work in our world today, and in particular, the economic and political dominance of another story: what economist Kate Raworth calls the 'twentieth century neoliberal story' (she also refers to it as a 'play' and a 'show', with a script and cast of characters) (Raworth, 2017, p. 68). This story of neoliberalism, first told before World War II, then sustained and worked on after 1945 by a small but well-funded group of economists, began to be heard increasingly loudly from the 1970s and to gain widespread attention and influence in the 1980s, with its adoption by the Reagan presidency in the USA and the Thatcher premiership in the UK and the subsequent spread of neoliberal policies around the world. Since then, neoliberalism has 'transformed British, American, and global politics' (Steadman Jones, p. 329), and 'sunk its roots deep into everyday life' (Mirowski, 2013, p. 28).

Today, as British environmental activist George Monbiot describes,

> the story told by neoliberalism . . . dominate[s] our political and economic systems, and almost every aspect of our lives . . . seeping into our language, our understanding of the choices we face and our conception of ourselves.
>
> (Monbiot, 2017, p. 29)

Yet like all dominant discourses, so pervasive has the story become that many simply treat it as natural, as telling self-evident truths, as a statement of immutable fact rather than a work of fiction.

So what is this story, both powerful and invisible? Monbiot offers this concise summary of what he calls 'the most powerful political narrative in circulation today':

> [The story told be neoliberalism] defines us as *competitors*, guided above all other impulses by the urge to get ahead of our fellows. This urge, it argues should be cultivated and encouraged. Our democratic choices are best exercised by *buying and selling* – a process that automatically rewards merit and punishes inefficiency. By discovering a natural *hierarchy of winners and losers*, 'the market' creates a more *efficient* system than could ever be devised through planning or design.
>
> Defined by the *market*, defined as a market, human society should be run in every respect as if it were a *business*, its social relations reimagined as *commercial transactions*, people redesignated as *human capital*. The aim and purpose of society is to *maximise profits*.
>
> (ibid., p. 30; emphases added)

The story of neoliberalism, therefore, is about how life in all its many facets – including personal relationships – can and should be reduced to economic relationships, based on the constant exercise of competition, choice and calculation by individuals, each one understood to be a unit of human capital and to act in life as 'homo economicus' or economic man or woman. This economically rational and self-interested subject is 'malleable rather than committed, flexible rather than principled' (Ball, 2013, p. 139), constantly striving to maximise her or his economic advantage (returns) in a world made up by multiple markets of competitive providers. Indeed, market fundamentalism, a belief in and commitment to markets as the answer to everything and as 'the supreme area of human activity, development and growth' (Steadman Jones, 2014, p. 270) lies at the heart of neoliberalism.

Neoliberalism offers us a world of relentless competition, constant choice and calculation, and unremitting pursuit of personal advantage. This is a world of winners and losers, of insecurity and inequality, neoliberalism regarding inequality as 'a necessary and unavoidable evil' (Steadman Jones, 2014, p. 338) because it spurs everyone on to ever-greater effort, efficiency and productivity. It is a world, too, of low taxes, limited government, privatisation of the public, and 'the wholly inappropriate importation of free markets into the provision of public services, such as health care provision, education, and housing' (ibid., p. 268). Put simply, public bad, private good. This is a world in need of strong human technologies to maximise efficiency and hence returns by increasing the accuracy of calculations about the best choices to make and by enhancing control to ensure these best choices deliver on their promise. This is a world summed up in the motto of McKinsey's, the global management consultants: 'everything can be measured, and what gets measured gets managed'. (It is, perhaps, worth a moment to reflect on the assumptions, the values and the hubris that lie behind this statement by an organisation that depends on measurement and management, as well as its potential consequences if enacted in, say, early childhood education.)

The story of neoliberalism is not confined to the immediately economic; or rather, it reduces everything to the economic. Every aspect of life – the social, the cultural, the aesthetic, the emotional, the political – is swallowed up by the economic, to be subsumed under the economic rules, relationships and practices of neoliberalism. The story, indeed, claims to provide the answer to 'life, the universe and everything',[3] and it is within this vast sweeping narrative of neoliberalism that it becomes possible to think of education not only as just another marketized product (as in the story of markets) but also as just another investment, the returns on which can be quantified and predicted, in large part through realising the full potential of human capital – if, that is, the basic material, children, are made subject to correct technologies and strict management (as in the story of quality of high returns). 'Homo economicus' and 'human capital' are just two sides of the same neoliberal image of the individual as an essentially economic being striving to survive in an essentially economic world.

Contesting dominant discourses

To contest such dominant discourses requires, first of all, understanding them for what they are – just stories, which like all stories can be analysed, questioned and criticised. You need to understand what they are and what they are trying to do, succinctly explained by the Portuguese sociologist Boaventura de Sousa Santos: '[dominant discourses are] the successful globalisation of a particular local and culturally-specific discourse to the point that it makes universal truth claims and "localises" all rival discourses' (Santos, 2004, p. 149). So always remember that today's dominant discourse was yesterday's local folk tale, a fringe narrative that originally had few tellers or listeners. Always remember, too, the Emperor's New Clothes, and don't let the confident tones and sweeping claims of the storytellers dull your senses and blunt your critical faculties. Having said that, I appreciate that achieving critical understanding can be easier said than done, especially when surrounded by people and documents telling the same story over and over again, treating it as holy writ, without a hint of doubt or an acknowledgement that other stories exist.

But once over that hurdle, and it is a big one requiring you first to doubt the Emperor's New Clothes, it is possible to start questioning and contesting the current dominant discourses. A good place to start, therefore, is to ask that question, why? Why today do we talk so much in the way that we do about early childhood education? This is to 'relativize' and 'historicise' the story of markets and the story of quality and high returns, in other words to treat each one as 'a particular local and culturally-specific discourse' that has managed to break out and go global thanks to a particular historical conjuncture of conditions and forces. When we do this, we can look into what these conditions and forces are (e.g. neoliberalism); and we can also understand that far from being the Truth, these stories are just two of many possible stories that can be told about early childhood education.

Having asked why, contesting can then take another step: to look more critically at dominant discourses. One angle of approach is to ask if a dominant discourse is credible even in its own terms. Does it actually do what it claims?

In *Transformative Change and Real Utopias in Early Childhood Education*, a book in the *Contesting Early Childhood* series, I looked at the story of markets and how it works out in practice (Moss, 2013). I concluded that the admittedly patchy evidence is not convincing: 'at best it can be said that the case for markets in early childhood education, judged in their own terms, is not proven' (ibid., p. 52). Stephen Ball and Carol Vincent, in one of the very few studies undertaken into an actual local market in early childhood services, are blunter in their conclusions: the 'childcare market [in the UK] just does not work like markets are supposed to . . . and indeed it is a very inefficient market' (2006, p. 38). This should not perhaps surprise us, given the underwhelming record of free market neoliberalism more generally, described by the historian of neoliberal politics as a 'faith-based policy' whose 'commitment to markets was rarely subjected to detailed empirical examination and criticism' and which has left 'politicians and officials operat[ing] as if under a spell' (Steadman Jones, 2014, p. 333).

In the same book, I come to the same conclusion for the story of quality and high returns. On closer examination, I find the story's claims to be unproven, indeed incredible. Like the story of markets, the story of quality and high returns is more fairy tale than factual documentary, a fairy tale I just don't believe. Why? Because, despite the endless research studies quoted by storytellers in support of their story, it just does not hold up once you step back and look at the bigger picture. The Emperor turns out to have no clothes!

Most of the studies used to give credence to the story come from just one country, the United States. Yet despite many research studies, usually local, and many early intervention projects, the United States shows little sign of the predicted high returns, when viewed nationally, and has a persistently poor record when it comes to the health and welfare of its citizens – despite being one of the richest countries in the world, measured by per capita GDP. Internationally, the United States has one of the highest levels of child poverty among OECD countries (OECD, 2018). Furthermore, child poverty is little changed since 1965 when the national early intervention programme, Head Start, was initiated, with young children (under 5 years) continuing to experience the highest rates of poverty in the population; viewed over time, fluctuations in child poverty seem to be due more to fluctuations in the economy and other policy measures, such as income redistribution.

Current events in the USA give ample evidence of a society that is deeply divided, full of discontent, and with many of its members feeling excluded, angry and alienated. What's going on? Why does the story of quality and high returns not seem to come true? Because other things have been going on that have far more impact on children, families and society than any number of early intervention programmes.

Jobs, or rather good jobs, have dwindled and earnings have stagnated, with the fruits of economic growth going to the top 1%. Nobel prize-winning economist Joseph Stiglitz has described this surge of inequality, what he terms the 'Great Divergence':

> Between 1980 and 2013, the richest 1% [in the USA] have seen their average real income increase by 142% (from $461,910, adjusted for inflation, to $1,119,315) and their share of national income double, from 10% to 20%. The top 0.1% have fared even better. Over the same period, their average real income increased by 236% (from $1,571,590, adjusted for inflation, to $5,279,695) and their share of national income almost tripled, from 3.4 to 9.5%. Over the same 33 years, median household income grew by only 9%. And this growth actually occurred only in the very first years of the period: between 1989 and 2013 it

shrank by 0.9% . . . In the first three years of the so-called recovery from the Great Recession of 2008–2009 – in other words, since the U.S. economy returned to growth – fully 91% of the gains in income went to the top 1%.

(Stiglitz, nd, pp. 1–2)

The situation has not improved since (Alvaredo, Chancel, Piketty, Saez and Zucman, 2017). Internationally, the US is now one of the most unequal societies in the OECD club of rich nations. In a 2011 report titled *Why Inequality Keeps Rising*, the OECD notes that the US 'has the fourth-highest inequality level [among 34 member states] in the OECD, after Chile, Mexico and Turkey. Inequality among working-age people has risen steadily since 1980, in total by 25%' (OECD, 2011b). This growth of inequality has taken place under a regime of neoliberalism that views inequality as 'a necessary and unavoidable evil' (Steadman Jones, 2014, p. 338).

Inequality might be considered an evil in its own right; but its malign influence is felt far and wide. In their landmark book *The Spirit Level: Why More Equal Societies Almost Always Do Better*, British epidemiologists Richard Wilkinson and Kate Pickett deploy a mass of evidence to support their argument that inequality 'seems to make countries socially dysfunctional across a wide range of outcomes' (Wilkinson and Pickett, 2009, p. 174). They go on to argue that

> [t]he evidence shows that reducing inequality is the best way of improving the quality of the social environment, and so the real quality of life, for all of us (including the better-off). . . . It is clear that greater equality, as well as improving the wellbeing of the whole population, is also the key to national standards of achievement and how countries perform in lots of different fields. . . . If you want to know why one country does better or worse than another, the first thing to look at is the extent of inequality. . . . And if, for instance, a country wants higher average levels of educational achievement among its school children, it must address the underlying inequality which creates a steeper social gradient in educational achievement.
>
> (ibid., pp. 29–30)

This conclusion, based on many years of research into inequality across a range of countries, is echoed by the former head of Sure Start, a major early intervention programme in England, reflecting on her experience:

> I believe that without significant redistribution of wealth across social classes, where you are born and who your parents are will remain a significant determinant of life chances. . . . The expectation [of Sure Start]

that early years services, however wonderful, could affect overall inequality was unrealistic. This shift will come from wider social reforms.

(Eisenstadt, 2011, pp. 160–161)

So, once we look more closely and bring some critical thinking to bear, the dominant discourse begins to look less convincing. It looks, indeed, like an instance of magical thinking, where complex and fraught situations can be wished away with a wave of the wand. Indeed, this was the view of the American psychologist Edward Zigler, one of the architects of the US early intervention programme Head Start, when he wrote a short article in 2003 to mark that programme's 40th anniversary and which he titled '40 Years of Believing in Magic Is Enough'. Zigler concluded that

[t]here is no magical permanent cure for the problems associated with poverty. . . . Expecting the achievement gap to be eliminated [by early intervention] is relying too much on the fairy godmother. . . . Are we sure there is no magic potion that will push poor children into the ranks of the middle class? Only if the potion contains health care, childcare, good housing, sufficient income for every family, child rearing environments free of drugs and violence, support for parents in all their roles, and equal education for all students in school. Without these necessities, only magic will make that happen.

(Zigler, 2003, p. 10)

Closer and critical enquiry also makes the dominant discourse appear not only incredible but dangerous too. Here are three reasons why I say this. First, the story of quality and high returns reinforces an individualistic view of cause and effect, adopting that 'methodological individualism' already encountered in the discussion of HCT, the doctrine that 'places the individual at the centre and emphasizes the human agent over social structures' (Tan, p. 3). We may not actually want to blame the poor directly for the trouble they cause themselves and others, but by adopting the story of quality and high returns we implicitly say the problem does in fact lie with them and the solution rests in changing them, their attitudes and behaviour, without regard to anything going on outside and beyond them. We look to a technical fix to cure these shortcomings of the poor, leaving the remainder of us to get on with life undisturbed. In doing so, it seems to me that the story of quality and high returns colludes with the status quo, distracting attention from the much more difficult and contentious work that is needed to reduce inequality, exclusion and injustice. Such work calls for fundamental changes in society, the redistribution of income, wealth and power, changes likely to face fierce opposition from powerful vested interests (who, in the US and elsewhere, have increased their influence over government through their ability to fund politics and lobby politicians, while at the same time finding ever more ingenious ways to avoid paying their fair share of taxes).

Second, there is a very real prospect of the story of quality and high returns leading to ever greater control and governing of both children and the adults who work with them, in the search for ever more effective human technologies applied ever more precisely and consistently, essential conditions, it is argued, for achieving high returns. For this is a story essentially of prescription, predictability and regulation, with carefully calculated inputs and closely specified outputs leaving no room for the unexpected and surprising, for wonder and amazement, qualities that, as we shall see in Chapter Four, are highly valued in the early childhood education of Reggio Emilia, an experience that tells a very different story.

Which brings me to a third and final reason why this particular dominant discourse is so dangerous. The story of quality and high returns is focused on means (effective technologies) rather than ends, such as what do we want for our children, here and now and in the future, which of course also raises profound questions about the type of community, society and world we want to see. Instead, the story of quality and high returns presumes a future of more of the same – only better managed – and a process of 'future proofing' children to fit this world of ever increasing competition, consumption and calculation. Early childhood education is assumed to play a key role in this process, contributing to squeezing every last drop of human capital from *homo economicus* to ensure survival in an environment of cut-throat competition.

Yet, such a world is arguably not only undesirable (is this what we really want for our children and our societies?) but unsustainable, faced by multiple environmental crises and the possibility of technology wiping out many jobs with a longer-term prospect of most humans losing their economic usefulness altogether (Harari, 2016).[4] To focus on means at the expense of ends feels short-sighted and thoughtless.

The story of quality and high returns tells of an early childhood education that is, first and foremost, a technical practice, a matter of finding the right technologies to ensure high returns. The ends – be they readiness for school, learning goals, the realisation of human capital, a competitive labour force – are taken-for-granted, unexamined givens, the focus of the story being on means, on what works, what human technologies will ensure ends are met and those tantalising profits from investment delivered. But, and this will be the subject of Chapter 3, from my perspective education is not primarily a technical practice; it is first and foremost a political practice. It starts from asking political questions, defined by Belgian political scientist Chantal Mouffe as 'not mere technical issues to be solved by experts . . . [but questions that] always involve decisions which require us to make choices between conflicting alternatives' (Mouffe, 2007).

I have already raised some of these questions – for example, what do we want for our children? – and will suggest others in Chapter 3. The point to make now, however, is that political questions require us to think deeply about the fundamentals of education. But the facile claims of the story of quality and high returns, with its attention directed to identifying effective human technologies to achieve taken-for-granted ends, divert us from this difficult but urgent and exhilarating task.

Meet the resistance movement

I referred earlier to a 'resistance movement', a global community of people who do question and contest the dominant discourses in early childhood education and offer a rich array of alternative perspectives and narratives. Who or what is this movement? It is a diverse and complex entity, made up of many actors impelled by many different desires, perspectives, values and interests. It occupies many different spaces and finds expression in many different forums.

Some members are inspired by the work of previous educators, people such as Froebel, Montessori, Dewey, Freinet, Freire and Malaguzzi; others by more contemporary projects, such as the municipal schools of Reggio Emilia. Cultural diversity plays an important part, through the contribution of educators from or working with, for example, First Nations in Canada or Maori communities in New Zealand, whose socio-cultural approaches to early childhood education recognise, value and celebrate the traditions and knowledges of such diverse and distinctive communities. Yet others are enthused by the different perspectives opened up by working with a diversity of disciplines (for example, philosophy, sociology, political science, feminist and childhood studies) and theorists (for example, Bakhtin, Foucault, Derrida, Levinas, Deleuze, Barad, all of whom appear in the *Contesting Early Childhood* series and some of whom will appear again later in this book).

The voices of this resistance movement, with their 'alternative narratives' and 'multitude of perspectives and debates', are not hard to hear if you choose to listen. They can be found speaking clearly in many different places – though very rarely in the discussion papers or policy documents of think tanks, national governments or international organisations, which seldom invite their presence. These places where the resistance movement can be heard include: the Reconceptualising Early Childhood Education group with its annual international conference (Tobin, 2007; Bloch, 2013; see also http://receinternational.org/) and the AERA's Critical Perspectives on Early Childhood Education SIG (https://sites.google.com/site/cpecesig/home); many books, for example in the *Contesting Early Childhood* or the *Critical Cultural Studies of Childhood* (www.palgrave.com/gp/series/14933) book series, or *Reconceptualizing Early Childhood Care and Education: Critical*

Questions, New Imaginaries and Social Activism: A Reader (Bloch, Swadener and Cannella, 2018), as well as many academic articles, for example in the journals *Contemporary Issues in Early Childhood* and *Journal of Pedagogy;* a growing number of undergraduate and postgraduate courses that intro-duce alternative stories to their students, and of doctoral theses undertaken by students who are attracted by these same stories; and networks for those interested in past pedagogical traditions or current pedagogical projects, for example the many national networks for people interested in Reggio Emilia. Not to forget the instances of groups campaigning against manifestations of dominant discourses and for alternatives, such as (to give an example close to home for me) 'More Than a Score', a coalition of organisations and individu-als connected to primary education working together to change the English government's extremely prescriptive and standardising policy on assessment and accountability (https://morethanascore.co.uk/who-we-are/).

The diverse members of this resistance movement are drawn to ques-tion and contest dominant discourses, such as the story of quality and high returns, for many reasons. They may well be averse to such stories, for some of the same reasons that I have outlined earlier. They may find other stories more desirable and pleasing, while most have fundamentally different per-spectives on life to those who tell the story of quality and high returns (or the story of markets), seeing the world through different lenses and making very different meaning of it. Put another way, they have chosen to occupy a different paradigmatic position – and it is to the issue of paradigm that I now turn.

Questions – yours and mine

At the end of each chapter I will offer some questions you might find interest-ing and useful to discuss. But the most important questions are those that you (individually or as a group) have after reading this and other chapters in the book. So, for each chapter, and before moving to my questions, I would like you to think about and discuss:

- What questions for you as a reader (or for us as a group) does this chapter raise?
- What did you find particularly thought provoking, interesting or important?
- What did you really disagree with? What would you like to contest with the author?
- What did you find difficult to understand?
- What did you want to know more about?
- How might you work on the difficult bits? And on the bits you want to know more about?

As I say, your questions are most important. But if you have time after asking and discussing those, here are some other questions you might want to consider:

- How do you react to the idea of storytelling in early childhood education, as a way we try to make sense of things, or weave reality? Does it work for you, or does it seem wide of the mark?
- Have you ever felt like the child in the Emperor's' New Clothes? When and why? What did you do? What did you wish you had done?
- I have talked about the 'story of markets' and the 'story of quality and high returns' as dominant discourses. Do you agree or disagree? Are you aware of other dominant discourses in early childhood education? If so, what are they?
- Who, in your experience, are the loudest voices telling the dominant stories in early childhood education?
- I have given some examples of 'human technologies' in early childhood education. Are there other examples you can suggest?
- What other members of the resistance movement do you know of?

Notes

1 To give just one example of the moribund state of democracy in early childhood education, take the case of the International Early Learning and Child Well-being Study (IELS) proposed by the Organisation of Economic Cooperation and Development (OECD). This proposal for a cross-national assessment of 5-year-olds across four 'early learning domains', using standardised measures, was first mooted in 2012, with a decision to proceed taken in 2016 after several years of discussion and preparatory work involving OECD and member state governments. Knowledge of these plans only leaked out to the wider early childhood community in summer 2016, i.e. after the decision to proceed had been taken behind closed doors, and, at the time of writing (early 2018), many people still remain unaware of what is going on even though the main study is about to begin. Despite many concerns that have been voiced since summer 2016, no attempt has been made by OECD or member state governments to open up the proposal to debate and contestation or to consider alternative approaches to developing cross-national work on early childhood education. For more on the IELS, see the OECD's website (www.oecd.org/edu/school/international-early-learning-and-child-well-being-study.htm) and a number of critical responses (e.g. Moss et al., 2016; Moss and Urban, 2017). I return to IELS later in the chapter.

2 The OECD obviously hopes that the IELS will grow to equal the spread of PISA and add to its mesh of international testing, which extends from early childhood through 15-year-olds (PISA) to higher education (Assessment of Higher Education Learning Outcomes, AHELO) and adult social skills (Programme for the International Assessment of Adult Competencies, PIACC). At the time of writing, only three countries – England, Estonia and the USA – have signed up to the first round of the IELS, hardly sufficient to give the exercise credibility. OECD's hope must be that more countries will sign up after the first round.

3 Followers of Douglas Adams' comedy science fiction masterpiece *The Hitchhiker's Guide to the Universe* may recognise this phrase. In this surreal sci-fi book, a group of hyper-intelligent beings demand to learn the Answer to the Ultimate Question of Life, The Universe, and

Everything from the supercomputer, Deep Thought, specially built for this purpose. It takes Deep Thought 7.5 million years to compute and check the answer, which turns out to be 42. Deep Thought points out that the answer seems meaningless because the beings who instructed it never actually knew what the Question was.

4 I recognise that the future of employment and jobs is very contentious; doom-laden scenarios, such as Harari's, may prove too pessimistic and over dramatic, and automation may benefit us all overall. But this will require societies and citizens prepared to exert democratic control over the process, for the common good, in other words to focus on ends – achieving and realising the common good. Without such active and democratic intervention, the results are likely to be harmful overall, with 'the most likely outcome of automation [being] an increase in inequalities of wealth, income and power' (Roberts, Lawrence and King, 2017, p. 3).

Chapter 2

The importance of paradigm

Why is there a 'multitude of perspectives and debates' in early childhood today? Why are alternative narratives being told? Perhaps the most important reason is to do with '***positionality***': how the many individuals and organisations involved see and understand the world (including early childhood education) from different positions. These positions may be due to innate individual differences, such as gender, age, ethnicity, mother tongue, disability, sexual orientation and so on – a young, lesbian Maori woman may well view the world differently to an ageing, heterosexual white Englishman such as the author. These positions may also be due to personal affiliation to particular groups, such as a profession, academic discipline, political party or social movement. And then again, they may be due to ***paradigm***, whose positioning effects are both powerful and often invisible – or at least unrecognised.

Different paradigmatic positions produce very different perspectives and discourses because they produce very different ways of seeing and understanding things. Yet the importance of paradigm is seldom, if ever, acknowledged in today's dominant discourses in early childhood education, for example by those who tell the story of quality and high returns or the story of markets. Indeed, as we shall see, it is difficult for these dominant discourses to acknowledge the possibility of different perspectives, since they believe that theirs is the only way of seeing and understanding the world. These stories, their narrators imply, are just how things are, telling it as it is – rather than just being a particular take on things, the result of viewing things in a particular way from a particular position.

In this chapter, I want to introduce paradigm to readers unfamiliar with the concept, providing examples that will hopefully make its meaning clearer. Running through the chapter is a theme: that paradigm is of central importance to the relationship any of us has with early childhood education (or, indeed, with any other aspect of life). In my view, that importance confronts us with the necessity of thinking about and then choosing a paradigmatic position, a choice that each one of us should acknowledge and take responsibility for making. Once aware of paradigm, choice and responsibility become inescapable.

What is paradigm?

Paradigm is a basic belief system through the lens of which we see, interpret and make sense of the world and our experiences in it; it can be thought of as a world view or a mindset. This system consists of an assemblage or bundle of ideas, assumptions and values that we each hold and may be unquestioningly reproduced through upbringing and education – or challenged and changed through those same processes. Paradigm affects our thinking about every-thing, including *ontology (What is reality?), epistemology (How do you know something?)* and *methodology (How do go about finding out?)*. The central point to make is that things that seem self-evident and natural viewed from one paradigmatic position – with a particular mindset or through a particular lens – appear nothing of the sort when viewed from another position.

At this stage, I should make an admission. I only came to an understanding of paradigm and its great importance in middle age and only then because I had the good fortune to work with someone who provoked me to confront the issue. Before that I was accustomed to view the world from a particular paradigmatic position (positivism, of which more later), without really think-ing about it or appreciating that there were alternatives. Yet as time passed, my unconsidered paradigmatic position increasingly failed me; in particular, it prevented me finding a satisfying answer to a problem that was increas-ingly baffling me ('the problem with quality', also more of which later). Being confronted by my colleague with the issue of paradigm and being forced to think and make a choice opened up new ways of understanding the problem and of finding my own answer. So, by urging on readers the importance of paradigm, I speak from experience, my main reservation being that I wish I had engaged with the issue far earlier.

Indeed, with a background as a historian, I should really have done so, because history is full of examples of paradigms and, indeed, of paradigmatic shifts, when whole communities or societies come to see life and the world in a quite different way, with a different mindset. Let me give an example of paradigm, wholly unconnected with early childhood or even contemporary debates about paradigm, but which appeals to me as a historian. It provides a stark instance of how a changed paradigm can completely alter the way the world is seen by a group of people. It comes from a book called *The Inven-tion of Science* by British historian David Wootton. He begins the book by comparing how a well-educated Englishman would have viewed the world in 1600 with his counterpart in the 1730s (and these were times when a good education was largely confined to men). The former believes that

> witches can summon up storms that sink ships at sea. . . . He believes in werewolves, although there happen not to be any in England – he knows they are to be found in Belgium (Jean Bodin, the great sixteenth-century French philosopher, was the accepted authority on such matters). He

believes Circe really did turn Odysseus's crew into pigs. He believes mice are spontaneously generated in piles of straw.

He believes in contemporary magicians: he has heard of John Dee, and perhaps of Agrippa of Nettesheim (1486–1535), whose black dog, Monsieur, was thought to have been a demon in disguise. If he lives in London he may know people who have consulted the medical practitioner and astrologer Simon Forman, who uses magic to help them recover stolen goods. He has seen a unicorn's horn, but not a unicorn.

He believes that a murdered body will bleed in the presence of the murderer. He believes that there is an ointment which, if rubbed on a dagger which has caused a wound, will cure the wound. He believes that the shape, colour and texture of a plant can be a clue to how it will work as a medicine because God designed nature to be interpreted by mankind. He believes that it is possible to turn base metal into gold, although he doubts that anyone knows how to do it. He believes that nature abhors a vacuum. He believes the rainbow is a sign from God and that comets portend evil. He believes that dreams predict the future, if we know how to interpret them. He believes, of course, that the earth stands still and the sun and stars turn around the earth once every twenty-four hours. . . . He believes in astrology, but as he does not know the exact time of his own birth he thinks that even the most expert astrologer would be able to tell him little that he could not find in books.

Fast forward a century and a quarter, and the well-educated Englishman sees a very different world, partly because he literally sees it through a new lens.

Our Englishman [of the 1730s] has looked through a telescope and a microscope; he owns a pendulum clock and a stick barometer – and he knows there is a vacuum at the end of the tube. He does not know anyone (or at least not anyone educated and reasonably sophisticated) who believes in witches, werewolves, magic, alchemy or astrology; he thinks the *Odyssey* is fiction, not fact. He is confident that the unicorn is a mythical beast. He does not believe that the shape or colour of a plant has any significance for an understanding of its medical use. He believes that no creature large enough to be seen by the naked eye is generated spontaneously – not even a fly. He does not believe in the weapon salve or that murdered bodies bleed in the presence of the murderer.

Like all educated people in Protestant countries, he believes that the Earth goes round the sun. He knows that the rainbow is produced by refracted light and that comets have no significance for our lives on earth. He believes the future cannot be predicted. He knows that the heart is a pump. He has seen a steam engine at work. He believes that science is going to transform the world and that the moderns have outstripped the ancients in every possible respect. He has trouble believing in any miracles, even the ones in the Bible.

What has led to this profound change in perspective? Wootton describes the transformation as the 'Scientific Revolution', which has not only brought about a transformation in people's lives but also a transformation in how human beings understand and think about the world and mankind's place in it. As a result of this revolution, or at least its beginning stages, the educated Englishman of the 1730s had a very different mindset to his forebear, which caused him to make meaning of the world in very different ways and with very different conclusions.

Now this is a very particular example. The changes wrought in seeing and understanding the world are clearly huge and easily grasped; for the hypothetical 'educated Englishman' living in the 1730s (and indeed for us today), the world of 1600 now seems alien and hard to credit. Moreover, we are looking here at a change in mindset over time, how over a century or more the 'educated Englishman' came to see things differently; this is a historical account of paradigm change.

But different paradigms may, and do, co-exist. Indeed, they did in 1730s Europe. Change wrought by the scientific revolution was not uniform. Its impact was most felt on the 'educated' (as opposed to the majority who had little or no education), on Englishmen (as opposed to their Continental counterparts, or at least those in Catholic countries; we don't know how far the changes were experienced by English women). By the early 18th century, different people in different positions and places saw and understood the world in different ways, from very different paradigmatic positions. Moreover, we are considering here only one part of the world, Europe. Elsewhere, the world may, indeed will, have been seen through very different lenses.

Positivism and postfoundationalism

I want to look now at paradigm in the present day, or at least *some* paradigms found in contemporary *Western* culture – I lack the knowledge and experience to explore paradigm in other contemporary cultures but recognise that elsewhere there is a rich diversity producing different ways of seeing the world.

The American sociologist Patti Lather talks about 'paradigm proliferation', and has developed a 'paradigm chart' on which she maps out five broad paradigmatic positions, under headings that suggest their main ambition: 'predict', 'understand', 'emancipate', 'deconstruct' and 'next?' (see Table 2.1) (Lather, 2006). She uses this chart 'in my teaching of qualitative research to help students begin to map the field' (ibid., p. 36). As she says in the notes accompanying the table, 'all these paradigms operate simultaneously today', but they appear in a historical sequence. I will consider and contrast two of the paradigmatic positions on the chart, ***positivism*** and ***postfoundationalism***

Table 2.1 Revised paradigm chart

Predict	Understand	Emancipate	Brk Deconstruct	Next?
*Positivist Mixed methods	*Interpretive Naturalistic	*Critical Neo-Marxist	Poststructural Postmodern	Neo-positivism
	Constructivist Phenomenological	< Feminist > Critical race theory Praxis-oriented	Queer theory < Discourse analysis >	
	Ethnographic	Freirian participatory action research		
	Symbolic/ Interaction		Postcolonial	Post-theory
			Post-Fordism	Neo-pragmatism
	Interpretive mixed methods		Posthumanist	Citizen inquiry
			Post-critical	Participatory/ dialogic Policy analysis
		Gay and lesbian theory		
			Postparadigmatic diaspora (Ohn Caputo)	
		Critical ethnography	Post everything (Fred Erickson)	Post-post

Notes:
* Indicates the term most commonly used; < > indicates cross-paradigm movement. Brk (Break) Indicates a shift from the modernist, structural, humanist theories/discourses on the left to the postmodernist, poststructural, posthumanist theories/discourses on the right. In the post theories, all concepts (language, discourse, knowledge, truth, reason, power, freedom, the subject, etc.,) are deconstructed. Though all these paradigms operate simultaneously today, there is a historical sense to their articulation. August Comte (1778–1857) proposed positivism in the nineteenth century; social constructivism is often dated from Peter Berger and Thomas Luckmann's (1966) book, the Social Construction of Reality. The emancipatory paradigms grew from the Frankfurt School and the social movements of the 1960s and 1970s; and the post paradigms, from the critiques following the Second World War, include those of Michel Foucault (1926–1984), Jacques Derrida (1930–2004) and Gilles Deleuze (1925–1995). Paradigm shifts occur as reaction formations to the perceived inadequate explanatory power of existing paradigms. Therefore, someone who works in emancipatory paradigms, for example, is often aware of the theoretical assumptions as well as the critiques of positivism and interpretivism. Note also that some theories that start out in one paradigm change considerably when they are taken up in another; e.g. poststructural feminism is considerably different from liberal, emancipatory feminism. Conventional science is positivist, but when science's assumptions are rethought in interpretive or post paradigms, it is not the same; i.e. science is not the same in all paradigms in terms of ontology, epistemology and methodology.

Source: Lather, 2006

(the umbrella term I use for the raft of 'post theories' listed in Lather's fourth column), which come under Lather's 'predict' and 'deconstruct' headings.

In dwelling on just these two paradigmatic positions, I could be considered guilty of simplification and reduction. My defence is that space is limited and that these positions are particularly influential in early childhood education today and in generating that 'multitude of perspectives and debates' that I discussed in the previous chapter. Moreover, they fall on either side of what Lather describes in the 'Notes' for the Table as a 'break', indicating a fundamental shift in thinking: on one side are 'the modernist, structural, humanist theories/discourses . . . [on the other] the postmodernist, poststructural, posthumanist theories/discourses'. Last but not least, Lather's other positions are there to be accessed and worked with by those who want to delve further into this important subject.

Positivism

We live, it is argued, in a period of resurgent positivism – or what some term 'neo-positivism' or 'repositivization' (Lather, 2006). These terms, the 'neo' and 're' of positivism, reflect the long history of positivist thought, its ups and downs and its resilient capacity to adapt and survive. Positivism is often dated to the first half of the 19th century and the work of a French philosopher Auguste Conte (1797–1857), one of the founders of the discipline of sociology. It has been strongly contested at different times, for example by interpretive, critical and postmodern critiques dating from the post-war years, which relate respectively to the 'understand', 'emancipate' and 'deconstruct' labels in Lather's chart. However, positivism has bounced back again from the 1980s onwards, hitched to the coat tails of neoliberalism's ascendency.

What is positivism, this paradigmatic position that is currently so prominent, not least in the dominant stories of today's early childhood education? As Lather's label – 'predict' – suggests, positivism expresses a desire to predict and therefore to control and a belief that this is possible if correct procedures and techniques are correctly applied. Central to the positivist position and its belief in prediction and predictability is the idea that there exists an objective reality out there that can be discovered, then accurately represented and communicated by language. Put another way, positivism believes in the possibility of revealing, through the application of scientific methods, knowledge that is value- and context-free, an objective Truth (singular), and the further possibility of discovering universal and systematic theories and laws on the basis of this knowledge – theories and laws that permit replicability and hence prediction. In this way, scientific knowledge can transform the world.

This view of the world is imbued with a number of assumptions, assumptions that also express what is valued in the positivist paradigm: universality, objectivity, certainty, stability and closure – in short, the importance and the possibility of being able to reach a final and correct conclusion, free of context and perspective, untroubled by positionality: the assumption that only knowledge produced by science and its approved methods can be true; the assumption that language is transparent in its meaning, so that communication is a process of transmitting unambiguous meaning; and the assumption that the world, or at least the social world, including human beings, can be understood as a system of separate variables, each one of which can be studied and acted on in isolation, expressed in quantitative research by the idea of 'controlling' for other variables in order to understand the discrete effect of one particular, separate variable; it is not, we might say, a paradigm at ease with complexity, inter-connectedness or life's irreducible messiness. As Elizabeth St. Pierre has argued:

> Many of these ideas [associated with positivism] illustrate an age-old desire to get below the messy, contingent surface of human existence to a pristine, originary foundation, a bedrock of certitude . . . [which persists] because of the romance of an orderly, progressive, predictive empirical science based on fact devoid of value as the final arbiter.
>
> (St. Pierre, 2012, p. 493)

A major actor in this paradigm is the 'disinterested, rational subject who can uncover "objective" knowledge' (St. Pierre and Pillow, 2000, p. 6). This subject is epitomised by the figure of the scientist assuming a dispassionate and expert stance, with a 'god's eye view' from above the world that enables her or him to represent reality accurately and authoritatively. This subject of positivism is privileged as the producer of true knowledge, uninfluenced by power or politics, context or contingency, and with the ability through such work to provide society with scientifically derived solutions to its problems and ills – evidence of what works.

I have already hinted at the relationship between positivism and neoliberalism, suggesting that the positivist paradigm has gained renewed vigour in step with the rise to prominence of neoliberalism as an economic and political regime. The two complement and support each other. As St. Pierre explains, neo-positivism and neoliberalism share

> goals of producing knowledge that is value-free, mathematized and "scientific", and used in the service of free market values, economic rationalism, efficiency models . . ., outsourcing, competitive individualism, entrepreneurship and privatization. In this ideology, everything must be scientized and reduced to the brute (value-free) data of mathematics for the purpose of control.
>
> (St. Pierre, 2012, p. 484)

One might also add that positivism's dispassionate scientist is the close relative of neoliberalism's self-interested *homo economicus*, both expected to make rational, objective and quantified calculations, both capable of reducing the world and life to numbers in the interests of predictability and control – we are back to McKinsey's dictum that 'everything can be measured, and what gets measured gets managed', a quintessential positivist statement of belief.

The positivist paradigm may, therefore, face opposition from those who similarly contest neoliberalism. But the paradigm is also contested for other reasons, in particular for assuming a ***unified theory of science***. What is that? It is the belief, sometimes known as 'scientism', that the assumptions and methods of the natural sciences (e.g. physics, chemistry, biology) are appropriate and essential to all other disciplines, including the humanities and the social sciences; in other words, a belief that all sciences – be they natural or social – can be treated as similar, sharing the same assumptions about objective knowledge and universal laws and using the same methods of scientific investigation. British political philosopher John Gray sets out this central positivist tenet:

> The project of unified science means that the social sciences are no different in their methods from the natural sciences. Both seek to discover natural laws. The only genuine knowledge is that which comes from scientific inquiry; and every science – including the social sciences – aspires to the generality and certainty of the laws of mathematics.
>
> (Gray, 2009, p. 271)

Thus, Comte believed that nothing can be known that cannot be quantified and 'envisaged a unified science in which all of human knowledge would be reduced to a single set of laws' (ibid., p. 271). This belief was based on 'the notion that there is an existing order in the social world – underlying laws and regularities – just as there is in the natural world . . . [and] that the laws of the social world are scientifically comprehensible' (St. Pierre, 2012, pp. 487–488). The natural and the social, in short, are of a piece.

Such beliefs in the possibility of a unified science persist today among those adopting a positivist paradigm, whose basic assumptions can be summarised as follows:

> 1) The aims, concepts and methods of the natural sciences are applicable to the social sciences; 2) the correspondence theory of truth which holds that reality is knowable through correct measurement methods is adequate for the social sciences; 3) the goal of social research is to create universal laws of human behaviour which transcend culture and history; and 4) the fact/value dichotomy, the denial of both the theory-laden dimensions of observation and the value-laden dimensions of theory create the grounds for an 'objective' social science.
>
> (Lather, 1991, p. 172)

However, there are strong grounds for questioning the equivalence of natural and social sciences. The basic problem lies in the intrinsic difference between the natural world and the social world. The Danish economic geographer Bent Flyvbjerg argues that the natural science approach, with the high value it attaches to prediction, has not and cannot work in the social sciences, and to try and make it do so is simply a waste of time and effort, the problem being people, families, communities and societies and the proactive ways in which they behave:

> Regardless of how much we let mathematical and statistical modelling dominate the social sciences, they are unlikely to become scientific in the natural sciences sense. This is so because the phenomena modelled are social, and thus "answer back" in ways natural phenomena do not.
>
> (Flyvbjerg, 2006, p. 39)

John Gray similarly argues that we cannot study the human and social world in the same way we study the natural or physical world because

> social objects are not like stars or stones, which exist independently of how humans think about them; social objects are partly created by human perceptions and beliefs, and when these perceptions and beliefs change, social objects change with them. . . . [W]e can never have objective knowledge of society, if only because our shifting beliefs are continuously changing it.
>
> (Gray, 2009, p. 110)

The problem then is that there are no constants and regularities in the social world, only movement and diversity, innumerable contexts and complexities. It is a world of unavoidable messiness that makes the search for immutable laws and reliable predictions a wild goose chase. Not surprisingly, John Gray argues that 'it is doubtful if the various forms of social studies [including economics] contain a single law on a par with those of physical sciences' (ibid., pp. 272–273).

The paradigm of positivism, with its mindset of assumptions, beliefs and values, and the world view to which they give rise, is the subject of incredulity in some quarters. Its assumptions and beliefs seem highly contestable if not simply unbelievable. But such questioning goes further in that some adopt a paradigmatic position that is very different to that of positivism, with a rejection of much that it holds to be true and an embracing of much that it disdains. Let me offer one such alternative position, which is attracting a substantial following among what I have termed the resistance movement in early childhood education, while recognising and emphasising that it is *an* alternative, not *the* alternative.

Postfoundationalism

But first, a brief word of caution. In practice, paradigmatic labels may encompass an assortment of variants, with a basic shared core of ideas but some differences in emphasis and perspective. So, if I label as 'postfoundational' a paradigm that takes a very different position to positivism, this should be understood as embracing a variety of theoretical perspectives including postmodernism, poststructuralism, postcolonialisms, posthumanism and other 'posts' listed in Table 2.1 – perspectives that share the same position but focus their gaze on different subjects or through differing lenses.

The broadly defined postfoundational paradigm challenges the basic tenets, or foundations, of positivism. Postfoundationalism recognises the inevitability in the social world of complexity and context, uncertainty and provisionality, subjectivity and interpretation – but also values them. The world consists of inter-connections and entanglements and cannot be divided into discrete, measurable and controllable variables. Language is no longer a transparent and neutral tool for representing and expressing an objective and true description of reality, acting as the servant of reality. Instead, the language we use actually constitutes or constructs reality – hence the importance of discourses, the ways in which we make meaning of things by the ways in which we talk about them (the 'discursive' role of language), and the way that dominant discourses strive to govern how we make meaning or weave reality through the language that they use. In short, different language creates a different reality; and if you want to change how you think and understand things, you need to find a new language for thinking and talking about them; I illustrate this in Chapter 4, where I contrast vocabularies for early childhood education that appear in the story of quality and high returns and in the narrative of Reggio Emilia. This understanding of the constitutive role of language has been termed the 'linguistic turn'.

The role of language and discourse contributes to the paradigms of positivism and postfoundationalism having very different views on epistemology – in other words, the two paradigms have very different understandings of what knowledge in the *social* world is. Thus, postfoundationalists,

> building on critical philosophies of science, reject the possibility of absolute truths and universally ordered systems of knowledge. Instead, knowledge is understood as produced by an 'economy of discourses of truth' and meaning emerges from the interaction of competing knowledges. Some knowledges justify and support dominating meanings and practices while other knowledges, usually marginal, challenge hegemonic discourses. . . . This perspective doesn't make scientific knowledge 'untrue'. Rather, *it demands that we understand Truth in a different way, as the contingent product of particular, situated ways of comprehending the world and not as something that is absolute and immutable which pre-exists*

social relations and awaits discovery. . . . [T]he central issues become those of understanding the conditions in which certain discourses or world-views are privileged and how the distinctions they produce between true and false can be contested.

(Otto, 1999, p. 17: emphasis added)

From this perspective, therefore, there are knowledges and truths, not Knowledge and Truth. For there is not and cannot be some position outside the social world – no 'god's eye view' – from which objective, stable and universal knowledge can be revealed to the dispassionate scientific observer, who can then represent this newly discovered reality accurately and objectively, and use it, in turn, to build universal and predictive laws. Viewed instead from a postfoundational position, the knower, the person who wants to know the social world, is inextricably part of and bound up in that world, which she or he sees and comprehends from a particular position and with a particular perspective. Knowledge of the social world is unavoidably subjective, consequently partial and perspectival, and provisional, because there can never be a final and comprehensive knowing. So, in a world of multiple local practices, perspectives and knowledges, rather than there being one (singular) Truth, to which all subscribe, there are socially constructed (plural) truths reflecting how things seem viewed from different perspectives and within different contexts.

Postfoundationalism, therefore, adopts a ***social constructionist*** approach to ontology (What is reality?) and epistemology (How do you know something?), in which the social or human world and our knowledge of it are socially constructed, a process in which all of us, as human beings, are active participants in relationship with others:

Social construction is a social process, and in no way existent apart from our own involvement in the world – the world is always *our* world, understood or constructed by ourselves, not in isolation but as part of a community of human agents, and through our active interaction and participation with other people in that community. For these reasons, knowledge and its construction is always context-specific and value-laden, challenging the modernist belief in universal truths and scientific neutrality.

(Dahlberg, Moss and Pence, 2013, p. 23)

Reverting to the doubts expressed earlier about the possibility of a 'unified science', a social constructionist approach 'begins with the premise that the human world is different from the natural, physical world and therefore must be studied differently' (Klenke, 2016, p. 21). It adopts, therefore, not only a different approach to ontology and epistemology, but also a different methodology (How do you go about finding out?). You will find an example of a social constructionist approach, expressed as a question, 'What is your image of the child?', and methodology, pedagogical documentation, in Chapter 4, when I discuss the early childhood education in Reggio Emilia.

At this point it is important to make three points. First, keep remembering we are talking here about the social world and social science rather than the natural world and physical science. Postfoundationalists are not seeking a unified science.

Second, and especially topical as this book is being written when terms such as 'post-truth', 'alternative facts' and 'fake news' are daily making the headlines, we must distinguish between data and facts and knowledges and truths. Data and facts can be objectively true: Paris is the capital of France, the Holocaust occurred in the Second World War, global warming is happening now and human activity is a major cause, to give three disparate examples. 'Knowledge' is the meaning we make of things, how we construct or weave reality; we use data and facts in this process, but which data and which facts and how we use them will vary individually and between groups. So, when it comes to 'facts' we can speak of the Truth (though sometimes that truth changes as new information comes to light); when it comes to knowledge of the social world we need to speak of competing truths.

Third, postfoundationalism relativises, because there can be no one objectively right answer in a social world of multiple perspectives – but this should not be confused with anything goes, a world of aesthetic and moral equivalence. Being positioned in a postfoundational paradigm does not mean being unable to evaluate and arrive at a conclusion or judgement; it does not mean giving up on making aesthetic or ethical choices. We can and must, though it is demanding on us to have to do so. For we must take responsibility for this process and for our choices; we cannot abdicate responsibility to someone or something else, some supposedly universal code or neutral yardstick or objective expert, claiming universal knowledge and truth. This is the conclusion of the Polish sociologist Zygmunt Bauman (1925–2017), in his writing about 'postmodern ethics' (which I discuss further in the next chapter). He emphasises the greater, not lesser, responsibility that the postfoundational paradigm brings with it, insisting that to adopt this position offers no easy way out from making choices, but rather the 'prospect of a greater awareness of the moral character of our choices; of our facing our choices more consciously and seeing their moral contents more clearly' (Bauman, 1995, p. 7).

Relativising in postfoundational paradigm is not, therefore, a cop-out, as some would suggest. Quite the contrary, for it demands more of us. Deciding what we think is right or good – for example, in early childhood education – is inescapable. The buck stops with us.

One further point of difference should be noted between positivist and postfoundational paradigms: the relationship between knowledge and power. From the positivist perspective, knowledge can and should stand apart from power; the aim being to keep distance, assert independence, defend against manipulation and censorship, in sum to avoid the contamination and corruption of power. Under these conditions, it is possible, indeed necessary, to seek for and find a single, objective and universal real truth.

But from a postfoundational perspective, this is wishful thinking. Knowledge and power are inextricably inter-twined in a symbiotic relationship. Power functions through knowledge, working with those (partial, perspectival) knowledges that support its agenda, further its interests and increase its effectiveness, while what (partial, perspectival) knowledge is deemed true knowledge is a function of power and the knowledges it favours and legitimises. Under these conditions, and in the words of Australian academic Glenda MacNaughton in *Doing Foucault in Early Childhood Studies: Applying Poststructural Ideas*, her book in the *Contesting Early Childhood* series, 'knowledge can never be free from ideology, because all knowledge is biased, incomplete and linked to the interests of specific groups' (MacNaughton, 2005, p. 22). There are many different knowledges and claims to truths, for example about the child and early childhood education, each vying for influence and power, each bidding to be taken up as *the* truth, leading to questions such as whose knowledge counts and gains power and whose knowledge is marginalised and suppressed.

So, just as certain expert voices provide stories about early childhood education that chime with the beliefs and desires of neoliberal governments and organisations, so too the adoption of these stories by such powerful institutions validates, amplifies and disseminates these same expert voices. In this interaction between social scientists and policymakers, knowledges that resonate with and support the world view and goals of the powers that be are included, validated and used in policy making, while other knowledges that don't (for example, from the resistance movement) are excluded. It is, as Trisha Greenhalgh and Jill Russell argue, a sort of power play hidden behind the mask of 'evidence-based policy-making':

> The selection and presentation of evidence for policy making, including the choice of which questions to ask, which evidence to compile in a synthesis and which syntheses to bring to the policy making table, should be considered as moves in a rhetorical argumentation game and not as the harvesting of objective facts to be fed into a logical decision-making sequence. . . . The very expression 'evidence-based policy making' suggests there are technical solutions to what are essentially political problems.
>
> (Greenhalgh and Russell, 2006, pp. 1, 2)

In this relationship of knowledge and power, experts and powerful institutions rely on each other, leading to an inter-dependence that leaves little room for mutual questioning or contesting and marginalises many knowledges – a case, you might say, of you scratch my back and I'll scratch yours.

A short postscript

Before moving on to consider paradigm in early childhood education, I want to add a postscript to this discussion by making clear what paradigm is not – or rather one of the things that it is not. In the past, I have found that people sometimes equate paradigm with methods chosen in research, in particular whether researchers choose to work with 'quantitative' or 'qualitative' methods; for example, collecting and analysing large data sets drawn from large samples, or working intensively with a handful of cases, perhaps using material from semi-structured interviews. Such differences are methodological rather than paradigmatic.

It is true that a positivist is more likely to rely on quantitative methods, applying statistical techniques to the analysis of numbers, while the postfoundationalist is more likely to be found working qualitatively, striving to interpret complex material generated from interviews or other sources, eschewing numbers and statistical techniques. But there is no reason why a positivist might not use more qualitative methods, or a postfoundationalist quantitative methods, in both cases to complement other methods of working. In other words, both may use 'mixed methods'.

Paradigmatic difference shows itself not in the methods used but in the assumptions about the knowledge produced. Positivists will believe that they are representing the world as it truly is, or at least that they are getting increasingly close to this goal of revealing the true state of things: the data, they may say, shows or tells us certain realities. Postfoundationalists will believe that they are achieving a partial interpretation of the world, an interpretation that they acknowledge is made from a particular perspective but which they hope will prove satisfying and useful to others; they hope their interpretations will help generate fresh understandings, provoke new thinking and open new directions for future research or policy. The difference made by paradigm, therefore, is epistemological rather than methodological.

Paradigm in early childhood education

Early childhood education is no more immune to paradigm than any other field of human activity. More than 25 years ago, Mimi Bloch (1992), one of the founders of the Reconceptualising Early Childhood Education movement, argued that early childhood work in the United States, whether in publications, conferences or universities, was closely tied to a positivist paradigm in both theory and method, with all its attendant beliefs, including the possibility of universal, decontextualised theories, a social world reducible to a system of separable variables, and a meaningful distinction between theory and practice. While fellow American early childhood researcher and Reconceptualist Jo Tobin has argued that

> although post-structural theorists such as Michel Foucault, Mikhail Bakhtin, Judith Butler, Frederic Jameson, Michel de Certeau, Jean

Baudrillard, Jacques Derrida, Gayatri Spivak, and Homi Bhabha have written little or nothing about young children, their theories beg to be applied to early childhood education.

(Tobin, 2007, p. 29)

Positivism rules, OK!

I shall show in later chapters how such theorists, working within a postfoundational paradigm, have in fact been applied to early childhood education. But for the moment I will take another example to illustrate the importance of paradigm in early childhood education: how viewing the world from different paradigmatic positions produces very different understandings. The example is about '*quality*' and the argument is simple: the concept of 'quality' makes sense viewed from a positivist paradigm but not from a postfoundational paradigm.

Although I have not actually done a word count, my guess would be that 'quality' is one of the most used words in early childhood education today. It is spoken and written about by everyone and everywhere, and invariably used in a taken-for-granted way, as something that is unquestionable and self-evidently desirable. It seems to hold the key to good things happening in early childhood education, and not least to those high returns on investment that I discussed in Chapter 1. Viewed from this perspective, the only problem with quality is essentially technical – how do we define quality and how do we get it? What mix of 'human technologies' is most likely to 'deliver' high returns?

Yet for me, 'quality' – both the concept and word itself – is deeply problematic, and not just at a technical level, leading me to conclude some years ago that I would no longer choose to work with 'quality'. What is the 'problem with quality' as I see it? And how did paradigm assist in resolving the problem, at least to my satisfaction? To answer these questions means going back a bit in time.

Interest in the concept of 'quality' in early childhood education, and its importance for practice and outcomes, proliferated from the 1980s onwards. Again, we should ask why? – why did people begin to talk so much about 'quality' at that time? And why has it grown to today's crescendo of 'quality' talk? My answer would be that 'quality' emerges as part of the resurgent positivist paradigm, which as we have seen also got its second or third wind from the 1980s onwards with the triumph of neoliberalism. 'Quality' is a positivist concept that serves the interests of managerialism, an essential component of a neoliberal world.

Let me explain my thinking. The search for high returns in a competitive marketized society calls for the setting of performance standards as well as of precise and measurable outcomes for assessing performance, enabling a constant drive to improve performance. These standards need to be expert derived, evidence based and reliably measurable; they must, too, be universal, objective and stable. Which is where 'quality' comes in, for 'quality' is short-hand for a standard of technical performance against which early childhood services can be evaluated, at any time and in any place, a standard waiting 'out there' to be discovered, revealed and measured by experts deploying scientific methods. Using such methods, 'quality' can be measured and compared around the world, the same measure used (perhaps with some small variants, in a passing nod to context) in Beijing, Bangalore, Berlin and Boston. Put slightly differently, 'quality' is a technology of normalisation, establishing norms against which performance can be assessed, so shaping policy and practice; a technology of distance, claiming to be able to compare performance anywhere in the world, irrespective of context; and a technology of regulation, providing a powerful tool for management to govern at a distance through the setting and measurement of norms of performance.

But come the 1990s and 'quality' in early childhood education, for some at least, began to seem less straightforward – the problem with quality, it appeared, went beyond the technical to the philosophical and political. In particular, there was a growing awareness of context, complexity, plurality and subjectivity. Writers on quality increasingly argued that:

- quality was a *subjective, value-based, relative* and *dynamic* concept, with the possibility of *multiple perspectives* or understandings of what quality is;
- work with quality needed to be *contextualised*, spatially and temporally, and to recognise cultural and other significant forms of *diversity*;
- the *process* of defining quality – who is involved and how it is done – was itself contested, with questions asked about how that process had operated in the past, in particular the dominance of a small group of experts to the exclusion of a wide range of other stakeholders with an interest in early childhood institutions.

This short extract from two American writers published in 1996 gives a flavour of these emerging arguments:

> The subcultures and plurality of values in societies often mean that no one definitive definition of quality exists. It is a relative concept that varies depending on one's perspective. . . . Indeed, quality is both a dynamic and relative concept so that perceptions of quality change as a variety of factors evolve.
>
> (Bush and Phillips, 1996, pp. 66–67)

Where these lines of argument seemed to lead was the possibility of there being multiple definitions of 'quality', constructed from different perspectives and in different geographical contexts and subject to change over time, with each definition owing at least as much to values and contexts as to any notion of objective scientific discovery. From this realisation emerged the new 'problem with quality'. The most immediate manifestation of this emergent problem was the prospect of 'quality' becoming meaningless and useless. For if, instead of 'one definitive definition of quality', there were to be many different definitions of 'quality', each one constituted from a different set of perspectives, then communication, comparison and assessment would become impossible; quality would lose its value as a technology of normalisation, distance and regulation, no longer able to serve as a managerial tool. Instead of a single, universal and objective benchmark, early childhood education would face a chaos of competing and contrasting subjective claims. No one would know any longer what 'quality' meant.

Underlying this chaotic prospect, however, was a more profound problem: an unease that what had been approached as an essentially technical issue of expert knowledge and measurement might, in fact, be a philosophical and political issue of conflicting values and meanings. Rather than discovering the truth and, with it, certainty, the early childhood world was confronted by the prospect of multiple perspectives and ambiguity and the very real possibility of consensus replaced by dissensus. The critique by the American philosopher of education Bill Readings of the concept of 'excellence' in relation to 'quality' and early childhood institutions:

> Measures of excellence raise questions that are philosophical in that they are fundamentally incapable of producing cognitive certainty or definitive answers. Such questions will necessarily give rise to further debate for they are radically at odds with the logic of quantification.
>
> (Readings, 1996, p. 24)

This was the confused and confusing position facing Gunilla Dahlberg, Alan Pence and myself when we came together to write *Beyond Quality in Early Childhood Education and Care* (Dahlberg *et al.*, 2013). Published in 1999, the book confronted the emergent 'problem with quality' and did so by adopting a different paradigmatic position: postfoundationalism or, as the sub-title of the first English edition put it, 'postmodern perspectives'. This repositioning proved to be vital, enabling us to come at the 'problem with quality' from a quite different direction and gain new insights into the problem.

Our conclusions were as follows:

- 'Quality' is a concept with a very particular meaning, inscribed with specific assumptions and values, and the product of a particular paradigmatic position, i.e. positivism, and as such it is neither natural (self-evident) nor neutral (objective);
- The concept of 'quality' cannot be reconceptualized to accommodate context, complexity, values, diversity, subjectivity, multiple perspectives

and other features of a world understood to be both uncertain and diverse – the 'problem with quality' cannot be addressed by struggling to reconstruct the concept in ways it was never intended to go;

• If context, complexity, values, diversity, subjectivity and multiple perspectives are deemed important, indeed unavoidable, then it is necessary to adopt a different paradigmatic position, one which values, welcomes and is at ease with them, for example postmodernism (or, more broadly, postfoundationalism);

• If you do this, then you can work with a different concept, 'meaning making'. Rather than an expert-led search for a universal standard and method of measurement, 'meaning making' is about building and deepening 'understanding of the early childhood institution and its projects, in particular the pedagogical work – to make meaning of what is going on' (ibid., p. 112). This meaning making always occurs in relationship with others, in participatory processes of co-construction, processes that involve dialogue, reflection, contestation and interpretation;

• Making or constructing meaning and deepening understanding in this way is valuable in its own right. But people may choose to continue by making judgements (evaluations) about the work so understood, judgements that are made in relation to the wider questions of what we want for our children here and now and in the future – questions which must be posed over and over again and which need to be related to even larger questions about "what is the good life?" and "what does it mean to be a human being?" (ibid., p. 113);

• Whereas the concept of 'quality' ends with a decontextualised and objective statement of fact, often expressed as a number based on scores from a rating scale, the concept of meaning making calls for a continuous process of reflection and interpretation that may result in occasional judgements of value, judgements for which the judges must take responsibility 'rather than hide behind statistical pretension to objectivity' (ibid.). The concept of 'quality' might be said to lead to a form of managerial accounting, whereas the concept of 'meaning making' is much nearer to the idea of democratic accountability.

The 'problem with quality' was resolved, at least to our satisfaction (though it remains a problem throughout the early childhood field, where most people find it impossible to get beyond 'quality' and its positivistic foundations). It turns out that 'quality' is a choice, not a necessity; you don't have to work with the concept, though you may choose to do so. Adopt a positivist position and you can aspire to find, measure and work with a universal, stable and objective standard, 'quality', a technical exercise ending in a quantified statement of fact, for example a score for an early childhood centre. Adopt a postfoundational position, and, acknowledging context, multiple perspectives and subjectivity, you construct or make meaning, in relationship with others; you undertake a political exercise ending in a judgement of value about how an early childhood centre relates to a co-constructed ideal of good early childhood education.

In the former case you may well work with a rating scale, which assesses how far the subject of evaluation, for example a kindergarten or school, conforms to the defined standard of quality. In the latter case you may work with a tool such as pedagogical documentation, where processes and practices in the school or kindergarten can be made visible and therefore subject to discussion, reflection, argumentation and, ultimately, provisional interpretation and even judgement. In the former case, you may end up with a score or set of scores and a belief that you have arrived at an objective, definitive and final statement of fact; in the latter case, you are more likely to be engaged in a continuous process of making meaning about different facets of the kindergarten or school, making judgements of value that are acknowledged to be perspectival, partial and provisional.

Two very different approaches, starting from two very different paradigmatic positions. It's your call. You choose.

Meeting across the paradigmatic divide?

What this example hopefully demonstrates is the importance of paradigm for how we understand early childhood education, so that different paradigmatic positions lead to the adoption of quite different concepts, understandings and practices. I have posed two contrasting paradigmatic positions, while suggesting there may be many more. What I do not want to suggest is that one position is intrinsically better than another – that the right-thinking person must obviously go for this or that paradigm. I have personally made a choice about the paradigmatic position I have taken up because I find that position appealing and resonant, more in tune with my hopes and desires for education. But I realise there are other positions and respect those who choose one of the alternatives.

But what I do want to suggest, and I am here re-stating an earlier plea, is that you should be aware that you face a choice and that you acknowledge, always, that you have made a choice from among a number of alternatives. One of the biggest problems in early childhood education today, as I see it, is how those who view the field from the paradigmatic position of positivism and who usually subscribe to the dominant discourses, in particular the story of quality and high returns, neither acknowledge that they have taken a position, and therefore see things from a particular perspective, nor acknowledge the existence of any other positions. It's easy to confirm this prevailing narrow focus. Check out any reports on early childhood education produced by or for governments, think tanks, international organisations or similar bodies and see if you find any reference to paradigm and paradigm proliferation and diversity (e.g. 'we have chosen to adopt a paradigmatic position of positivism in our approach to this policy report, appreciating that other positions exist, and have made this choice because . . .'). Or look in the references for any mention of books in the *Contesting Early Childhood* series, or any other publications from what I have called the resistance movement, who by and large have chosen not to adopt a positivistic position; it is as if they, and the stories they tell, simply do not exist and don't merit even refuting.

I am uncertain whether the absence of such references, along with the accompanying failure to acknowledge the 'multitude of perspectives and debates' in early childhood education, is because the positivists who shape policy and the public perception of early childhood education are unaware of alternative paradigms and the work they inspire – or because they are aware but dismiss the alternatives with disdain as wrong-headed or even dangerous. Or perhaps most positivists simply find other paradigms unintelligible (by contrast, most postfoundationalists understand the positivist position very well, having been exposed to it over many years or indeed having occupied that position at some stage of their lives). Elizabeth St. Pierre raises this last possibility, noting that what seems clear and coherent within one paradigmatic position may not be intelligible within another, then goes on to ask a very important question:

> How does one learn to hear and 'understand' a statement made within a different structure of intelligibility [i.e. from a different paradigmatic position]? At the least, this question shifts prevailing attitudes by assuming that the burden of intelligibility lies as much with the reader as with the writer, a position contrary to that of those who chide postmodernism for 'deliberate obfuscation over clarification' (Constas, 1998, p. 38). For some reason, these readers expect postmodernism to be readily accessible and coherent within a structure it works against.
>
> (St. Pierre, 2000, p. 25)

Whatever the reason, the marginalisation of alternative viewpoints by the positivist powers that be has, I believe, deeply troubling consequences for early childhood education. Instead of being a field full of diverse communities who, despite their differences, manage to engage with and talk to each other and in which a multitude of perspectives and debates and many different stories can be heard, we are looking at a field that has been riven by a paradigmatic divide. On either side of the divide are different camps, showing little sign of wanting to engage and talk with those on the other side, essentially ignoring each other and following their own lives undisturbed by the other. We are all the poorer for this state of division and non-communication. (For a fuller discussion of the paradigmatic divide in early childhood education, see Moss, 2007.)

The marginalisation of paradigm by the positivist dominant discourse and its proponents has another unfortunate consequence: the depoliticization of early childhood education. For, early childhood education, I contend, is first and foremost a political and ethical practice, meaning it starts with political and ethical questions, one of which is 'What paradigmatic position do you take?' To ignore paradigm and to take one's paradigmatic position for granted is, in effect, to deny that a political choice is being made, a political choice closely bound up with ethics. It is to reassert the importance of such political and ethical practice to the contesting of early childhood that I now turn.

Questions – yours and mine

Don't forget to share and discuss the questions you have after reading this chapter, including the ones I suggested at the end of Chapter 1.

Here though are some of my questions to you:

- Do you think you have a paradigmatic position which shapes how you see and understand things? What is it? How do you think you have come to have this position? Has your position changed over time?
- Take an issue in early childhood education, for example, curriculum, assessment or working with parents: how might these issues be understood and implemented from different paradigmatic positions?
- What is your response to the (postfoundational) idea that in the social world there are many truths and many knowledges?
- Is 'quality' a concept that you choose to work with? Do you think there can be an objective, stable and universal standard of early childhood education?
- Should paradigm be introduced into the education of people wanting to work in early childhood education? If so, when and how?

Chapter 3

Politics and ethics as first practice

I have argued that the dominant discourses in early childhood education can be contested on various grounds; that they claim too much, not working even in their own terms; that they are dangerous, leading to greater governing of children and adults alike; and that they only make sense viewed from a particular paradigmatic position. In this chapter I want to add two further grounds for contestation: politics and ethics. I will argue that early childhood education is, first and foremost, a political and ethical practice, meaning that it is built on answers to political questions, questions that are by their nature contestable, and also on relationships, which call for the choice of a relational ethics, an ethics that guides how we should relate to each other. By contrast, the two dominant discourses I have highlighted treat early childhood education as primarily a technical practice.

The issue in contention, therefore, is *what is first practice in early childhood education?* Where do we start from in education? Do we start with technical practice, seeking 'evidence-based' answers to technical questions about the most effective means to use, technical questions such as 'What works?' or 'What is quality?' Or do we start with political and ethical practice, that is by asking political questions that are, to reiterate the words of Belgian political scientist Chantal Mouffe (2007), 'not mere technical issues to be solved by experts . . . [but questions that] always involve decisions which require us to make choices between conflicting alternatives'. These include questions about relational ethics in the practice of early childhood education; but answers to all political questions involve a strong ethical dimension – about what a good education is.

What is first practice in early childhood education?

Both the story of markets and the story of quality and high returns start with technical practice. *Technical practice* is their first practice. They take purposes and ends – an education for predetermined outcomes and high returns on investment, and an education based on the marketized delivery of services – for granted, as settled and uncontestable. The 'whys' and the 'whats' are simply assumed in these stories, reserving their full attention for the 'hows': how do we get high returns? how do we create and operate a market? The result is recurring studies to identify which combination of technologies ('quality') gets the best predetermined outcomes and enquiries into how to make the 'childcare' or 'education' market work better. Increased effectiveness is the order of the day.

Gert Biesta, a Dutch philosopher of education, contests this priority given to technical practice, arguing that it favours

> a technocratic model in which it is assumed that the only relevant research questions are questions about the effectiveness of educational means and techniques, forgetting, among other things, that what counts as 'effective' crucially depends on judgments about what is educationally desirable.
>
> (Biesta, 2007, p. 5)

By raising the notion of the 'educationally desirable', we are immediately into political territory, since there can be no one right answer to the question of what is desirable or good, only a variety of answers, some of which are conflicting. This means we must, each and every one of us, make political choices between often conflicting alternatives. The great Italian educator Loris Malaguzzi similarly chooses the primacy of the political when he insists that '[education is] always a political discourse whether we know it or not. It is about working with cultural choices, but it clearly also means working with political choices' (Cagliari, Castegnetti, Giudici, Rinaldi, Vecchi and Moss, 2016, p. 267). The political choices that he and others in Reggio Emilia have made are the subject of the next chapter.

I agree with Biesta and Malaguzzi. In my view, education is, first and foremost, a ***political practice***, building on political questions that call for choices to be made between often conflicting alternatives – 'working with political choices'. The denial of politics in favour of technical practice, as in today's dominant discourses, reflects in large part the pervasive neoliberal climate of the day, since as well as competition, calculation and choice, neoliberalism has a deep suspicion of politics in general and democratic politics in particular, preferring to leave decisions and governing to impersonal markets and (supposedly) dispassionate managers. In effect neoliberalism has long ago made its political choices and no longer wishes to discuss them, placing them in the locked drawer labelled 'taken-for-granted'. All that matters now is to identify and apply the correct human technologies to implement those choices.

But let us return to the political. What sort of political questions and, therefore, what sort of political choices might early childhood education involve? For Malaguzzi and the schools he worked with in Reggio Emilia, the subjects of the next chapter, the first such question has to be 'What is your image of the child?', arguing that a 'declaration [about the image of the child] is not only a necessary act of clarity and correctness, it is the necessary premise for any pedagogical theory, and any pedagogical project' (ibid., p. 374).

For Malaguzzi, the political choice was clear: 'We [in Reggio Emilia] say all children are rich, there are no poor children. All children whatever their culture, whatever their lives are rich, better equipped, more talented, stronger and more intelligent than we can suppose' (ibid., p. 397). The 'rich child' is born with immense and unknowable potentiality, having what Malaguzzi famously described as a 'hundred languages'[1] and making meaning of the world (learning) right from the beginning of life, as a protagonist, an active subject. The rich child, too, is a citizen with rights, those with disabilities being children with special rights, rather than a poor child with special needs.

The answer to the political question, the political choice made by Malaguzzi, is important; it is the basis of his educational thinking and practice. But equally important is his understanding that a choice has been made, a political choice made from a number of potentially conflicting alternatives. As such, as a clear and public statement, the choice made is contestable, it is subject to critique and disagreement. That is the nature of a political discourse; that is what makes education first and foremost a political practice.

Moreover, we can see here how Malaguzzi's politics is framed by paradigm. His question about the image of the child, it seems to me, follows from the adoption of a social constructionist position within a postfoundational paradigm. Gunilla Dahlberg, Alan Pence and I explored this relationship between paradigmatic position and political choice in *Beyond Quality in Early Childhood Education and Care*:

> From our postmodern perspective, there is no such thing as 'the child' or 'childhood', an essential being and state waiting to be discovered, defined and realized, so that we can say to ourselves and others 'that is how children are, that is what childhood is'. Instead, there are many children and many childhoods, each constructed by our 'understandings of childhood and what children are and should be'. Instead of waiting upon scientific knowledge to tell us who the child is, we have choices to make about who we think the child is, and these choices have enormous significance since our construction of the child and early childhood are *productive*, by which we mean that they determine the institutions we provide for children and the pedagogical work that adults and children undertake in these institutions.
>
> (Dahlberg *et al.*, 2013, p. 46; original emphasis)

In that book we outlined a number of different social constructions of the child: the child as knowledge, identify and culture reproducer, starting life as an empty vessel into which adults pour content; the child as innocent, needing protection from a corrupt world; the child as nature, or the scientific child of biological stages, with universal properties, whose development is a biologically determined process, following general laws; and the child as a component in labour market supply, who must be taken in hand to ensure an adequate labour supply and the efficient use of human resources. Our political choice, however, was none of these, but rather the child as co-constructor of knowledge, identity and culture. The other constructions, we argued, 'produce a "poor" child, weak and passive, incapable and under-developed, dependent and isolated'; whereas our answer to the question of what image, the child as co-constructor, produced a 'rich' child, 'born equipped to learn . . . active and competent, he or she has ideas and theories that are not only worth listening to, but also merit scrutiny and, where appropriate, questioning and challenge' (Dahlberg *et al.*, 2013, p. 54).

Your answer to this first political question will, therefore, be of the utmost significance – it will be productive because it will have profound consequences. It will generate other 'image' questions and influence your answers to these questions, questions such as 'What is your image of the educator?' and 'What is your image of the nursery, kindergarten or school?' But such 'image' questions do not exhaust the political choices to be made. Here are some other political questions that, in my view, are important in the building of early childhood education.

- What paradigmatic position is to be taken? This question recognises that paradigm is inescapable and that much else flows from the position that is chosen, both what questions are asked (e.g. what is your image?) and what answers are given (e.g. to questions about the meaning of knowledge).
- What is knowledge?
- What do we mean by education? What do we mean by care?
- What is/are the purpose/s of early childhood education? What is it for?
- What are the fundamental values of early childhood education?
- What ethics should we work with in early childhood education?
- What is the 'diagnosis of our time'? This question is lifted from the title of a book by the Hungarian sociologist Karl Mannheim (1893–1947). By asking this, we recognise the need to analyse and interpret the social, cultural, economic, political and technological conditions in which we are living, in order to create an education that is both relevant to the lives of children, families and communities and committed to working for a better life and world (though that itself implies one answer to another political question, 'What is the purpose of early childhood education?').
- What kind of society do we want? What do we want for our children, here and now and in the future?

In the next chapter, I shall give examples of how some of these political questions have been answered in one instance, the municipal schools for young children in the Italian city of Reggio Emilia. I shall demonstrate also how the answers to such questions are 'productive', as they produce or construct an early childhood education that is 'desirable' or 'good', terms I much prefer to 'quality', as they imply a choice has been made that is political and ethical – and, therefore, contestable, because different political choices will produce alternative and sometimes conflicting understandings of what is 'desirable' or 'good'. By contrast, 'quality' seems to hide behind a technical veneer, purporting to offer a criterion or norm that is objective, definitive and uncontestable.

There are two other points to be made about political questions. First, the list represents a personal view of what questions are important. You may agree with my choices or have different ones. Once again, the important point is to understand that there are choices to be made in early childhood education, choices between sometimes conflicting alternatives, in this case what political questions are important to ask.

Second, I have been guilty of simplification by suggesting that technical practice is first practice in the dominant discourses in early childhood education, in contrast to my contention that politics and ethics are first practice. Actually, it is rather more complicated. I have already claimed that the story of 'neoliberalism has long ago made its political choices and no longer wishes to discuss them, placing them in the locked drawer labelled "taken-for-granted"'. The same is true for the dominant discourses in today's early childhood education, which act *as if* technical practice were first practice. So, the dominant discourse of quality and high returns seems to give priority to technical practice with all its talk of 'quality',' evidence-based practice' and 'what works'; while the same is true for the story of markets, with all its talk of how to create effective markets.

But like any other educational discourse, any other story about early childhood, these stories are in fact built on political choices in answer to political questions. Behind their technical veneer, the story of quality and high returns and the story of markets are as political as any other story of early childhood education – and hence their political choices are just as contestable as those of any other story. The difference between my position and the storytellers of these discourses is this: I am upfront about political practice, while they just don't acknowledge the political dimension, pretending instead that their stories are natural and neutral, rather than the product of particular choices made and particular positions taken. They hide their political practice, and to find it you have to peel away the technical surface.

Let me give three examples of my reading of the political choices that hide behind the technical surface of the story of quality and high returns. The first example is of how the story of quality and high returns is built on a particular image of the child. This image, which I have already touched on, has been termed the ***scientific child*** and is constructed mainly through the lens of developmental psychology, a discipline that plays a major and taken-for-granted role in the story of quality and high returns, through its system of classifications and norms (e.g. developmental stages).

This is how Gunilla Dahlberg, Alan Pence and I described developmental psychology's 'scientific child' in our book *Beyond Quality in Early Childhood Education and Care*:

> [This child is] an essential being of universal properties and inherent capabilities whose development is viewed as an innate process – biologically determined, following general laws – unless, of course, the child has some abnormality. That, we say, is the way children of that age are, that is their nature, that is what they can and cannot do if they are 'normal'. Albeit simplified, one could say that this is *Piaget's child*, since Piaget's theory of stages has surely been very influential for this construction, even though Piaget himself never put much stress on stages (Dahlberg, 1985).
>
> This construction produces a young child who is a natural, rather than a social, phenomenon, abstracted and decontextualised, essentialized and normalised, defined either through abstract notions of maturity (Gesell and Ilg, 1946) or through stages of development. The influence of culture and the agency of children themselves are equally discounted, leaving 'the decontextualised individual who develops through natural and autonomous processes' (Vadeboncoeur, 1997, pp. 33–34). In this construction, 'the psychological classifications assigned to children have no particular time or space continuum – self-esteem, competence and creativity seem to exist outside history and social contexts' (Popkewitz, 1997, p. 33). The focus is on the individual child who, irrespective of context, follows a standard sequence of biological stages that constitute a path to full realisation or a ladder-like progression to maturity.
>
> (Dahlberg *et al.*, 2013, p. 49)

There are times, too, in the story of quality and high returns, especially when storytellers start talking about the need for early childhood education to 'ready' children to learn or to 'ready' children for compulsory schooling, when another image comes into view, again one I have already touched on: the child as knowledge, identity and culture reproducer, an empty vessel needing to be filled, a child born with nothing and needing to be loaded up with knowledge, values and identity, a child who needs to be taught how to learn.

What these images embedded in the story of quality and high returns share is an image of the 'poor' child, children defined in terms of what they cannot do or what they need to acquire, a child who is passively waiting for something to happen, whether by biological programming or through inculcation, a child who is lacking and needs to be readied. And they in turn produce a particular image of the educator and the nursery, school or kindergarten, the former as a technician, needing to follow prescribed steps to achieve prescribed outcomes, filling the empty vessel with the correct contents and in the correct way; and the latter as a sort of processing plant where correct technologies applied correctly by technicians can bring about predicted developments and ensure later high returns.

My second example of how a political choice is made but not acknowledged in the story of quality and high returns is an implicit understanding of education as a process of attaining certain defined and standardised developmental and learning goals, *en route* to re-producing knowledge of reality, a process in which the learner is 'independent and separate from other subjects as well as from the material environment, matters and artefacts in the world around them'. This assumes a representational view of knowledge, meaning that knowledge is understood to be an objective, stable and accurate representation of a pre-existing reality, a literal reproduction of the world. In this representational epistemology, learning is

> a process that progresses in a linear fashion from a stage of a lower degree of cognitive complexity and abstraction in the individual child's language construction, to an increasingly more advanced conceptual stage . . . Knowledge is understood as cognitive constructs in language . . . believed to represent pre-existing things and phenomena in reality. . . . [The learning subject] acts upon their world in order to discover the "laws of nature" and uncover its hidden truths. These universal laws stand above and transcend humans . . . we see ourselves as "beings-*in*-the world" (Barad, 2007, p. 160), who discover and learn about it, as we inhabit it as independent and free subjects and make use of it for our own benefit. Humans have, in line with this thinking, always sought a position of mastery over nature *in* the material world.
>
> (Lenz Taguchi, 2010, pp. 17–18)

What we end up with is an education that has been described scathingly as

> driven by uncreative thought . . . embracing a trivialised idea of learning and knowledge expressed through the economic logic, and the right input-output relation . . . [and] where we shall be measured, weighed, quality assured, predicted, supervised, controlled, evaluated.
>
> (Olsson, 2013, p. 231)

Instead of creative thought, we (children and adults) are locked into an idea of learning and knowledge that is 'about "thinking right" and about reproducing knowledge that already exists' (ibid.), where questions and answers are givens, and which leaves no space for invention, for the new, for the interesting, for the remarkable and for the surprising. It is an education of following 'rigid lines' rather than an education for generating 'lines of flight' – two concepts I shall return to in Chapter 6 when considering the ideas of Gilles Deleuze.

My third example of the implicit political choices in the dominant discourse of quality and high returns is a diagnosis of our time and a view of the future that presumes, without question, the desirability, inevitability and perpetuity of neoliberal capitalism and an accompanying rampant consumerism fuelled by a frantic search for novelty and status. In this diagnosis and long-term view 'there is no alternative', only more of the same. Faced by this necessity, the primary, indeed over-riding, purpose of education is economic, acting as a 'means to develop human capital rather than promote democratic learning or citizenship objectives' (Hyslop-Margison and Sears, 2007, p. 3), to create subjects who will be fit for purpose in a world defined by competition, individual choice and consumption. In these conditions, the particular task facing early childhood education as the first stage of lifelong learning is to start the process of preparing adults who will prove autonomous, enterprising and risk-managing, well adapted to a neoliberal workforce that must be competitive, flexible and compliant and to a neoliberal society of consumers who need to be calculating, insatiable and individualistic, so ensuring personal and national survival in a never-ending global rat race. The result: education as future proofing the child, for a future of more of the same.

A minister responsible for early childhood education in England has expressed this vision in a speech: 'The 21st century will belong to those countries that win the global race for jobs and economic advantage. In order for every adult to fulfil their potential, they need to be properly equipped with essential skills from the very beginning of their lives' (Truss, 2013). The government policy paper that accompanied this speech, the vacuously titled *More Great Childcare*, insisted that '[m]ore great childcare is vital to ensuring we [i.e. England] can compete in the global race' (Department for Education (England), 2013, p. 6). What do we want then for our children in this inevitable world of endless more of the same? The answer lying deep in the story of quality and high returns is to train them from birth 'to compete in the global race', to ensure they achieve a state of constant and unquestioning 'readiness' for whatever demands the market will make on them, always compliantly prepared for what may come next in a fast-moving global economy, never dwelling on the past or being in the present – and certainly not 'contesting the visions of the future that they are being presented with'.

The importance of ethical practice

One of the political questions posed earlier is 'What ethics should we work with in early childhood education?' Posing it as just one of several political questions may seem to place ***ethical practice*** as subsidiary to politics. But I want to argue that ethics is on a par with politics as providing the bedrock for education, hence that both politics *and* ethics are first practice. Indeed, it was this belief that led to the first book in the *Contesting Early Childhood* series, a book called *Ethics and Politics in Early Childhood Education*, written in 2005 by Gunilla Dahlberg and myself. In that book, we argued that ethics as well as politics are first practice in early childhood education and proposed three ethical approaches that we found particularly interesting and consistent with a postfoundational paradigmatic position. I offer them here as examples of possibility, not as a comprehensive list.

Postmodern ethics

'Postmodern ethics', which I have already touched on in the previous chapter, is the term used by Zygmunt Bauman to describe an approach that rejects an ethics of rules and regulations to be followed invariably and unquestioningly, an ethics that removes responsibility from the individual, who only has to follow the rules and regulations. Underlying this kind of ethics is a deep mistrust of individuals, who it is assumed can only act ethically if they have detailed codes telling them what they must do. Bauman associates this ethical approach with a quest for order, control and certainty.

Moving to what Bauman terms a postmodern position acknowledges that life is unpredictable and messy and that many ethical decisions cannot be clear-cut and certain. Adopting this position offers an opportunity to re-personalise ethics, so that the individual once again assumes the responsibility that comes from facing and making ethical choices rather than following universal codes. Ethics exists, Bauman argues, but without one foundational code to provide certain, neat and universal answers; we have, instead, to learn to live with ambiguity and ambivalence in an ethical system where 'must do' is replaced by 'it depends'. Here is Bauman setting out his basic idea:

> It is possible to give up on the grand narrative idea of a single ethical code, without giving up on the idea of moral responsibility as a regulative ideal. . . . Choices between good and evil are still to be made, this time, however, in the full daylight, and with full knowledge that a choice is being made. With the smokescreen of centralized legislation dispersed and the power-of-attorney returned to the signatory, the choice is blatantly left to the moral person's own devices. With choice comes responsibility. And if choice is inevitable, responsibility is unavoidable.
>
> (Bauman, 1995, p. 5)

You will see here a theme that runs through this book: that instead of falling back on some externally derived rule book, interpreting our role as applying the standards set out in that rule book, we are constantly faced by having to make choices about the right thing to do, about what is good, about for example what we think is a good/desirable early childhood education or the right relationships between all those, children and adults, who are involved in that education. Today, the word 'choice' has been hijacked by the story of neoliberalism, conjuring up an image of the autonomous consumer calculating her or his best buy, making a purchasing choice that best serves her or his interests – the informed consumer that we should all strive to be, making an informed choice between products offered to us by the market. But we can reclaim 'choice' as something less individualistic and economistic, for example in Bauman's terms as deciding what is the right thing to do in the circumstances and always bearing in mind our relationships with and responsibilities to others; furthermore, such decisions may often best be made in relationship with others, even if the final responsibility rests with us. Rather than the choice of the consumer, we are talking about the choice of the citizen, aware of the ramifications of her or his choice not only for her/himself but for others. (Of course, the citizen can also make individual calculative choices as a consumer, for example when buying groceries, although those consumer choices may also be influenced by ethical concerns, for example about the environmental or human costs of products.)

This idea of a re-personalised ethics, an ethics that turns its back on codes and rule books, can raise anxieties, not least about relativism (again) and competence. Bauman confronts both anxieties head on. Dispensing with codes and rule books that tell us with certainty what we must do does *not* mean that anything goes, that all views must be considered equivalent. It means, instead, that ordinary people must be more active in ethical practice, think for themselves (and in relationship with others), make ethical choices and take responsibility for those choices – not abrogate responsibility to some code or rule book ('all I did was follow instructions').

Are we up to this task? Can we shoulder this responsibility? Bauman thinks so, sharing the same confidence in human beings as does Malaguzzi, both believing in their innate capacities. Malaguzzi's 'rich child' born with a hundred languages is matched by Bauman's image of human beings as 'essentially moral beings' showing moral competence and who confront ethical issues from an early stage:

> Well before we are told authoritatively what is 'good' and 'evil' . . . we face the choice between good and evil: we face it already at the very first, inescapable moment of encounter with the Other. This means in its turn that, whether we choose it or not, we confront our situation as a moral problem and our life choices as moral dilemmas. What follows is that we bear moral responsibilities (that is, responsibilities for the choice between good and evil) well before we are given or take up any concrete responsibility through contract, calculation of interest or enlisting in a cause. What follows is that such concrete responsibilities are unlikely to exhaust and replace in full the primal moral responsibility which they strive to translate into a code of well tempered rules.
>
> (ibid., p. 2)

What Bauman describes is an ethics that, like life itself, is messy and complex, uncertain and ambivalent, with no 'foolproof recipe'. This is an ethics of responsibility that is far more demanding than an ethics of rule following but that is, at the same time, hopeful, since personal responsibility, having to think for yourself, is 'morality's last hold and hope' (ibid., p. 35). (An ethics of rule-following can lead to some awful consequences if the rules themselves turn out to be warped, for example the Holocaust, which was enabled by many people unquestioningly following the Nazi rule book.)

One immediate implication of 'postmodern ethics' for early childhood education is that we should beware of concepts like 'quality', because they seek a universal code or standard to which all should strive to adhere, removing from us the hard work of thinking. Instead, adopting this ethical stance, we should assume responsibility for deciding what we think is a good or desirable education, in doing so grappling with political questions that provide a framework to guide our ethical thinking. And in making choices we will both dialogue with others but also have to think about the sort of relationships we wish to see in a good early childhood education. For education is a relational practice, and relational ethics, how we should conduct those relations, are at its heart: ethics such as the ethics of care and the ethics of an encounter.

The ethics of care

An ethics of care, the second ethical approach I want to discuss, owes much to feminist scholars, though they have in turn drawn inspiration from other thinkers including Emmanual Levinas, who will figure prominently in the next section on the 'ethics of an encounter'. Like Bauman, also, they regard ethics as a creative practice, requiring the making of contextualised ethical decisions that do not simply involve applying universal codes or rules. 'It depends' is, again, a recurring theme.

Joan Tronto describes an ethics of care as combining two elements: 'a *practice* rather than a set of rules or principles . . . [involving] particular acts of caring and a *"general habit of mind"* to care that should inform all aspects of moral life' (Tronto, 1993, p. 127; emphasis added). That habit of mind includes several qualities or values: attentiveness (to the needs of others), responsibility, competence and responsiveness. Furthermore, caring, understood as an ethic, should be widely applied: it is, say Tronto and co-author Bernice Fisher, a 'species activity that includes everything we do to maintain, continue and repair our "world" so we can live in it as well as possible' (Fisher and Tronto, 1990, p. 19) – so care not only of other people, but also of communities, societies and the physical environment.

Selma Sevenhuijsen, another leading proponent of an ethics of care, distinguishes an ethics of care (which we might see as situated within a postfoundational framework) from the universalist ethics of the code or rule book. The former is concerned with responsibilities and relationships rather than rules and rights; the former is bound to concrete situations rather than being formal and abstract; the former is an active ethical practice rather than a set of principles to be followed. Finally, the individual or ethical subject in the ethics of care is different to the ethical subject of universalist ethics:

> The moral agent in the ethics of care stands with both feet in the real world. While the universalist ethicist will see this as a threat to his independence and impartiality . . . the care ethicist sees this precisely as a crucial condition for being able to judge well. . . . [For the] ethics of care demands reflection on the best course of action in specific circumstances and the best way to express and interpret moral problems. Situatedness in concrete social practices is not seen as a threat to independent judgement. On the contrary it is assumed that this is exactly what will raise the quality of judgement.
>
> (Sevenhuijsen, 1998, p. 59)

Key words here are 'reflection', 'specific circumstances' and 'situatedness', 'interpret' and 'judgement'. Like the ethical subject in Bauman's postmodern ethics, the ethical subject in the ethics of care is a protagonist who must grapple with context, complexity, ambiguity and uncertainty to decide what it means to relate to the Other in a caring way, applying the qualities of attentiveness, responsibility, competence and responsiveness to decide when and how best to practice acts of caring. She or he may, of course, engage with others in deciding how to 'judge well', but the responsibility for that judgement is, ultimately, personal.

Apart from its value in shaping relational ethics in early childhood education, I find that an ethics of care also helps to clarify a recurring issue in early childhood: the ***relationship between education and care***. This relationship remains, in most countries, highly problematic, with the early childhood system split between 'education' and 'childcare', leaving many services and workers defined in terms of 'childcare'. These 'childcare services' or 'childcare workers' are then seen, first and foremost, as providing care, which is widely viewed and treated not as an ethic but as a commodity – attention to children's physical needs and safety, often understood as purchased in the market by parents so they can go out to work. This split approach to early childhood is invariably associated with the 'childcare' part of the early childhood system being devalued and treated in an inferior way, compared with the education part, whether it be 'childcare workers' having lower levels of education or scandalously poor pay and other working conditions or the funding of 'childcare services' being reliant on substantial parental contributions (which, of course, makes it harder to improve the situation of the workforce).

Working with an ethics of care, we can define a different relationship between education and care. Education, broadly defined, is recognised as a central purpose of all early childhood services, while care, defined as an ethic rather than a commodity, is recognised as a key component of relationships in education. Put another way, care as an ethic should permeate *all* education services, as relevant in compulsory schooling or universities as in early child-hood education. (An ethic of care can and arguably should, following the same argument, permeate any other service or organisation, from hospitals and prisons to factories and offices.) Of course, early childhood services (like schools and other services for children) must adapt their opening hours to parental working hours – but important as that is, it is not central to their identity and purpose. So if we start talking about an 'ethics of care', we can stop talking about 'childcare services', acknowledging that an ethics of care is important for all children, irrespective of their parents' employment, and all services.

An ethics of an encounter

This ethical approach is associated with Emmanuel Levinas (1906–1995), a French philosopher of Lithuanian Jewish origin who emerged as a leading thinker in France in the 1950s. Largely ignored until the mid-1980s, today Levinas is considered one of the greatest French philosophers of the 20th century. His concept of the ethics of an encounter has radical implications for early childhood education, challenging much of the way this is conceptual-ised and practiced today, for it requires a fundamental rethinking of relation-ships that lie at the heart of educational practice.

Levinas's starting point is how in Western thought knowledge readily becomes a will to know. In other words, the knower, that is the person want-ing to know, is determined to make sense of someone or something through applying her or his own system of understandings, concepts and categories. It is that moment when I (the knower) think that I know someone or some-thing because I can fit the someone or something into my system, my way of viewing and understanding the world – that 'oh! he/she/it is just like . . .' moment. In my will to know, I have come to the Other with my typical ways of knowing and made sense of the Other by applying them. The process can be described like this:

> as soon as I finish a conversation with another person, as soon as I pause to reflect, I have the opportunity to think. Once I think, I will try to under-stand what my discussion partner is saying in categories already familiar to me. . . . *Essentially I will translate the vocabulary of the other into my vocabulary, imposing my ideas of what the other has said. In this way, I have reduced the otherness of the other (his alterity) to the sameness of my thought.* I do not allow the other to appear in her light, but the light I lend to her.
> (Diedrich, Burggraeve and Gastmans, 2003, p. 42; emphasis added)

For Levinas, this will to know exacts a high price, as the knower assimilates the Other into the knower's way of seeing and thinking. Or, in Levinas's vivid term, the knower 'grasps' the Other and so makes the Other into the Same. By doing this, I banish uncertainty and ambivalence for order and predictability, mastering the Other by making her/him/it part of my world. This involves oppression, even violence, forcing the unknown Other into concepts, categories and classifications that I can understand and use to control and, in the process, denying their otherness: as Robert Young puts it, 'when knowledge or theory comprehends the Other, the alterity of the latter vanishes as it becomes part of the same. . . . In all cases the other is neutralized as a means of encompassing it' (Young, 1990, pp. 44, 45).

It is another example of a phenomenon already apparent to readers of this book – the urge towards universal and normative thinking characteristic of positivism and of its autonomous, rational and calculating subject, familiar, too, in the story of quality and high returns, where technical practice is deployed in the service of predetermined and standardised outcomes. Using my system of categories, I ask if the child before me can do a, b and c, not what can this child do, some of which may be quite outside my system and beyond my expectations.[2]

Levinas challenges this way of thinking, this will to know and to make the Other into the Same, in the ethical approach that he develops: the ethics of an encounter. The basis for this ethics is the absolute alterity and unknowability of the Other; this is a singular Other whom I cannot represent and classify into a category, an Other I cannot grasp by seeking to understand through imposing my framework of thought, my own perspective. Instead, my relationship with the Other must be one of respect for their absolute alterity or otherness, a recognition that they are a stranger 'whom it is impossible to reduce to myself, to my thoughts and my possessions'.

But the relation to the Other is not just a matter of respecting alterity, of not grasping, of not making them into the Same. It goes further. Levinas's ethic is also premised on absolute and infinite responsibility for the Other, an unconditional responsibility that has no expectation of returns, no element of calculation: 'I have to respond to and for the Other without occupying myself with the Other's responsibility in my regard' (Levinas, 1987, p. 137).

Levinas's ethic of an encounter can seem hard to get our minds around, so different is it to the prevailing ideas in our neoliberal world. He contests autonomy, calculation and returns and the urge to manage and govern others, foregrounding instead unbounded responsibility, inter-dependence and hospitality, an unconditional welcoming of the Other as stranger. But he also poses a more specific challenge to the current field of early childhood education: how to think another whom I cannot grasp. For the ethics of an encounter confronts educators with profound questions 'such as how the encounter with Otherness, with difference can take place as responsibly as possible – as something which the so-called "free thought" cannot grasp through categories, classifications and thematizations' (Dahlberg, 2003, p. 270).

Can we imagine an early childhood education that avoids categories, classifications and thematizations, in curricula or modes of assessment or any other respect? Can the educator respect the otherness of the children with whom she works, resisting the temptation to grasp that alterity by 'pigeon-holing' them into her own mental schema? Can she hold herself open to the unexpected and the unknowable, the perplexing and the wondrous? This is difficult at any time, but particularly so when the story of quality and high returns is so dominant, with its desire for certain outcomes to be attained by control, classification and calculation.

Some common themes

A number of themes link these three ethical approaches, common threads that appear in each, all of which contest core ideas in the dominant discourses of early childhood education, not to mention the hyper-dominant discourse of neoliberalism. First, they are all concerned with responsibility, in particular what it means to be responsible for the Other (e.g. what it means for the teacher to be responsible for the child). Bauman, for example, is strongly influenced by Levinas when he proposes that responsibility for the Other is the central challenge of postmodern ethics. Or, to take another example, responsibility is an important part of the habit of mind required for an ethics of care. Responsibility, except to the self, is hard for an autonomous, self-interested *homo economicus* to assume, for it involves notions of both dependency and inter-dependency; we cannot live thinking only of ourselves (or just thinking about our nearest and dearest), for we are unavoidably part of wider relationships in which each one of us depends on others.

Second, all three approaches recognise that responsibility entails respect for otherness. Tronto, echoing Bauman and Levinas, concludes that 'questions of otherness are at the heart of contemporary theory' (Tronto, 1993, p. 58). The quality of responsiveness in the ethics of care is important here because excessive control of the Other is recognised as a major risk in relationships of care – care can smother or grasp the Other. In such relationships, often involving inequality and vulnerability, it is important to try and understand what is being expressed by those in a vulnerable position rather than assuming you know by imagining yourself in a similar situation. Responsiveness, says Tronto, 'suggests a different way to understand the needs of others rather than to put ourselves into their position. . . . [O]ne is engaged from the standpoint of the other, but not by presuming the Other is exactly like the self' (ibid., p. 135). Or in Levinas's phrase, the carer must try to avoid grasping the cared-for.

Third, all three approaches reject calculative and rational thinking in relations with the Other. Ethics, in Bauman's view,

> begets an essentially unequal relationship: thus inequality, non-equity, this not-asking-for reciprocation, this disinterest in mutuality, this

indifference to the 'balancing up' of gains and rewards – in short, this organically 'unbalanced' and hence non-reversible character of 'I versus the Other' relationship is what makes the encounter a moral event. . . .

[M]orality is endemically and irredeemably non-rational – in the sense of not being calculable, hence not being describable as following rules that are in principle universalizable. The moral call is thoroughly personal; it appeals to my responsibility, and the urge to care thus elicited cannot be allayed or placated by the awareness that others do it to me, or that I have already done my share by following to the letter what others used to do.

(Bauman, 1993, pp. 48–49, 60)

A multitude of debates?

I have spoken so far about stories and perspectives and will have more to say about them. But what about the multitude of debates referred to in the remit for the *Contesting Early Childhood* series? They should follow from the priority given to political and ethical practice, a priority for which this chapter has argued. To ask political questions that provoke alternative answers, questions such as 'What is your image of the child?' or 'What is the purpose of education?' or 'What are the fundamental values of education?' invites debate. As, too, does an ethical practice that, rather than following a rule book, calls for making ethical choices, in response to that recurring dilemma in life expressed in the phrase 'it depends'.

There are debates in early childhood education, but not perhaps as many as there could or should be. In particular, they are lacking between followers of the dominant stories and those who adhere to what I have termed the resistance movement. That paradigmatic divide, which I referred to in the previous chapter, cuts off such debates between the mainstream and others, with the former focused on improved technical practice (What works? How to improve 'quality'?) and unaware of or uninterested in political questions and ethical issues. That leaves debates within and among the resistance movement, but important as these are, they are not enough.

Politics, ethics, responsibility, otherness, non-rationality. We have come a long way from the dominant discourses in early childhood education, whether the more local story of markets or the more widespread story of quality and high returns, stories that, in close relationship to positivism and neoliberalism, prioritise technical practice and are imbued with calculation, categorisation and control; stories that are about universal standards, procedures and rules – but stories that are so preponderant today that it can sometimes seem impossible to imagine what other stories might sound like and how they might be enacted in practice. But there are alternatives, other stories about early childhood education that have been enacted in practice, and I turn now to consider one of them: the municipal schools and early childhood education in Reggio Emilia in Italy, a living example of an educational project that tells a very different story.

Questions – yours and mine

Don't forget to share and discuss the questions you have after reading this chapter, including the ones I suggested at the end of Chapter 1.

Here though are some of my questions to you:

- What for you is the bedrock or starting point of early childhood education – technical practice, political and ethical practice, or something else?
- What are your political questions?
- Choose a political question, it doesn't matter which; what is your answer or political choice?
- Take an official document and look for a declaration of the image of the child, i.e. an explicit statement. Can you find one? If yes, what image is offered? Do you share that image? If you can't find such a statement, why do you think that is? Reading the document, do you think that the authors of the document have an implicit image of the child in their minds? Do you share that image?
- What ethical approach do you think should guide early childhood education?
- How do you understand alterity or Otherness? Can you think of an instance when you tried to 'grasp' the Other, to make the Other into the Same' – even if you were not aware at the time of doing so?
- How can educators relate responsibly to children, recognising their 'otherness'? How might educators try to understand what a child can do without resorting to measures using predefined categories?

Notes

1 The 'hundred languages of childhood' refer 'to the different ways children (human beings) represent, communicate and express their thinking in different media and symbolic systems; languages therefore are the many fonts or geneses of knowledge' (Vecchi, 2010, p. 9). The 'hundred' is arbitrary, a provocation to think about the many ways children and adults can represent, communicate and express themselves and to highlight the equal dignity that should be given to all languages. These languages range from the many visual languages that there are, such as drawing, painting and sculpture, through music and dance, to a wide range of scientific languages, reading and writing, and much else besides.

2 A specific example is given in the book 'Listening to Four Year Olds', where the author Jacqui Cousins recounts such an encounter with Sonnyboy, a boy from a traveller background whose knowledge was outside the school system's and beyond its expectations (Cousins, 2003).

Chapter 4

Reggio Emilia

A story of democracy, experimentation and potentiality

Reggio Emilia has become an international phenomenon of early childhood education, the subject of worldwide attention and admiration. What is Reggio Emilia, and what is its place in contesting early childhood? Reggio Emilia is a modest-sized city in Northern Italy, about 70 kilometres to the west of Bologna, one of a string of cities that lie on an east-west axis along the valley of the River Po. But when people in the early childhood field talk about Reggio Emilia they are referring to something special that has evolved in that city over the last 50 years or so: a network of 'municipal schools' for young children and the early childhood education that takes place within them.

Tens of thousands of people from around the world have visited these schools or seen the travelling exhibition – *The Hundred Languages of Childhood* – about these schools, and many of these observers agree that something important, exciting and special has been taking place. In this chapter, I will discuss what makes these schools and the education they provide so important, exciting and special and how they constitute one of the 'alternative narratives of an area that is now made up of a multitude of perspectives and debates' – a narrative that contests the dominant 'story of quality and high returns' (as well as the 'story of markets'). The chapters that follow this one are different in character, being about theorists and theories that contribute to that 'multitude of perspectives and debates' that the *Contesting Early Childhood* series seeks to explore – and which enable the creation of alternative narratives. Indeed, it will become apparent that Reggio Emilia's alternative narrative carries within it some of the concepts and ideas of Foucault, Deleuze and posthumanism.

But I will start by saying why, in my view, this relatively small, local project matters so much, its significance reaching well beyond Reggio Emilia's city limits.

Why does Reggio Emilia matter?

The first thing to say is that Reggio Emilia is not important for providing a transferable programme or universal blueprint that, properly applied, can provide a panacea for early childhood education worldwide. Instead, it seems to me that the education undertaken in the municipal schools is best under- stood not as an 'approach', implying a generalisable model, but as a **local cultural project** that has emerged from a very particular time and place, the time being the 1960s and 1970s and the place being Reggio Emilia in the region of Emilia Romagna, a place with a very particular history and political, cultural and social context. Let me explain further this history and context.

Although much had changed in the intervening years, Reggio Emilia in the 1960s, when its first schools opened, was still dominated by memories of 20 years of authoritarian fascist rule, beginning in 1923 and culminating in five years of war, Nazi occupation and a bloody resistance struggle. The end of that dark age in 1945, following the Liberation, left a terrible legacy of human loss, psychological scarring and material destruction, but it also opened up to a new period of great expectations and excitement and a deter- mination to rebuild a better society. This is captured in these words by Loris Malaguzzi (1920–1994), a leading figure in Reggio Emilia's project and one of the great educational thinkers and practitioners of the 20th century, look- ing back to that time towards the end of his life:

> I remember these were times [after the Liberation of Reggio Emilia from Nazi occupation, in April 1945] when everything seemed possible. . . . At that time, after the war, after the grief, and after the ruins, there was a very strange phenomenon, impetuous and strong, it made possible a great longing, great fervour and great excitement. It was the ridiculous capacity of being able to think anything, and to think that anything could be physically realised.
>
> (Cagliari *et al.*, 2016, p. 415)

So, despite the dreadful legacy, the post-war period was a time of hope and optimism, given expression by the city's active local authority (the *comune*), which had great confidence in its capacity to improve the lives of its people in many ways. Malaguzzi himself, having trained as a teacher and a psycholo- gist, and after a period as a teacher in state schools and adult education (he taught in a cooperative college educating former partisans and prisoners of war whose schooling had been interrupted by the war), devoted the rest of his life to working for the *comune*, in summer camps, in a centre for school- children with psychological problems and in the city's municipal schools for young children. His work in these schools was to be influenced not only by his previous employment but also 'by his participation in the struggles of democratic and progressive movements and by various examples of coopera- tive education' (Catarsi, 2004, p. 8).

The schools in Reggio Emilia not only emerged in this historical context but in a local political context of active left politics, a strong cooperative movement and an unwavering commitment to democracy. Asked what had prompted the people of Reggio Emilia to create their early childhood education, the mayor of the city during the 1960s

> replied that the fascist experience had taught them that people who conformed and obeyed were dangerous, and that in building a new society it was essential to safeguard and communicate that lesson and nurture and maintain a vision of children who can think and act for themselves.
> (cited in Dahlberg *et al.*, 2013, p. 12)

The first municipal school in Reggio Emilia, for 3- to 6-year-olds, was opened by the *comune* in 1963, followed by many other schools in later years, including for children under 3 years; the local project was a 0–6 school system. Malaguzzi was first appointed as consultant to these schools, then subsequently director. Reggio Emilia today has a network of 47 municipal schools, run either by the city itself or by cooperatives under agreements made with the city. These are not the only schools in the city – others are provided by the national government and by church bodies – but it is the municipal schools that have brought Reggio Emilia onto a world stage, with their reputation for creativity, experimentation and participatory democracy.

Reggio Emilia was and is not alone in developing such an innovative local cultural project. Other cities in northern and central Italy also opened municipal schools for young children in the 1960s, in what has been called a 'municipal school revolution' (Catarsi, 2004, p. 8), all of these *comuni* deciding to take responsibility for the education of their young children in the absence of state action and dissatisfied with the church schools that were the only provision in those days. Although over the years some of these *comuni* have handed their schools over to the state to run, mainly as a way to save money, others like Reggio Emilia continue to provide their own municipal schools, and other towns and cities apart from Reggio Emilia have also established international reputations for their work.

Nor was Reggio Emilia alone in the sense of coming up with its local project all on its own; the city's early childhood education did not drop out of the sky but was influenced in its formation by previous and contemporary educational pioneers. We could say, and I will return to explain this concept further, that Reggio Emilia co-constructed its education project in relationship with others – just as, today, we might think of other places co-constructing their local educational projects in relationship with Reggio Emilia and others. Read Malaguzzi, for instance, and you will find constant references to the influences on his thinking, be they individuals (such as Dewey, Freinet, Piaget, Vygotsky, Bruner)[1] or disciplines (such as psychology, cybernetics or neuroscience). There was also constant exchange with other towns and cities embarked on similar local projects, and with other important contemporary figures in education from Italy and beyond. Reading, border crossing and dialogue fuelled Malaguzzi and his colleagues with ideas, enthusiasm and energy.

Reggio Emilia, therefore, has not existed in isolation, but it has evolved a distinct identity; it has made political choices and taken responsibility for them. But if Reggio Emilia is not a transferable programme or an approach that can be franchised, why is it important? Should this local cultural project, which has grown out of a very particular context, matter to the rest of us? I think it should for several reasons.

First, it shows what can be achieved by local communities or groups with the courage and imagination to engage in what Roberto Unger has termed 'democratic experimentalism', which he describes as

> an innovative collective practice, moving forward the qualitative provision of the services themselves. That can no longer happen in our current understanding of efficiency and production by the mechanical transmission of innovation from the top. It can only happen through the organisation of a collective experimental practice from below. . . . Democracy is not just one more terrain for the institutional innovation that I advocate. It is the most important terrain.
>
> (Unger, 2005b, pp. 179, 182)

If Reggio Emilia and other Italian cities have achieved something special educationally, 'a collective experimental practice from below', then so too can some (not necessarily all) other communities, given the right conditions. The results will not be the same as Reggio Emilia, because the contexts and conditions differ, though they may have something in common, sharing some images, values and practices with Reggio – cousins, one might say, rather than identical twins. Distantly related (or not related at all), but still something new, innovative and hopeful, another alternative narrative. Democratic experimentalism cannot be legislated for, but it can surely happen in some places, where conditions are right. Indeed, it can and has happened, as there are numerous other examples of innovative local projects in early childhood education, in other parts of Italy and far beyond.

Second, Reggio Emilia challenges the 'dictatorship of no alternative' so avidly sought by the dominant discourses in early childhood education, in particular the story of quality and high returns and the story of markets. It brings hope to early childhood education. For this Italian city shows that there are alternatives; it has created its own narrative, what I have termed, in *Transformative Change and Real Utopias in Early Childhood Education*, a 'story of democracy, experimentation and potentiality', and by so doing has proven other worlds are possible, where other stories can not only be told but enacted, and not only enacted but sustained. Reggio Emilia is, of course, not the only example of what might be termed radical or progressive democratic education – many others have and do exist, across educational sectors, and they are all important. But it is, I think, by far the most extensive in scale and long lasting of such examples, demonstrating the viability and achievability of alternatives given sufficient attention to the conditions needed for them to thrive.

Third, it gives the lie to the story of markets. For here is an exemplary system of early childhood education, renowned for its innovative and very good pedagogical work, that is provided by public authorities, not private businesses, and that is based on cooperation between centres and democratic participation by citizens, not competition and individual choice. Of course, public provision and cooperation is not a guarantee of exemplary education, but neither is it inevitably worse than markets; indeed, given the right conditions, it is likely to be far better.

Finally, as we saw in the previous chapter, Reggio Emilia demonstrates the importance of working with political questions as a basis for building up early childhood education. They do so explicitly, being quite upfront about doing this: for, to repeat Malaguzzi's clearly stated view, education is 'always a political discourse whether we know it or not. It is about working with cultural choices, but it clearly also means working with political choices'. By doing so, by asking and answering political questions, by making political choices, Reggio Emilia acts as a provocation to the rest of us. Why do we often find it hard to recognise that education is, first and foremost, a political practice? What are our political questions? Do we agree with Reggio Emilia's political answers?

What I want to do in the remainder of this chapter is explore Reggio Emilia's politics of early childhood education, which constitute its alternative narrative. I will not attempt a comprehensive account; for those who want to know more, there are three books by authors from Reggio Emilia in the *Contesting Early Childhood* series (*In Dialogue with Reggio Emilia* by Carlina Rinaldi (Rinaldi, 2006); *Art and Creativity in Reggio Emilia* by Vea Vecchi (Vecchi, 2010); and *Loris Malaguzzi and the Schools of Reggio Emilia*, a selection of Loris Malaguzzi's speeches and writings (Cagliari *et al.*, 2016); and other publications that provide valuable insights (for example, Giudici and Krechevsky, 2001; Edwards, Gandini and Forman, 2012; Giamminuti, 2013). Rather I plan to take you on a short journey that will demonstrate how answers to political questions connect one to another, the one leading to the next in a chain, to form a distinctive local cultural project, an alternative narrative of early childhood education.

Reggio Emilia's politics of early childhood education

What do we mean by learning? And what pedagogy do we work with?

The starting point for this journey is the question 'What is your image of the child?' – a question which, as we saw in the previous chapter, was for

Malaguzzi 'the necessary premise for any pedagogical theory, and any peda-gogical project'. We have already seen how the educators in Reggio Emilia answer this: the rich child born with a hundred languages; the child as pro-tagonist and citizen; the child of unknowable potentiality, an idea perfectly captured in these words of the 17th-century Dutch philosopher Baruch Spi-noza (1632–1677): '[W]e never know in advance what a body can do.' This rich child is learning from birth itself, not needing to be readied or prepared to learn at some later age. But what then, from Reggio's political perspective, is learning?

Learning is understood from a social constructionist perspective. It is a process of co-construction or meaning making, always in relationship with others, as Carlina Rinaldi, who succeeded Malaguzzi as director of Reggio's municipal schools, explains.

> Learning does not take place by means of transmission or reproduction. It is a process of construction, in which each individual constructs for him-self [sic] the reasons, the 'whys', the meanings of things, others, nature, events, reality and life. The learning process is certainly individual, but because the reasons, explanations, interpretations, and meanings of oth-ers are indispensable for our knowledge building, it is also a process of relations – a process of social construction. We *thus consider knowledge to be a process of construction by the individual in relation with others, a true act of co-construction.* The timing and styles of learning are individual, and cannot be standardized with those of others, but we need others in order to realize ourselves.
>
> (Rinaldi, 2006, p. 125: emphasis added)

Such learning works through processes of theory building:

> For adults and children alike, understanding means being able to develop an interpretive 'theory', a narration that gives meaning to events and objects of the world. Our theories are provisional, offering a satisfactory explanation that can be continuously reworked; but they represent some-thing more than simply an idea or a group of ideas. They must please us and convince us, be useful, and satisfy our intellectual, affective, and aesthetic needs (the aesthetics of knowledge). In representing the world, our theories represent us.
>
> (ibid., p. 64)

But theories must be more than just pleasing and convincing to each theory builder. They must also be tested out with others. Hence the importance to learning of relationships with others, both other children and adults, and the centrality to education of working within small groups; for education is, Malaguzzi insists, 'collective and social'.

Relationships matter in another sense: the relations created between different languages enabling 'learning processes [to] take place in which several languages (or disciplines) interact together' (Vecchi, 2010, p. 18). Vea Vecchi, Reggio Emilia's first *atelierista* (an educator with an arts background working with teachers in a school), develops this theme further when she writes of the necessity

> to design and plan our school environments, the materials used, procedures practised, the professional development of educators and the things proposed with children so that there is a real possibility of the hundred languages being able to develop through the synergies created, and of the observations and documentation we produce being capable of carefully viewing this interweaving of languages.
>
> (ibid.)

Elsewhere, Vecchi further emphasises the importance of relationships in education and the danger of education undermining rather than strengthening relationships:

> When we are born we are a whole, and the whole of our senses strains to relate with the world around us in order to understand it. Very quickly, however, we find ourselves 'cut into slices', a phrase used by Loris Malaguzzi to define the state of separation in our culture and which forces us to pursue knowledge on separate paths. . . . We need to reflect seriously on how much individual and social damage is being caused by education and culture which prefer to separate than to work on connections.
>
> (Vecchi, 2004, p. 18)

Relationships, interconnections, interdependency – all key to appreciating Reggio Emilia's understanding of learning and education.

Viewed from this perspective, learning does not follow a linear pathway, with progressive and predictable stages. Rather, it proceeds by fits and starts and unexpected deviations, involving lines of flight (a concept I return to in Chapter 6) leading off in unpredicted ways provoked by encounters with difference as new connections are made and new theories are tested with others. Rather than a staircase, where one step follows another in sequence, the knowledge that learning constructs is more like a tangle of spaghetti (Malaguzzi's metaphor), with no beginning and no end, but where you are always *in between*, and with openings towards many other directions and places. Put another way, knowledge is understood to be about the creation of something new, of new properties 'that have never existed before and, more importantly, are inconceivable from what has come before' (Osberg and Biesta, 2007, p. 33). As we shall see later, unpredictability, amazement and wonder are important values in Reggio Emilia's early childhood education.

For the rich child to learn through processes of co-construction calls for a particular pedagogy: what in Reggio Emilia is termed a ***pedagogy of relationships and listening***. A pedagogy of relationships acknowledges the centrality of interaction and dialogue between children and adults in the construction of knowledge (and hence, too, the importance of relational ethics), but also the importance of relationships between languages. While a pedagogy of listening acknowledges the importance of 'listening to thought – the ideas and theories, questions and answers of children and adults. It means treating thought seriously and with respect; it means struggling to make meaning from what is said, without preconceived ideas of what is correct or appropriate' (Rinaldi, 2006, p. 15). Adopting this pedagogy, a school should be, first and foremost,

> a context of multiple listening. This context of multiple listening, involving the teachers but also the group of children and each child, all of whom can listen to others and listen to themselves, overturns the teaching-learning relationship. This overturning shifts the focus to learning; that is, to children's self-learning and the learning achieved by the group of children and adults together.
>
> (ibid., p. 67)

A pedagogy of relationships and listening is enacted, first and foremost, through ***strategy and projects***, not programmes. A programme, with its focus on premeditation and prediction, creates 'caged-in' experience, stifles creativity and originality, and leads to closure rather than keeping meaning open. Programme, Malaguzzi argues,

> rests on a theory of certainty that does not belong to us . . . I think every attempt at programme, especially in the first part of children's lives, is an attempt against nature, against that indeterminate and undetermined part of genetic legacy, against the strategic part, the designing part of the organism, of the brain, of children's human condition.
>
> (Cagliari *et al.*, 2016, p. 336)

If programme 'contains a certainty of prescription', strategy has 'a capacity for flexibility, a capacity for attention, reflection and for changing attitude . . . the capacity to deal with situations and problems by letting go of our old ways of putting things together' (ibid., p. 335) – a capacity that finds expression in project work, which entails a

> flexible approach in which initial hypotheses are made about classroom work (as well as about staff development and relationships with parents), but are subject to modifications and changes of direction as the actual

work progresses . . . [growing] in many directions without an overall ordering principle, challenging the mainstream idea of knowledge acquisition as a form of linear progression.

(ibid., p. 357)

The pedagogy of relationships and listening calls for and requires further particular political choices to be made in answer to other political question, starting with 'What are the fundamental values of education?'

What are the fundamental values of education?

One of the most fundamental values chosen by the municipal schools in Reggio Emilia is *democracy*. This is expressed in the way the schools are run and managed, with nonhierarchical staff groups and management committees whose members are elected by staff and parents. But it is also expressed in the everyday life of the schools, in the relationships of children and adults, and in a pedagogy built on listening, dialogue and mutual respect. Such democracy is, for John Dewey (1859–1952), philosopher and educational reformer, primarily a way of living together, embedded in the culture and social relationships of everyday life; it is 'a personal way of individual life . . . [signifying] the possession and continual use of certain attitudes, forming personal character and determining desire and purpose in all the relations of life' (Dewey, 1976, p. 225). This is democracy understood not only as a way of governing affairs, but also as an approach to living and relating, a relational ethic and a culture that can and should pervade all aspects of everyday living, not least in the school, where it is 'a way of being, of thinking of oneself in relation to others and the world . . . a fundamental educational value and form of educational activity' (Rinaldi, 2006, p. 156). As I have already suggested, this commitment to democracy is rooted in a strong reaction to the experience of dictatorship and oppression.

Other values sustain, I think, the choice of image of the child and the chosen understanding of learning and knowledge. The first of these I have already touched on: the value of *inter-connectedness*, expressed by Malaguzzi in this excerpt from a conference speech that he gave towards the end of his life:

Think of interconnecting, the great verb of the present and the future . . . bearing in mind that we live in a world no longer made of islands, but in a world made of webs. In this image there is the construction of children's thinking and the construction of our own thinking. A construction that cannot be made up of islands that are separate, but which belong to a great archipelago, to a great web, in which interference, interaction, inter-disciplinarity is the constant.

(Cagliari *et al.*, 2016, pp. 349–350)

This value is given expression, as we have seen, in the attention paid to relationships between people and between languages. It also leads to dismay at the prospect of dis-connecting, of how children are born whole and with a hundred languages yet all too often find themselves 'cut into slices' by schools, forced 'to pursue knowledge on separate paths'.

The next two fundamental values I want to highlight are **uncertainty** and **wonder**. Both are important because they lead to a welcoming of the unexpected, the surprising, the not knowing of what a body can do, and lead us away from focusing our gaze on what we expect, on the prescribed programme with its predetermined outcomes, the known quantity. Both welcome the singularity or otherness of the individual and militate against wanting to grasp and make the Other into the Same through processes of classification and standardisation. I am here also alluding to Reggio Emilia's answer to the question 'What ethics?' – which can, I think, be interpreted as an ethics of an encounter.

Malaguzzi describes teaching as 'a profession of uncertainty'. But this is not meant as a concern or criticism; it is not a sign of weakness. Quite the contrary, for he goes on to say that, in his view,

> uncertainty should be freed of its small degree of negativity and any denials of its virtuous nature; it must be brought back as a constituent element of our lives, of our relations with ourselves, with others and with nature . . . as a constituent element of our growth. . . . Uncertainty can be turned into something positive when we start to test it and see it as a state of ferment, a motor of knowledge.
>
> (Cagliari *et al.*, 2016, p. 334)

If you recognise and value uncertainty, you are open to an emergent learning, where something new and unexpected can appear from a pedagogy of relationships and listening and be welcome, rather than clutching at the security of what is already known and expected. Malaguzzi's use of the word 'motor' is significant, suggesting that uncertainty propels movement in learning, a dynamic approach to knowledge creation.

Such learning is also more likely to happen and be welcomed when wonder or amazement are valued. Malaguzzi would ask visitors 'Has anything made you wonder today?' reflecting the importance he attached to education creating the unexpected, the unpredictable and the surprising, something new that makes us think and see the world in a new light. For him, Reggio Emilia's

> strength in resisting for so many years comes precisely from this fact that every other week, every other fortnight, every month, something unexpected, something that surprised us or made us marvel, something

that disappointed us, something that humiliated us, would burst out in a child or in the children.

(Cagliari *et al.*, 2016, p. 392)

The opposite of wonder, the antithesis of Reggio Emilia's pedagogy, is to be found in an education built on the certainty and rigidity of developmental stages,[2] learning goals and other predetermined outcomes, and consequently working with what Malaguzzi dismissively calls a 'prophetic pedagogy', which

[k]nows everything beforehand, knows everything that will happen, does not have one uncertainty. . . . It contemplates everything and prophesies everything, sees everything to the point that it is capable of giving you recipes for little bits of actions, minute by minute, hour by hour, objective by objective, five minutes by five minutes. This is something so coarse, so cowardly, so humiliating of teachers' ingenuity, a complete humiliation for children's ingenuity and potential.

(Cagliari *et al.*, 2016, pp. 421–422)

A focus on the value of uncertainty and wonder may give the impression of a chaotic and rudderless education, in which anything goes. But this would be misleading. The early childhood education in Reggio Emilia is driven by a desire to understand learning processes and the potentiality of people and pedagogy, and this requires the rigour of two other values: ***research*** and ***experimentation***. So, while 'our own aptitude for marvelling when faced with the facts of our daily professional life is to be valued', so too is 'a desire to interrogate these facts and obtain answers by subjecting them to methodological observation and experiment' (ibid., p. 124). The two words – research and experimentation – appear regularly throughout the writings of Malaguzzi, Vecchi and Rinaldi, indicating their central importance to the Reggio Emilia project and a refusal to surrender research and experimentation to academics. That is why Carlina Rinaldi has

written so often about the teacher as a researcher. As I wrote, it's not that we don't recognise your [academic] research, but we want our research, as teachers, to be recognised. And to recognise *research as a way of thinking, of approaching life, of negotiating, of documenting.* . . . But can you find a university teacher who can learn from a practitioner? Very rarely! That is why Malaguzzi was never recognised and I think will never be recognised as a researcher. But to do good practice means to continue to do research, to continue the theory, and this is what they [universities] don't challenge. But we [in Reggio] are, first of all, researchers.

(Rinaldi, 2006, p. 192; emphasis added)

Research involves certain rigorous ways of working: documentation, analysis, reflection, interpretation, argumentation. Research is practice, something you do. But, before that, it is a value that, in the words of Carlina Rinaldi, 'shapes a way of thinking, of approaching life, of negotiating, of documenting'.

Experimentation as a value is not about 'the lifeless controlling of all parameters as well as working with an expected outcome' (Olsson, 2009, p. 27); it is not about building and testing new technologies to be applied to children or adults; nor about comparing intervention A against intervention B. Rather, for Reggio Emilia it is about the importance of bringing something new to life, 'that which is not yet known', something that is interesting and remarkable, whether that something is a thought, knowledge, a project, a service or a tangible product. Experimentation expresses a willingness, a desire in fact, to invent, to think differently, to imagine and try out different ways of doing things. It is driven by a longing to go beyond what already exists, to venture into the not yet known, to be surprised and not to be bound by the given, the familiar, the predetermined, the norm. Experimentation is open-ended (avoiding closure), open-minded (welcoming the unexpected) and open-hearted (valuing difference). In summary, we can say that experimentation means trying out theories and testing them to see if they work; which means experimentation needs to be the subject of research, as do many other aspects of education.

Research and experimentation are values not only for teachers, but also for children. They are intrinsic elements of a pedagogy of relationships and listening, forming important means for theory building and testing: children 'want to do research for themselves, try, make mistakes, try again, marvel, understand, imitate now so as not to imitate later. They want to discover the causes and the relations between things and facts' (Cagliara *et al.*, 2016, p. 239). They do this, in Reggio Emilia's pedagogy, through the process of building or evolving a project, in which initial hypotheses are made, shared, listened to and contested, so modified and refined as the actual work progresses. This is the project as a pedagogical tool for combining experimentation and research.

The rich child with a hundred languages; learning as the co-construction of new knowledge; a pedagogy of relationships and listening; valuing democracy, inter-connectedness, uncertainty and wonder, experimentation and research – all these answers to political questions call in turn for a particular image of the teacher.

What is the image of the teacher?

The 'rich' child, an active subject co-constructing knowledge and identity, born a learner and with a hundred languages, requests a 'rich intelligence in others, rich curiosity in others, a very high and advanced capacity for fantasy, imagination, learning and culture in others' (ibid., p. 397). In short, the image of the rich child needs to be complemented by the image of the ***rich***

teacher: multi-lingual, since 'the hundred languages of the children have to become the hundred languages of the teacher' (Rinaldi, 2006, p. 195); and with a capacity for amazement and surprise, since 'to be capable of maintaining this gift of marvelling and wonder is a fundamental quality in a person working with children' (Cagliari *et al.*, 2016, p. 392).

An important task for this teacher is creating rich opportunities and environments for children and their learning, opportunities and environments where the unexpected and wonderful are more likely to occur. This understanding of the teacher's role is expressed by Aldo Fortunati, an Italian educator from another important local cultural project in the Tuscan town of San Miniato, part of that network of communes that took part in the Italian municipal school revolution:

> An active and constructive child stimulates the teachers to place more attention on the organisation of opportunities than on predefining objectives. . . . [The role of the teacher is] removed from the fallacy of certainties and [reassumes] the responsibility to choose, experiment, discuss, reflect, and change, focusing on the organisation of opportunities rather than the anxiousness to pursue outcomes, and maintaining in their work the pleasure of amazement and wonder.
>
> (Fortunati, 2006, pp. 34,38)

Note here the suspicion shared with Reggio Emilia of predefined objectives and of certainty and the same valuing of wonder and amazement.

Yet while this teacher does not impose herself on the child, is not a transmitter of predefined knowledge, neither is she[3] just a passive onlooker. Rather the teacher is a protagonist participating actively in the co-constructive learning process. Adults, Malaguzzi observes, 'have a permanent historical role in education, and so there is no pedagogy of *laissez faire* or letting things pass, or of cancelling the principles of reality for principles of pleasure' (Cagliari *et al.*, 2016, p. 223). Education is realised 'through processes where adult protagonisms and children's protagonisms fuse together', which means there should be no 'deference to children, whom it is presumed have their own development programme and must avoid contamination from any perspective' (ibid., p. 354). In a television interview towards the end of his life, Malaguzzi takes these points further:

> The project in our schools is one that aspires to giving the greatest value possible to the child, which means crediting children with resources, with talents and with potentials that are much richer than we think; and letting children represent themselves with the richness of their intelligence, of their languages, of their openness to things, in a way that above all is conducive to their capacity for self-direction, self-learning and self-organisation.

This absolutely does not mean excluding the role of the adult, who is capable of seeing, listening and understanding: of much listening, of introducing themselves into a state of permanent interaction with children; offering them learning situations of great diversity, in the sense of being able to give them time – and time is an extraordinarily important entity in a situation where everyone is robbing children of time.

(ibid., p. 412)

The teacher, then, is a listener, a creator of rich learning environments, a giver of time, a respecter of otherness. But the teacher must also be prepared to challenge, contest and confront children; to question their theories, to offer alternative possibilities, to provoke their thinking. For Malaguzzi, there is a balance that must be struck between 'the concept of total ungovernability on the one hand, which is a pedagogy of the contingent; and of absolute and total governability on the other, which is a pedagogy of necessity' (ibid., p. 318): in other words, neither simply responding all the time nor continually working towards predetermined outcomes.

The image of the teacher has other facets, shaped by Reggio Emilia's fundamental values. The importance of a democratic education calls for a ***democratic professional***, a teacher comfortable with working collaboratively and non-hierarchically with others; supportive of democratic methods of managing the school in all its aspects, pedagogical as well as administrative; someone who welcomes diversity, of values, of ideas, of understandings, and who, in the words of the Brazilian educationalist Paulo Freire (1921–1997), 'respect[s] positions opposed to my own, positions that I combat earnestly and with passion' (Freire, 2004, p. 66). The educator as democratic professional may offer her 'reading of the world', but at the same time her role is to 'bring out the fact that there are other "readings of the world", different from the one being offered as the educator's own, and at times antagonistic to it' (ibid., p. 96) – and that, therefore, there are political choices to be made. Three *pedagogistas* (workers with a psychology or pedagogy degree, each of whom supports a small group of municipal schools, and found in many Italian *comuni*) from Reggio Emilia put this clearly when they argue that

> participation, in fact, is based on the idea that reality is not objective, that culture is a constantly evolving product of society, that individual knowledge is only partial; and that in order to construct a project, especially an educational project, everyone's point of view is relevant in dialogue with those of others, within a framework of shared values. The idea of participation is founded on these concepts; and in our opinion, so, too, is democracy itself.
>
> (Cagliari, Barozzi and Giudici, 2004, pp. 28–29)

Last, but not least, the image of the teacher is as a ***researcher and experimenter***, embodying the values of research and experimentation but also practicing research and experimentation in their everyday work – though never as an isolated activity, but always in relationship with others. The municipal schools '[desire] pedagogical research as a permanent method realised together by teachers, auxiliary workers, families, citizens' (Cagliari *et al.*, 2016, p. 222), with research understood (to return to the words of Carlina Rinaldi) as 'a way of thinking, of approaching life, of negotiation, of documenting'.

When the rich child and the rich teacher come together, what sort of institution do they require and request? What is the image of this early childhood institution?

What is the image of the early childhood institution?

The first thing to stress is that the image of the early childhood institution in Reggio Emilia is a *school for young children* – not a substitute home nor a 'childcare' service nor a 'kindergarten'. Malaguzzi (and others who participated in the municipal school revolution in Italy) regarded terminology as crucial to creating a new image for the early childhood institution, contesting the term commonly used for church-run schools in 1960s Italy – the *scuola materna* or motherly school, with the image evoked of a substitute family and teachers as motherly figures[4] – and arguing instead for the term *scuola dell'infanzia*, school for young children.[5] By using this term, Malaguzzi insisted that Reggio Emilia's early childhood institutions were, first and foremost, for education and for children, not primarily places to park children while their parents were at work, not 'childcare' services, though school opening hours should, naturally, take account of parents' needs: 'our feeling is hours should be based on the principle that schools are offered as a social service for families as well as being tools for children's education. The time children spend in school must therefore be assessed in relation to real family situations' (Cagliari *et al.*, 2016, p. 212). Meeting the needs of working parents was, therefore, necessary, but not particularly interesting or central to the identity of schools.

The *scuola dell'infanzia* is understood to be a *public* institution and a *public* space, constituting a place of encounter between citizens, a forum and a community resource. It is in and of its neighbourhood and must be open to all citizens of that neighbourhood, parents certainly, but also others without young children, just as the neighbourhood should be open to children from the school.

> Schools (and the areas in which they are located) should identify opportunities for relations with the *territorio* [local area] as a source of inspiration, didactics and contents. Piazzas, streets, buildings, people's houses, cultural, recreational and sports institutions, monuments, shops, offices, rivers and woods, factories and places where men and women work all form a vast reading book that can orientate educational activities; and they are all there to be explored and done, where children, teachers,

parents and citizens can rediscover a new dimension, the genesis and history of their relations and behaviour, the reasons for their condition and the duality of culture. Then we will no longer have schools that are separate buildings with a modest yard as their outer boundary.

(ibid., pp. 228–229)

Given this basic image of the school, what are these institutions for? Clearly for education-in-its-broadest-sense, involving learning as an emancipatory process of meaning making and self-formation, but also paying attention to all aspects of children's health and well-being, a holistic view of education. But for Malaguzzi schools have other inter-related roles. They are, as I have already outlined, places of research and experimentation. Being open to all children and families, they are places for building inclusion, solidarity and community, not only within the school but between the school and its surrounding *territorio*. They are places where values and culture are both reproduced and created, their influence spreading beyond the school into the surrounding city: values such as democracy and solidarity, research and experimentation, and a culture of childhood, imbued with the image of the rich child and recognition of children's rights. And they are places for renewing and enacting democratic practice, a 'living centre of open and democratic culture, enriched and informed by social encounters' (ibid., p. 180).

Democracy runs through the everyday life and relationships in the school, in its management and in its relationship with families, who 'must be taken from a passive position as pure consumers of a service and brought to an active, direct presence and collaboration' (ibid., p. 113). This helps distinguish Reggio Emilia's schools from more traditional schools, giving them 'a democratic, open, anti-dogmatic, socialising profile' compared 'with an authoritarian, isolating, dogmatic, privatising nature' (ibid., p. 205). As this contrast suggests, Reggio Emilia's insistence on the early childhood institution as a school is also about reclaiming the image of school, turning away from a widely held negative image of the school as an isolated and enclosed space of control and constraint, and moving towards the school as an open place of emancipation and participation. Given the negative image of the school that still seems widespread today (that often shocked look among adults if you argue for young children's right to education in schools), Reggio Emilia's work of reclamation is unfinished.

Overall, then, the image is of a school as a place of many projects and possibilities, of unknown potentialities, of co-construction based on wide and complex interconnections. The school as a forum, a construction site, a workshop and a permanent laboratory – just some of the metaphors used by Carlina Rinaldi for this image of the rich school (Rinaldi, 2006). The school as a place of cooperation and solidarity, between children, all members of staff (teachers and others), parents and other citizens, but also itself as part of a network of cooperation and solidarity for mutual benefit. All this is the antithesis of the image of the school in the dominant discourses, as an enclosure where technologies can be applied for the effective production of predetermined outcomes and as a private business competing with others in the market place for the custom of individual parent-consumers.

Reggio Emilia: vocabulary, paradigm and conditions

Vocabulary

I have argued that Reggio Emilia can be understood as a local cultural project, the project being a community, in this case a city, taking on responsibility for the education of its young children. I have also suggested that it can be understood as offering an alternative narrative, a story of democracy, experimentation and potentiality so very different to the current dominant stories of quality and high returns and of markets. But it's not just that the storyline itself, the unfolding narrative, is very different. So, too, is the language used. These stories deploy very different vocabularies, a reminder of the power of language in how we construct meaning of the world – the constitutive role of language, the appreciation of which was at the heart of the 'linguistic turn' in Western philosophy in the mid-20th century.

The language of the dominant stories is instrumental, calculative and economistic, technical and managerial, dull and lifeless. It is replete with prosaic words such as 'evidence based' and 'programmes', 'quality' and 'outcomes', 'development' and 'learning goals' 'investment' and 'human capital', 'markets' and 'businesses', 'rating scales' and 'assessment systems', 'readying' and 'returns'. The language heard in Reggio Emilia's story is very different, more emotional, poetic, emancipatory and metaphorical, using words such as 'projects', 'potentialities' and 'possibilities'; 'uncertainty' and 'subjectivity', 'wonder' and 'surprise'; 'images', 'interpretations' and 'meaning making'; 'research' and 'experimentation', 'participation' and 'democracy'.

The point being made here is, again, not to tell you what vocabulary you should use, any more than I wish to tell you to which story you should subscribe. My take on language is personal, and you may well disagree. What I do want to do is to draw attention to the importance of language and the choices that can and should be made about what words to use. One of the problems of contesting dominant discourses is that it can seem so hard to imagine a different way of talking about early childhood education, a way in which words like 'quality', 'development' and 'readiness' don't crop up all the time, hijacking the narrative. But Reggio Emilia and further examples of alternatives to be given in the next three chapters demonstrate that we can talk about early childhood education in quite different ways. To return to this book's recurring theme: we have choices!

Paradigm

I hope it is clear from my discussion that Reggio Emilia offers a rich example of an education that acknowledges, openly and explicitly, political and ethical practice as first practice. The municipal schools understand that education confronts us with alternative and often conflicting answers to political questions and requires of us to decide what approach to relational ethics we choose to adopt. But what about my other earlier argument about the importance of paradigm, how it has a profound impact on how we see and understand things, not least education and knowledge? What paradigmatic position does Reggio Emilia take? How does it view the world?

In the book *Beyond Quality in Early Childhood Education and Care*, Gunilla Dahlberg, Alan Pence and I argue that Reggio Emilia has evolved a 'pedagogical practice located in a philosophical perspective which in many respects seems to us postmodern' (Dahlberg *et al.*, 2013, p. 129); in other words, it seemed to us that it was situated in a postfoundational paradigm. Subsequently, Carlina Rinaldi conceded that Reggio Emilia might be 'postmodern in its perspectives . . . because to be postmodern means to challenge'. But she added a major caveat: 'we are not for postmodernism, because "isms" are risky. Because they simplify and lock you in prison again' (Rinaldi, 2006, p. 182). A clear warning note sounded about Reggio Emilia's reluctance to attach labels to its project.

In *Beyond Quality in Early Childhood Education and Care*, we went on to argue that 'the Reggio experience and the work of Loris Malaguzzi . . . have challenged the dominant discourses of our time', calling in evidence for this statement how they have chosen 'to adopt a social constructionist approach' (Dahlberg *et al.*, 2013, pp. 128, 129), a claim more readily conceded by Reggio Emilia. We have already seen Carlina Rinaldi describe learning as a process of social construction. Here is Loris Malaguzzi looking back in 1990, four years before he died, on the experience and choices of the municipal schools.

> It is clear our choices have been in the direction of currents of thinking that define children first and foremost as disposed to and active in constructing the self and knowledge through social interactions and interdependencies: that as much as possible we have tried to hold together processes that are biological, political, cultural and – in the spirit of the times – also ecological. The webs of our inspiration connect up with constructivist and socio-constructivist theories; theories that generate a creative conception of development and knowledge.
>
> (Cagliari *et al.*, 2016, p. 377)

At the same time as Reggio Emilia has leant towards postmodernism and social constructionism, while avoiding partisan commitment, there has been a consistent questioning of the positivist paradigm, not least for its failure to address the complexity, inter-connectedness and uncertainty of life. Speaking in 1987 about new understandings of knowledge processes and ways of knowing, Malaguzzi identified himself with

> contemporary critiques and studies of positivist and post-positivist scientific theories, which for the whole of the nineteenth century and part of the twentieth, seemed committed to classifying, ordering, dividing and generalising the disciplines; to celebrating *laws* that were attributed with completeness, absoluteness, eternity, predictability, and the valued quality not only of being capable of guaranteeing research methods and results but also explaining and generalising phenomena.
>
> (ibid., p. 320; original emphasis)

Running through this statement, and much else in Reggio Emilia's project, is a deep distrust and distaste for positivism's desire to separate and to disconnect, and the value it attaches to linearity and continuity, universality and certainty, all in the interests of predictability and mastery.

Conditions

A final point about Reggio Emilia and its story of democracy, experimentation and potentiality. A theme of the *Contesting Early Childhood* series and indeed this book is that alternative stories, with their differing perspectives on early childhood education, can not only be told – they can also be enacted, that is they can be and are being put to work in practice. Examples will follow in later chapters, but Reggio Emilia is perhaps the most striking, both for its scope (a network of 40-plus schools) and duration (continuing for 50-plus years and still going strong). It provides a vivid exemplar of a **real utopia**, a concept that figures prominently in a book in the series, *Transformational Change and Real Utopias in Early Childhood Education: A Story of Democracy, Experimentation and Potentiality*.

The term 'real utopia' has been coined by the American sociologist Erik Olin Wright to describe utopian projects that combine three criteria: desirability, viability and achievability. Desirability is all about setting out a desirable vision of the future, envisaging how things could be done differently and better – what do we want? But this, for Wright, is the easy part of working with utopias, and not nearly good enough by itself. Real utopias need two extra ingredients: viability and achievability. Viability is about designing new policies and institutions based on desirable principles, and which respond

> to the perpetual objection to radical egalitarian proposals "it sounds good on paper, but it will never work". . . . [The exploration of viability focuses] on the likely dynamics and unintended consequences of the proposal if

it were to be implemented. Two kinds of analysis are especially pertinent here: systematic theoretical models of how particular social structures and institutions would work, and empirical studies of cases, both historical and contemporary, where at least some aspects of the proposal have been tried.

(Wright, 2007, p. 27)

Viability, then, is about being able to describe how a desirable vision might be realised, how you might do it in practice, with local cases providing one form of evidence. Achievability takes that to the next level, being about the process of widespread transformation and the practical political work of strategies for social change: 'It asks of proposals for social change that have passed the test of desirability and viability, what it would take to actually implement them' (ibid., p. 27) – how, for example, to pass from the isolated example to the regional or national level, what conditions might be needed to generalise the desirable vision. Wright argues that these three criteria are 'nested in a kind of hierarchy: Not all desirable alternatives are viable, and not all viable alternatives are achievable' (Wright, 2006, p. 96).

What Reggio Emilia offers is a strong contemporary case of viability for an alternative, radical education, and some elements of achievability – though limited because of its local nature. And here Reggio Emilia does offer a transferable lesson, that desirable visions can be made viable and possibly achievable if we combine vision with answering a key technical question: under what conditions is this vision achievable? This is what Reggio Emilia has brought off so impressively: an inspirational vision of children's education combined with an intense practicality. As a leading scholar of Reggio Emilia has commented:

> Many experiences or reforms have failed or are failing as a consequence of organizational adaptation to the [pedagogical] idea itself. Malaguzzi was able to seamlessly unite the ideas of a project with a strong organization that made its evolution possible. This organization is not neutral, but already the result of the selection of content and educational goals. . . . *The organization is a determining factor for the success of a project. Malaguzzi knew this very well.*
>
> (Hoyuelos, 2013, p. 216: emphasis added)

Space precludes going at great length into the conditions that have enabled the Reggio Emilia project to succeed, with one exception: they can be read about in detail elsewhere. For the moment, suffice it to say they involve paying detailed and consistent attention to: the built environment of the municipal schools, both inside and out; the continuing professional development of all workers and establishing good working conditions for them (including proper pay); building group working within the schools and providing strong external support to these groups through a team of *pedagogistas* and psychologists; the introduction of ateliers and *atelieristas* in the schools; creating a system of democratic social management for schools, involving the participation of representatives of workers and families; and the evolution of pedagogical documentation.

I will say more about **pedagogical documentation**, because it crops up in subsequent chapters, so merits a fuller introduction here. Pedagogical documentation can be described as a process of making processes (such as learning) and practices (such as project work) visible and therefore subject to reflection, dialogue, interpretation and critique. It involves, therefore, both documentation itself through the production and selection of varied material (e.g. photographs, videos, tape recordings, notes, children's work etc.) *and* discussion and analysis of this documentation in a rigorous, critical and democratic way – always in relationship with others. It represents, writes Spanish *atelierista* Alfredo Hoyuelos,

> an extraordinary tool for dialogue, for exchange, for sharing. For Malaguzzi it means the possibility to discuss and to dialogue 'everything with everyone' (teachers, auxiliary staff, cooks, families, administrators and citizens). . . . [S]haring opinions by means of documentation presupposes being able to discuss, real, concrete things – not just theories or words, about which it is possible to reach easy and naïve agreement.
>
> (Hoyuelos, 2004, p. 7)

This 'extraordinary tool' can serve a range of purposes: continuing professional development for teachers; fostering participation by families and communities in the work of the schools; research, especially into learning processes; participatory evaluation; and, as we shall see in the next chapter, enabling the deconstruction of dominant discourses as a prelude to constructing new discourses. Documentation assumes that everyone can participate, including children themselves, and that everyone will bring their own perspectives to the table, perspectives that are necessarily subjective, partial and provisional but nevertheless valuable; and perspectives that can be questioned and contested by others, a process leading to the co-construction of new perspectives, new understandings, new knowledge.

Two final words on this subject. I have emphasised the importance of subjectivity, both as an epistemological concept (i.e. we cannot know the social world objectively, only from our own perspective) and as a value (i.e. the great importance of individual perspectives as an expression of otherness and diversity). But if subjectivity is to fulfil its potential and not deteriorate into sloppy thinking and, worse, bias and prejudice, then it needs to be rigorous; it needs to be what Patti Lather calls 'rigorous subjectivity'. In other words, our views, our interpretations, our understandings need to be shared with others and made subject to questioning and contestation, potentially leading to reconsideration and new perspectives.

Second, as Gunilla Dahlberg emphasises in *Beyond Quality in Early Childhood Education and Care*, pedagogical documentation should not be confused with 'child observation'. The latter, she argues, is a 'technology of normalisation', whose purpose 'is to assess children's psychological development in relation to already predetermined categories produced from developmental psychology and which define what the normal child should be at a particular age' (Dahlberg *et al.*, 2013, p. 146). Pedagogical documentation, by contrast, 'is mainly about trying to see and understand what is going on in the pedagogical work and what the child is capable of without any predetermined framework of expectations and norms'. Moreover, it makes no claim to objective truth, to being a correct representation of reality, but instead acknowledges inescapable subjectivity, starting with the choice of what to document, and the co-construction of meaning; we are, says Gunilla Dahlberg, 'a long way from the idea of child observation as a true record, an actual representation of the child and his or her development' (*ibid.*, p. 147).

What emerges here, from pedagogical documentation and other organisational conditions that have been put in place over the years in Reggio Emilia, is what has been termed a ***competent system***, which is a system of

> reciprocal relationships between individuals, teams, institutions and the wider socio-political context . . . [that provides] support for individuals to realise their capability to develop responsible and responsive practices that respond to the needs of children and families in ever-changing societal contexts.
> (Urban, Vandenbroeck, Lazzari, Van Larer and Peeters, 2012, p. 21)

Such a system includes inter-connected organisational features that can strengthen and sustain a complex and demanding early childhood education, an education of uncertainty and wonder. Combine a good story with the good conditions of a competent system, and there is no limit to what may be achieved.

Reggio Emilia has connected up a number of elements to create an important alternative narrative, the whole local project based on an understanding of education as a political practice. Woven into that narrative and shaping the way the story is told are many influences, historical and contemporary, from a variety of disciplines and individuals – a 'multitude of perspectives and debates'. In the next three chapters, I turn my attention from an educational project that demonstrates that there are other pedagogical stories to be told in order to explore some philosophical perspectives that, though not directly about education, are nevertheless helping to shape thinking and practice in early childhood education, stimulating and enhancing alternative pedagogical stories. They might be thought of as examples of the rich raw material available to those who want to question dominant discourses and compose their own narratives.

Questions – yours and mine

Don't forget to share and discuss the questions you have after reading this chapter, including the ones I suggested at the end of Chapter 1.

Here, though, are some of my questions to you:

- Do you know of other local cultural projects (in a centre, a community, a country) that have evolved through innovative pedagogical work?
- What do you like about the early childhood education in Reggio Emilia? Do you have reservations or dislikes?
- Malaguzzi wrote that in 1945 he and others felt that 'everything seemed possible'. Do you feel that way today? If not, why do you think that is?
- Can you name and discuss some of the hundred languages of childhood? Try to name ten for starters.
- Take one of the political questions set out in this chapter and the political choice made by Reggio Emilia in response to the question. How do you respond to that choice? What would your political choice be?

Notes

1 These names only scratch the surface of individuals whose work Malaguzzi knew and admired; he read prodigiously. At a conference towards the end of his life, in 1993, he discussed how

> our references go from Piaget's genetic epistemology (but not the pedagogical interpretations that have been made to derive from it) to experimental theories of complexity: from Morin to Varela, Bateson to Von Foerster and Prigogine, from Mugny to Doise and Moscovici. And never ever forgetting Dewey, Wertheimer, Wallon, Claparède, Vygotsky, Bronfenbrenner, Hawkins, Arnheim, Gombrich, Papert, H. Gardner; and for the area of the neurosciences Edelman, Rosenfield, Levi Montalcini, Dulbecco and others we will mention later.
>
> (Cagliari *et al.*, 2016, p. 377)

2 In a speech in 1991, Malaguzzi talks about 'the problem of stages'. He continues:

> Let us take them and throw them out of the window. Perhaps we do not have time to speak ill of stages today, but there are several aspects here to convince us that breaking flow into stages means submitting to the rules of the municipal police. But we will not be subjected.
>
> (ibid., p. 409)

3 I use 'she' here because early childhood teachers, and other workers, are overwhelmingly female, even in Reggio Emilia, and despite Malaguzzi being an advocate of more male

teachers, to the extent even of challenging the Italian state, which in the early days of Reggio's schools forbad male workers in early childhood services.

4 This terminology survives today in France, where schools for 3- to 6-year-olds are still called *écoles maternelles*.

5 The term 'scuola dell'infanzia' is applied in Reggio Emilia to schools for children from 3- to 6-years-old; schools for children under 3 years are called 'asilo nido' (literally, a protective nest). I use the term 'scuola dell'infanzia' to refer to both types of school.

Chapter 5

Michel Foucault

Power, knowledge and truth

Michel Foucault (1926–1984) was a French philosopher, historian of ideas, social theorist and literary critic. He undertook specific studies of madness, health, crime, sexuality, knowledge and identity, but not of education – though there are references to education and the school throughout his work. So why include him in a book on early childhood education?

Because of his ideas or perspectives on power, and its relationship to knowledge and truth, and indeed to subjectivity – our identity, who we think we are. These perspectives have attracted increasing interest among those working in early childhood education, in particular for the insights they offer into the governing of both children and adults through processes of steering and shaping thought, talk, action and subjectivity. And though his analyses of power reveal its pervasive and insidious nature, a prospect that may leave the reader at times feeling disheartened, his work also considers how power may be contested, offering hope of resistance and change if we can bring critical thought to bear.

I shall end the chapter with two exemplars, one from Australia, the other from Sweden, of people working with Foucauldian concepts and ideas in early childhood education. The Australian exemplar is one of several such accounts contained in a book in the *Contesting Early Childhood* series by Glenda MacNaughton, whose title speaks to the relevance of Michel Foucault to early childhood education – *Doing Foucault in Early Childhood Studies: Applying Poststructural Ideas* (MacNaughton, 2005). I shall draw extensively on Glenda's work in this chapter, since she provides ample evidence of the relevance of Foucault to early childhood education and to the early childhood students whom she has taught.

Power, knowledge and truth

The focus of Foucault's thinking about power is relationships, and more specifically on the ubiquitous and inescapable presence of power relations. These relations are everywhere, and we can never be outside power – by which Foucault means we all participate in power relations, through which we are subjected to power by others but also exercise power on others; none of us can claim to be exempt. For in human relations

> whatever they are – whether it be a question of communicating ver-bally . . . or a question of a love relationship, an institutional or economic relationship – power is always present: *I mean the relationship in which one wishes to direct the behaviour of another.*
>
> (Foucault, 1987, p. 11; emphasis added)

For Foucault, therefore, we are all involved in the exercise of power, we are all trying to effect change in others, 'to direct the behaviour of another'. Of course, this may have good results. Foucault did not consider power to be necessarily bad or harmful, it may be productive and in a positive way. But it also means that we should not be naïve. Power is not something that some people exert over the rest of us, the world is not divided between those with and without power. We are all implicated in power relations.

Power, then, is local and diffuse. But this is not to say that all have equal power. There are great disparities in power relations, between individual and individual and between institutional power and the individual. Foucault was interested in how such institutional power – for instance, the power of gov-ernment and other organisations – operated, how it was effective. Central to his thinking was the ability of the more powerful to impose their ways of understanding, their perspectives, their view of things, their truths on others: for Foucault,

> power is a relationship of struggle to dominate the meanings we give to our lives. It is a battle to authorise the truth, because truths don't just happen, they are produced in our struggle to decide the meanings of our actions, thoughts and feelings.
>
> (MacNaughton, 2005, p. 22)

We are back here to Foucault's concept of 'dominant discourses', intro-duced in Chapter 1, the way that certain perspectives or stories claim to be the only way to think, talk and behave about a particular topic, subject or field, for instance the story of the Emperor's New Clothes, but also what I have termed the story of neoliberalism or, in early childhood education, the story of quality and high returns and the story of markets. Such dominant discourses think, talk and act as if they represent the incontrovertible truth, as if they provide the only valid meaning, as if they are the authorised version on the topic in hand: they act, to use another term coined by Foucault, as ***regimes of truth***. This usually happens once a particular discourse, or story, gets taken up by the powers that be, those institutions that exert great influ-ence on individuals, like the Emperor in Hans Christian Andersen's story or today's more mundane governing bodies. Glenda MacNaughton describes the process in the following terms:

> Truths about, for instance, normal gender development or normal sexuality resonate more powerfully in us and through us when they are institutionally produced and sanctioned. In Foucault's terms, institutionally produced and sanctioned truths govern and regulate us. . . . *Each field of knowledge, such as early childhood studies, health care or social work, expands by developing officially sanctioned truths that govern normal and desirable ways to think, feel and act.* For instance, the field of early childhood studies has grown through developing sets of truths about the normal and desirable way to be a child and an early childhood educator that are sanctioned and systematised by government, by professional associations and by the academy.
>
> (ibid., pp. 29–30; emphasis added)

Bearing in mind the distinction drawn earlier between natural science and social science and between facts and knowledge, Foucault is talking about there being different truths about knowledge in the social sciences, about the meanings that we give to the world, different meanings that reflect differences in position, perspective and interest among knowers. Given then that all such knowledge is partial and perspectival, the question is whose meanings or knowledges get to count and become accepted (widely, though not necessarily universally) as true, what regime of truth comes to govern a certain topic or field; which discourse dominates. How, in short, do 'some things come to count as true' (Ball, 2016, p. 1132).

Here we can pick up on the discussion from Chapter 2 about how, viewed from a postfoundational perspective, there is a tight and inescapable relationship between power and knowledge of the social world, a symbiotic relationship in which power feeds off certain knowledges while they in turn gain standing (and resources for further development) from their usefulness to power. Glenda MacNaughton again:

> Poststructuralists argue that it is impossible to have 'undistorted' knowledge free from the interests of the people it serves. Knowledge can never be free from ideology, because all knowledge is biased, incomplete and linked to the interests of specific groups of people. . . . [Poststructuralists] see the production of knowledge as a politically competitive endeavour in which different views about the world vie for power and the status of being the 'real' (or universal) truth about it. Poststructuralists challenge the idea that we can ever find the real truth about anything in our social world. For instance, they challenge the idea that we can discover or learn the real truth about young children's development and about good (and

bad) early childhood pedagogies. Instead, they believe that our knowledge about the world is inherently and inevitably contradictory, rather than rational, and, consequently, that many different truths about the child and about early childhood pedagogy are possible.

(ibid., p. 22)

Or put slightly differently, there are many different stories we can tell about children and early childhood education. But despite this diversity of possibilities, if we are not very careful one story or discourse will come to dominate and constitute a 'regime of truth', consisting of claims to real or true knowledge and best practice that are passed off as neutral (value-free), natural (incontrovertible) and, therefore, self-evidently (uncontestably) correct. This regime of truth 'generates an authoritative consensus about what needs to be done in that field and how it should be done' (ibid., p. 29).

Foucault, therefore, offers an understanding of how power works, both at the micro-level, through everyday power relations in which we are all involved, and through the effects of dominant discourses with their regimes of truth that assert that they are the one and only way to think, talk and behave. But he goes further by considering the ways in which institutional power actually operates on and through us. I will consider two of these now: discipline and governmentality.

Disciplinary power

Foucault identifies and analyses a fundamental shift in the exercise of institutional or state power, dating back as far as the 16th century. That shift involved a gradual movement from the sovereignty of the ruler, the absolute monarch, exercised through brute force, physical compulsion and fear, to a less violent but more effective form of governing populations, steering people in the desired direction without resort to violent coercion. This move was associated with a new goal of government, to maximise the productive potential of the whole population and hence the wealth of the nation, what Foucault termed 'bio-power': 'an explosion of numerous and diverse techniques for achieving the subjugation of bodies and the control of populations' (Foucault, 1978, p. 140), but in such a way as to minimise resistance.

These 'numerous and diverse techniques' were termed 'disciplines' by Foucault. Glenda MacNaughton lists several in her book, alongside examples of their application to early childhood education:

Surveillance: being – or expecting to be – closely observed and supervised in and through reference to particular truths. For example, an early childhood educator who expects to be observed and supervised by people who believe that high quality early childhood pedagogy equals developmentally appropriate practice will act in developmentally appropriate ways. [As another example, I have also instanced earlier the growing use of 'dataveillance' – surveillance via the collection and analysis of data – in 21st-century English early childhood education].

Normalisation: comparing, invoking, requiring or conforming to a standard that expresses particular truths about, for example, the developing child. For instance, observing children and comparing their behaviours with developmental norms.

Exclusion: using truths to establish the boundaries of what is normal, to include or exclude particular ways of being as desirable or undesirable and, in doing so, to define pathology. For instance, an early childhood educator who uses developmental truths will see non-developmental truths as inappropriate or wrong and exclude them.

Classification: using truths to differentiate between groups or individuals. For instance, an early childhood educator will talk about normal or delayed development by classifying children according to their stage of development.

Distribution: using specific truths to decide how to arrange and rank people in space. For instance, an early childhood educator will use developmental truths to assign children to different groups according to their stage of development.

Individualisation: using truths to separate individuals. For instance, an early childhood educator will use developmental truths to separate the individual children who are developing normally and those who are not.

Totalisation: using truths to produce a will to conform. For instance, an early childhood educator will use developmental truths to guide decisions about what all children should be like or should do at a given point in their life – e.g. all children should leave kindergarten able to tie their shoelaces.

Regulation: using specific truths to control ways of thinking and being by involving rules and limiting behaviours – often through sanctions or rewards. For instance, an early childhood educator will use developmental truths to decide the rules of behaviour that are appropriate for children at specific ages and stages of development, such as all children eighteen months of age need to sleep during the day.

(ibid., pp. 30–32)

Of these instances of disciplinary power, perhaps normalisation is the most fundamental. Establishing what is 'normal', what is the standard, what is expected is a central theme of many dominant discourses, and achieving the norm the goal of institutional or state power. Other disciplines, such as classification or exclusion, are means to that end. Disciplines, it could be said, determine what is normal, then apply techniques to shape individuals towards that norm and to assess if they have achieved conformity to norm.

Reverting to the discussion of ethics in Chapter 3, they are all techniques for 'grasping' the Other and making the Other into the Same, fitting the Other into a dominant matrix of standards and categories that becomes the predetermined outcome that all must strive to achieve and against which all are assessed.

Working with this Foucauldian frame, we can understand early childhood services, as well as schools, as having a particular image with a particular purpose in the story of quality and high returns: to act as enclosures where children can be efficiently and effectively subjected to disciplinary power, in order to achieve institutional norms, be it developmental stages, learning goals or standards of school readiness. Rather than asking what a child can or might be able to do, we ask can this child meet the norm, the desired outcome? Is this child 'normal'?

The different techniques of disciplinary power are exercised by the application of 'human technologies' such as those in modern day early childhood education that were discussed in Chapter 1. Foucault himself did not address himself to early education but does give a vivid example of how disciplinary power was deployed in the 19th-century French classroom through the human technology of the organisation of space and materials. In that environment, desks were arranged in a rectangle to form a single great table, under the constant surveillance of the teacher, who set performance standards, assessed pupils and moved their position on the table as performance improved or declined, a constant exercise of normalisation, classification, distribution and exclusion.

Governmentality

I have so far discussed how power works to shape and direct thinking and behaviour and achieve its desired results. It uses knowledges to construct dominant discourses, stories about a subject or topic that claim to be true, and therefore natural, neutral and necessary, and that marginalise or simply ignore other stories. It deploys disciplinary practices, working through human technologies, to control, govern and achieve compliance to the discourse.

But power also works in another, more insidious, way, what Foucault terms 'governmentality', by which he means how we come to embody the dominant discourse so that we govern ourselves according to its beliefs and assumptions, its desires and practices: in other words, how the dominant discourse or story becomes *our* story, its truth *our* truth, its desires *our* desires. Human technologies 'with aspirations for the shaping of conduct in the hope of producing certain desired effects' are still there, indeed are more potent than ever; but equally, if not more important, we discipline ourselves in the service of these 'desired effects'.

In the first book in the *Contesting Early Childhood* series, *Ethics and Politics in Early Childhood Education*, Gunilla Dahlberg and I introduced this concept of governmentality in which we govern ourselves through dominant discourses.

> [Dominant discourses] organise our everyday experience of the world, influencing our ideas, thoughts and actions. They exercise power over our thought by governing what we see as the 'truth', what we accept as rational and how we construct the world – and hence our acting and doing. Or rather, since we are inscribed in dominant discourses *we govern ourselves* through dominant discourses, *acting upon ourselves rather than being directly acted upon*. . . . So rather than an external force dictating to us, discipline often acts, discipline often operates through the *self govern- ing the self*. . . .
>
> Governmentality [therefore] refers to the way in which people and populations come to be governed or managed not through external coer- cion, but by more subtle and more effective practices. These practices work directly *on* us, steering us towards desired behaviour. But they also work *through* us, acting on our innermost selves, reaching to the inner- most qualities of being human: our spirit, motivations, wishes, desires, beliefs, dispositions, aspirations and attitudes. So though we are directly governed, the most important effect is that we govern ourselves – conduct of our own conduct – in ways that conform to the dominant regime.
>
> (Dahlberg and Moss, 2005, pp. 18–19; emphasis added)

The insidious nature of governmentality is its capacity to 'act on our inner- most selves', so we actually desire what the dominant discourse desires; its wishes are our wishes.

Lynn Fendler, an American professor of teacher education, provides a vivid example of this process of self-government: the influence exerted by develop- mental psychology in early childhood education on children and adults alike. Like Glenda MacNaughton and others, Lynn Fendler takes a critical attitude towards developmental psychology and associated concepts like 'developmen- tally appropriate', arguing that its findings or truths are not questioned or tested but unquestioningly accepted to form the basis for curriculum, assess- ment and practice. In this way, norms are established within a dominant concept of 'development' and 'the lives of individual children are evaluated with reference to that norm' (Fendler, 2001, p. 128). Fendler calls this a 'tech- nology of normalisation', a technology she terms 'developmentality' as a 'way of alluding to Foucault's governmentality, and focusing on the self-governing effects of developmental discourse in curriculum debates. Developmentality, like governmentality, *describes a current pattern of power in which the self disci- plines the self*' (ibid., p. 120; emphasis added).

In this way both children and adults govern themselves by aspiring to certain developmental norms, which are an 'analytical generalisation [that] takes precedence over the broad range of variations'. A generalised norm of developmental stages takes no account of culture or context, let alone individual difference, and leads us once again to the situation of measuring if a child can do a, b or c rather than striving to understand what it is that a particular child can actually do. Not surprisingly, given his perspective, Loris Malaguzzi was very critical of this norm, calling it the 'problem of stages' and urging their abandonment: 'Let us take them and throw them out of the window' (Cagliari *et al.*, 2016, p. 409). Rather than a regular, linear and sequential process of development, complete with normative stages, Malaguzzi speaks of an unpredictable and complex process of evolution: 'The unceasing evolution [of children] is not regular, we say it is *a-rhythmic* and *discontinuous*. Radically distinct stages do not exist in the children's evolution, neither is there a uniform, regular progress, as if we were simply dealing with quantitative growth' (ibid., p. 74). We can see Malaguzzi here resisting developmentality, refusing to be governed by the concept and associated norms of developmental psychology.

The insidious exercise of power through governmentality, this way that dominant discourses end up 'governing the soul'[1] by shaping our desires and aspirations, has a further effect: the capacity to shape not only our thought and behaviour but our subjectivity, working on our very sense of self, our identity, who we think we are. The relationship here is not just between power and truth but power, truth and self. Stephen Ball locates this relationship today within the wider context of a dominant neoliberal regime, which seeks to create individuals who are ideal neoliberal subjects, each expected to assume the identity of *homo economicus*, a self who is autonomous and self-managing, calculating and competitive, flexible and entrepreneurial. Consequently, subjectivity is 'a key site of political struggle in the context of neoliberalisation and neoliberal governmentality. . . . The question is what kind of self, what kind of subject have we become, and how might we be otherwise?' (Ball, 2016, pp. 1130, 1133).

To bring this back to my previous argument. If the story of quality and high returns tells of the necessity for the effective application of human technologies if defined objectives are to be achieved and high returns delivered, then the early childhood educator will not only govern herself to these ends. She must also come to understand herself, her subjectivity, her image, as a technician, highly skilled and conscientious no doubt, but nevertheless essentially an applier of technologies in the service of normalising children.

What can we do?

I warned earlier that Foucault's analysis of power and power relations could leave the reader feeling disheartened, struggling with a sense of powerlessness when confronted by the pervasive, insidious and deeply embedded forces of regimes of truth and the potent alliance of disciplines and governmentality.

But Foucault himself is not hopeless. He thinks that resistance and change are possible.

In the first place, dominant discourses, those expressions of institutional power, may be hegemonic, exercising a very strong influence and authority – but they never have the field entirely to themselves; they are never uncontestable and they are never uncontested. The dictatorship of no alternative that they try to be always faces opposition, people prepared to question regimes of truth and to insist that there are alternatives. They form what I termed, in Chapter 1, the resistance movement. For Foucault, resistance was inherent within relations of power, otherwise the relationship was simply one of master and slave. He stressed the importance and possibility of resistance and freedom in his later writings and interviews; he believed in the power of struggle and personally engaged in activism throughout his life both as a public intellectual and a private individual (Butin, 2001).

Three related strategies are of particular importance in resisting power: critique or critical thinking; deconstruction; and care of the self. Nor are these only means of resisting. They can also serve as means for creating something different.

British sociologist Nikolas Rose has a particularly vivid image of *critical thinking*:

> [It is] partly a matter of introducing a critical attitude towards those things that are given to our present experience as if they are timeless, natural, unquestionable. . . . It is a matter of introducing a kind of awkwardness into the fabric of one's experience, of interrupting the fluency of the narratives that encode that experience and make them stutter.
>
> (Rose, 1999, p. 20)

I like the images conjured up here. Being part of the awkward squad; asking questions all the time, in particular that favourite of 2-year-olds, 'Why?'; putting a spoke in the wheels that carry dominant stories forwards so smoothly and fluently; and making these same stories stutter when confronted by questions and scepticism about their claims to be timeless and natural. Foucault himself describes the process of critique as 'a matter of pointing out on what kinds of assumptions, [on] what kinds of familiar, unchallenged, unconsidered modes of thought the practices we accept rest' (Foucault, 1988b, p. 154). Or, to put matters a little differently, making visible the political choices that have been made and the reasoning behind these choices, especially when storytellers pretend there is no politics in their story, which also means unravelling and making visible the power interests and relationships that make a certain discourse dominant, that give a particular narrative its privileged position.

One aid to critical thinking is *deconstruction*, a concept and practice mainly associated with a French poststructural language theorist, Jacques

Derrida (1930–2004). Glenda MacNaughton offers an introduction to deconstruction:

> We can glimpse its meaning by looking at its two parts: 'de' (implies reversal or removal) and 'construct' (meaning to put something together). To deconstruct something is to take it apart, to 'unconstruct'. . . . [I]t refers to taking apart concepts and meanings in texts to show the politics of meaning within them. . . . [D]econstruction questions the meanings of words or concepts (ideologies, practices, texts) that are normally unquestioned. . . . It exposes the internal contradictions in particular systems of thought to question who benefits and how from the assumptions about our social world embedded in those systems of thought. As such, it helps us to scrutinise how our language choices fix power relations in specific regimes of truth.
>
> (MacNaughton, 2005, pp. 77, 78; emphasis added)

It is, if you like, a process of looking beneath the surface to what lies behind the veneer of fine words and confident assertions and asking awkward questions. Why the use of certain words and concepts – for example, in the story of quality and high returns, words like' quality', 'investment', 'returns', 'programmes', 'human capital' etc.? The tellers of this story chose these terms rather than others, so what do these language choices tell us about how they see the world, young children and early education? What values and assumptions do they express? Who gains from the choice of language, and how does this work? What political choices have been made, albeit implicitly? What, in short, is going on here?

But as MacNaughton points out, deconstruction is not just about criticising. It can also open us up to alternatives, to other ways of thinking, to wanting change, to 'a politics of possibilities' as we are 'drawn to "wonder" what other ways might be'. Because if we can shake ourselves free of a 'regime of truth', a dominant discourse, which insists there is only one way to think, see and do, we are open to other discourses, alternative stories, new ways of thinking, seeing and doing. Returning to the case of Reggio Emilia, Gunilla Dahlberg argues that the city's local cultural project was enabled by a process of deconstruction that preceded a process of reconstruction:

> What is so terribly impressive and exceptional about the Reggio experience and the work of Loris Malaguzzi is the way they have challenged the dominating discourses of our time, specifically in the field of early childhood pedagogy – a most unique undertaking for a pedagogical practice! This was achieved by deconstructing the way in which the field has been socially constituted within a scientific, political and ethical context and then reconstructing and redefining children's and teachers' subjectivities. That is, they have tried to understand what kinds of thoughts,

conceptions, ideas, social structures and behavioural patterns have dominated the field and how these discourses have shaped our conceptions
and images of the child and childhood, the way we interact with children
and the kind of environment we create for them.

(Dahlberg, 2000, p. 178)

In other words, to build something new in early childhood education, Reggio Emilia had first to deconstruct the regimes of truth that constrained what
they could think, say and do.

Towards the end of his life, Foucault consciously shifted his work from an
emphasis on technologies of discipline and domination – how power acts on
us – to an emphasis on 'technologies of the self' or '*care of the self*' (Ball,
2013). Now he was attaching more importance to how it may be possible
to constitute ourselves: that is, to the ways in which each of us can, in our
everyday lives, struggle against the effects of power on identity, and on how
we may construct our own sense of identity, of who we are, working on our
own subjectivity, on constituting our selves, since in Foucault's words 'the self
is not given to us, we have to constitute ourselves as a work of art'. We could
equate this with the discussions in the last chapter about the image of the
child or educator. Do we assume someone else's image, or do we struggle to
constitute, to create our own image?

Foucault, therefore, comes eventually to a view of the subject that finds a
place for both external forces and personal agency, so that the subject is

> both constituted and self-constituting in the relationships between dis-
> cursive practices (that determine what counts as true or false) and power-
> relations (the rationalities and techniques by which one governed the
> conduct of others) and ethics (the practices of self through which an
> individual constitutes itself as a subject).
>
> (Ball, 2013, p. 143)

Notice here how Foucault brings 'ethics' into his account, a practice of relational ethics, here meaning how one works on or cares for the self – care of
the self being an important part of the ethics of care discussed in Chapter 3.

Stephen Ball explores this issue further, arguing that if 'power acts upon
us in and through our subjectivity, then that is where our resistance and
struggle to be free should be focused' (Ball, 2013, p. 126). In an article titled
'Subjectivity as a Site of Struggle: Refusing Neoliberalism?', he uses the experience of several school teachers 'who attempt to wrest [their] self-formation
from the techniques of government and to make [themselves] intelligible in
different terms . . . thinking about how one is now and how one might be
different' (Ball, 2016, pp. 1135, 1136). These are teachers wanting to take
back more control of their own identities, of who and what they are, of their
sense of self.

The teachers in this example undertake this 'care of the self', the activity of shaping our own subjectivity, through the technique of what Foucault terms 'self-writing', a 'technology of the self' taking various forms. For the teachers in Ball's case, the forms of self-writing they practice include blogs, a thesis, conference papers and emails exchanged with Stephen Ball himself. Such writing becomes an act of what Foucault calls 'reflective indocility', of constituting the self as a work of art, of forming one's own subjectivity and freeing the self from an imposed subjectivity, someone else's image of who you are; at its simplest, this may mean the teacher resisting attempts to constitute her as a technician, someone whose job is to efficiently apply human technologies to predetermined ends, and instead exploring other possible identities and their meaning in practice. Returning to the idea of resistance, this is (in Ball's term) the exercise of 'the politics of refusal', a refusal both 'of the categories and norms which seek to represent us' and a 'renunciation of our "intelligible self" and a willingness to test and transgress the limits of who we are able to be' (ibid., p. 13) – so both refusal and exploration of alternatives. We could see this resistance as a political practice, involving an explicit political choice in response to the question 'What is your image of the teacher?'

By adopting a disposition to critical thinking and applying methods like deconstruction and care of the self, by not taking discourses and imposed subjectivities for granted but questioning and analysing them, we can disrupt regimes of truth, show that stories that claim to be fact are really fictions – and by such resistance, free ourselves to explore and produce different stories, to think differently and, as night follows day, come to desire change. Foucault puts the sequence of events vividly when he describes critical thinking as

> a matter of flushing out . . . thought and trying to change it: to show that things are not as self-evident as one believed, to see that that which is accepted as self-evident will no longer be accepted as such. Practising criticism is a matter of making facile gestures difficult. . . . *As soon as one no longer thinks things as one formerly thought them, transformation becomes very urgent, very difficult and quite possible.*
> (Foucault, 1988a, p. 155; emphasis added)

This is one of my favourite pieces by Foucault, for its directness, its confidence and its hope. For understood in this way, exercising freedom is the 'art of not being governed so much' by power (Foucault, 1990, p. 29) and in this way being able to think and speak for yourself, to explore and construct your meanings, your interpretations, your understandings of early childhood education and your identity and place within it. It is about asking not only 'Why?', but 'What if?' and 'How?'. It is about opening to alternative narratives and a multitude of perspectives and debates.

Doing Foucault in early childhood education: two cases

'I began to question my right to know the child'

I end this chapter with two cases of people working with Foucauldian concepts and ideas in early childhood education. What both have in common is making power and its effects visible and subject to scrutiny, through critical thinking and deconstruction, while at the same time exploring and constituting new possibilities. The first, drawn from Glenda MacNaughton's book, is a first-hand account by Kylie Smith from Australia, who at the time of writing was director of an early childhood centre in Melbourne and studying with Glenda.

From *Doing Foucault in Early Childhood Studies*, pp. 57–60

Critical reflection for me is about being ever vigilant in examining and making visible my subjectivities. I bring my unconscious to the conscious by asking myself why I speak and act in the ways I do and what are the effects for the people around me. The question I continually ask myself is: 'In whose best interests am I speaking and acting?'. Critical reflection for me is about taking time to locate and recognise the political, social and historical construction of the discourses I circulate. It is about recognising the discourses that I am drawn to and what is seductive about those discourses while I resist or silence other discourse. . . .

[Michel Foucault, Jennifer Gore, Gilles Deleuze and Bronwyn Davies] provide me with information about the construction of knowledge and with understandings of where that knowledge came from and why. This helps me to explore the political, historical and social construction of knowledge. Each time I read or reread a piece of theory it supports my critical reflection on whose knowledge informs my work and what the effects of different ways of understanding my work are for parents, colleagues and children. Further their theory draws me to consider the effects of my practice for children and parents and it supports me to be political by exploring these effects in order to critique my taken-for-granted truths that emerge within my taken-for-granted practices. . . .

I began to turn my gaze on myself when I began to read how Foucault believed that institutions used observation as a disciplinary apparatus. . . . I thought about how I turn my gaze on the child and how I turn parents' and other early childhood professionals' gazes on the child. I reflected that I do this so I can use their comments and my own knowledge to know the child. Using Foucault's challenging idea that 'observation is a disciplinary apparatus' I began to question my right to know the child. There are thoughts, questions, dreams and imaginings that I keep within myself that I have never shared with even the closest people in my life. Yet, I turn my gaze on the child expecting to know all of her. . . . I began to consider how I might see my practice differently by turning the gaze within to illuminate my subjectivities and their effects for children, parents and colleagues.

I can pinpoint the exact moment I began to critically reflect drawing on these ideas. I was outside in the playground at the centre talking with [a colleague] about the collection of data in her action research project that day. I had begun reading [Foucault's book] *Discipline and Punish: The Birth of the Prison* and was engaging with Foucault's idea of 'regimes of truth'. I had begun to consider how he used concepts of normalisation, surveillance, regulation, categorisation and totalisation [see pages 92–93] to explore how truth and power operate to limit and govern what we do and say and I began to see links between these ideas and the practices of observing children. While talking about these ideas and the issues emerging from the classroom . . . I suddenly thought that if the 'regimes of truth' circulate within my observation of the child what does that mean for parents?

I began to critically reflect on what observation means for parents by asking the question: 'How do I normalise and regulate parents' knowledge and practice?' Using this question I began to cast a shadow over my relationship with parents. I had always believed that I worked collaboratively with the parents who fit in my white middle-class understandings of the world. For the parents that didn't fit into this framework I worked to teach them what they needed to do to support their child, the teacher and the service so that they were seen as 'the good parent' rather than the 'difficult parent' or the 'parent who didn't understand'. . . .

The effects of using [poststructuralist] theorists to critically reflect are many. My relationships with parents and children have changed. I have less certainty that there is one correct answer. . . . Conversations now are about dialogue between people . . . [which is] about sharing questions, ideas, dilemmas and desires. . . . I no longer have the truth about the child, the parent or my own pedagogy. The effects of this uncertainty shift everyday. On some days, the uncertainty is liberating as I can explore possibilities rather than conform to the image of the good teacher. I learn about ideas, interests, beliefs and lived experiences that I knew nothing about . . . I ask questions rather than make knowing assessments and statements about the children and their actions . . . [which] become a basis for reflection and action. . . . However, some days uncertainty is problematic and frustrating. These days are usually the days when I'm feeling tired. . . . On these days I try to create space to write in my journal where I critically reflect [an example of self-writing]. I can usually bring focus to my thoughts by pondering the idea that there are always multiple truths but what are my bottom lines. My bottom lines are that people are treated in safe and respectful ways and that social justice is the platform from where I begin. . . .

In my current position the uncertainty, shifting, changing and contingent nature of my teaching due to critical reflection combined with action research means that every day is exciting and challenging. Every day there are new dangers and possibilities to explore, challenge and discuss – so every day there is something to do.

'The reconstruction of a new vision'

The second case, drawn from the book *Beyond Quality in Early Childhood Education and Care*, is the Stockholm Project, inspired by Reggio Emilia and working with Foucault's concepts and theories. This project involved four years of work with seven 'preschools' (the name given in Sweden to early childhood centres for 1- to 6-year-olds) in a community in Stockholm, the largest city in Sweden, and the teachers (or 'pedagogues') working in them. The project aimed 'to deconstruct the dominant discourses in the early childhood field, to be able to reconstruct other discourses' (Dahlberg *et al.*, 2013, p. 135). Gunilla Dahlberg, the researcher on the project, begins by discussing how early on in the Stockholm Project they decided to switch from thematic or project work to a focus on pedagogical documentation, before turning to reflect on the changes that the project brought about and affirming the value of problematizing and deconstructing dominant discourses in bringing these changes about. Above all, this way of working has enabled the teachers to 'develop their practice through struggling with a new construction of the child and themselves as pedagogues, and in this way to take more control over their own practice' (ibid., p. 144).

From *Beyond Quality in Early Childhood Education and Care*, pp. 141–145 (re-ordered)

During our work we have realized more and more that networking, combined with pedagogical documentation, have been key tools for opening up a process of analysis and self-reflexion, and hence for change to take place. . . . [W]e decided that we should start [the Stockholm Project] with thematic work, documenting what was done in the institutions and bringing the documentation into the network. We wanted to focus on, struggle with and reflect upon everyday pedagogical practice. But after a couple of sessions, we realized that thematic work was too far away from our ideas of change. It easily ran into documenting what we have always done, and not problematizing how we have constructed the learning child and the learning pedagogue. We also realized that documentation in itself was a very difficult tool to use; it needed training and new skills. So we changed tack, and decided that we would work with small-scale situations from the institutions, and observe and document them. We would 'swim in observations'.

This turned out to be very fruitful. With the help of different media and through working with observation and documentation of how children explore and co-construct the world and how their learning processes take place, the pedagogues in the project have begun to critically examine and develop their own pedagogical work. We have used documentation as a tool to understand how the child has been constructed in our early childhood institutions. It has helped us to answer the question: Do we see the child? What do we mean by saying 'to see the child'? This can be seen as a form of deconstructive work in relation to pedagogical practice – [we have analysed] what constructions of the child are behind the way we talk about the child and what kind of constructions are behind our way of relating to the child in our practice. How have these constructions shaped how the environment has been ordered? How has the whole pedagogical space been constructed? Are there other constructions to be made? Is this a pedagogical space for the 'rich' child, pedagogue and parent?

What we have found through concentrating our attention on documentation is that we have *not* ended up with our discussion of practice becoming more and more sophisticated, while the pedagogical practice itself remains virtually unchanged. We can easily learn a new language. . . . We can sit in networks and talk, and agree with each other as we always talk in a very abstract way, for example, when we discuss having a 'child-centred' perspective and a pedagogy which takes the 'perspective of the child'. But what does that mean? It is often surface-level talk. New words and concepts do not automatically change practice. A new understanding is not the same as new patterns of action. . . .

Pedagogical documentation has enabled us to avoid this happening. For if we document our practice and the child's learning we have concrete examples from practice to reflect upon. Pedagogical documentation opens up a possibility for moving back and forth between conceptual tools and practice. As well as deconstruction, documentation has enabled the pedagogues to develop their practice through struggling with a new construction of the child and themselves as pedagogues, and in this way to take more control over their own practice.

When the pedagogues started to listen to the children, and changed their pedagogical relationship, a new construction of the child and the pedagogue appeared. It was a child that, for example, could concentrate on an activity much longer than the pedagogues' earlier constructions had said he or she should be able to, and who was not as egocentric. The children in our project more and more start saying 'look what I can do and know', and the pedagogues are becoming more and more aware of the children's potentialities – what they actually can do and do do rather than what classificatory systems say they should do. The excitement that this has generated among the pedagogues is captured in this comment by one of them: 'I have been working with preschool children for 20 years now and I never thought children know and can do that much. I now have got another child in front of me'.

It is astonishing how changing the construction of the child has contributed to the production of a new practice. Malaguzzi once said about such change: 'in fact this is very simple, but there is someone who has made us think it is so difficult'. Through troubling the dominant discourses and constructions of the child one can open up for 'another child' – a child with lots of capabilities and a child that has got thoughts and theories that are worth listening to both from the perspective of other children but also from the perspective of the adult.

In our project it has become very obvious for us all how the constructions we have made of the child have enormous consequences for how we relate to children pedagogically, how we design and choreograph the milieu as well as how we relate to parents. If we have got a rich child in front of us instead of a problem child this influences everything. It functions as a language that in itself becomes productive. As the pedagogues in Reggio say: 'if we have a rich child in front of us, we also become rich pedagogues and we get rich parents'. We are able to take control over our own learning process and have the right to interpret the world, but also to negotiate interpretations with others. . . .

[E]arly childhood institutions and their pedagogical practices are constituted by dominant discourses in our society and embody thoughts, conceptions and ethics which prevail at a given moment in a given society. Therefore, to change a pedagogical practice, it is necessary to start by problematizing and deconstructing these discourses and to understand and demonstrate how they are related to what is going on in pedagogical practice. Reggio Emilia has helped us to do this and, by so doing, to create a space for the reconstruction of a new vision, offering alternative understandings of the child, the pedagogue and the early childhood institution. . . .

Through this process of deconstruction, we have come to understand how the identities of the child and the pedagogue have been constructed [in Sweden]. . . . We have gone on to analyse how these constructions have become productive in our pedagogical institutions: in our relations to children, to other pedagogues and in the way we have designed the environment, that is, the whole choreographing of the milieu.

This work has illuminated how these dominant discursive regimes and the practices they produce are tied to power. Right from the start, we found it was very difficult to get any tolerance for other ways of thinking about and understanding the field. This we have come to understand in relation to the ideas of Foucault. . . . Thus, we are often unaware that we embody a dominant discourse and the constructions it produces (the Idea enthroned as the Truth), or we are unconscious of the power that is connected to action, and that we are, in one way or the other, always participating in acts of power – for example, whether we permit children to have a lot of free, creative play, or permit them to choose by themselves from various Montesorri materials, or if we permit them to work with clay and observe and document their work. Categories and concepts function, too, as acts of power in Foucault's perspective. Reggio has helped us to see how we are not only inscribed, both as children and pedagogues, in dominant discourse, but also govern ourselves through these inscriptions.

It is important to emphasize that we are aware that constructions always embody power, and that this is true of the constructions that we have made of the child, and the pedagogical practices that we have produced from these constructions. This is something we never can get around. We cannot pretend to be free of power and to stand outside power relations, we are always within the knowledge/power nexus. Foucault said 'everything is dangerous', meaning that our constructions are always arbitrary and as such never neutral nor innocent. They always bear social consequences. . . .

Many people might consider this talk of power, problematization and (de)construction pessimistic and leading nowhere. However, from our experience in the project, together with the inspiration from Reggio Emilia, we have found them to be quite the opposite, causes for optimism and very productive. It is certainly true that adopting the perspective we have done carries risks and can produce no change at all. But it also bears possibilities and a potential for dynamic change. If we are subject to power, we also have power. If on the one hand conventions and social representations are embodied and always contain power, on the other hand as arbitrary constructions they can always be open for change. This is why it is so important to unmask and trouble the traditions that are embodied in institutions such as schools and early childhood institutions, and by so doing open up for new possibilities and a new space for change and hope. Here concepts and perspectives become tools for constructing alternative understandings and practices.

Through problematizing and deconstructing dominant discourses and constructions we can . . . interrupt the values underlying the practices that have been constructed. We can frame the practice in another way, by reinscribing ourselves in another discourse through reconstructing language and practice. In the project, using these methods, we have been able to open up a new space for the reinterpretation and reconstruction not only of the child, now understood as a co-constructor of knowledge and culture, but also of the pedagogue and of the early childhood institution. In that new space, we have also been able to understand the field of early childhood pedagogy from another perspective and to formulate alternative practices, or counter discourses, which could not be articulated in the previous dominant discursive regime. . . .

For us, therefore, the central questions in the project have become: How to get another construction of the child, knowledge, learning and the conditions needed for learning? How to reconstruct an early childhood pedagogy which has its starting point in the child's theories, hypotheses, dreams and fantasies and in a view of knowledge and learning as co-construction? How to border cross the project of modernity, holding out the prospect of a continuous and linear progress, certainty and universality, by recognizing uncertainty, diversity, non-linearity, multiple perspectives, temporal and spatial specificities? . . . [W]e have started to produce provisional answers to these questions, constructing a practice, or daring to play with a practice, which is more varied as well as more self-reflective about itself, its possibilities and its limitations and that does not hide away from uncertainty, multiple perspectives and relationships. . . .

From the start Reggio helped us to give authority and practical meaning to a construction of the 'rich' child and for that construction to inform the pedagogical work in the early childhood institutions. Our social constructionist perspective implies that child and pedagogue are seen as co-constructors of their own knowledge, their environment and themselves. Learning cannot be seen as an individual cognitive act, something that is taking place in the head of the child, but as a cooperative and communicative act. . . .

We can say that Reggio has helped us to create a crisis in our own thinking, and so helped us to transgress dominant discourses and practices. Through a critical inquiry and through a reflective practice we have been able to understand how our own thinking and practices are inscribed in dominant discourses, which has opened up a new space and helped us to understand that there are other possibilities – alternative discourses or counter-discourses. Working in relation to Reggio has helped us find critical and productive questions: How has the child, knowledge and learning been constructed in the Swedish context? Are there other ways of constructing the child and ourselves as pedagogues which can open up for an emancipatory practice in early childhood institutions? What tools and practices can help this deconstruction and reconstruction of dominant and counter discourses and different pedagogical practices?

Questions – yours and mine

Don't forget to share and discuss the questions you have after reading this chapter, including the ones I suggested at the end of Chapter 1.

Here though are some of my questions to you:

- Can you think of how in a relationship you have tried to direct the behaviour of someone else? Did social media play a part in this?
- Can you give examples, from your work in early childhood education, of the application of disciplinary techniques (as outlined on pages 92–93) to either children or parents or workers? Perhaps one of these, at least, could include the organisation of the physical environment.
- Do you have a right to know the child? If so, how far should that knowledge try to go?
- Does the idea of a 'politics of refusal' appeal to you, or does it not speak to your personal experience and current situation?
- How might you practice 'care of the self'? Have you ever done so? What happened when you did?
- Take one of the earlier excerpts– by Kylie Smith or Gunilla Dahlberg – and reread it. Choose a section that (a) you find difficult to understand and (b) you find particularly interesting and/or provocative. What is it about each section that makes it hard to understand/interesting or provocative?

Note

1 'Governing the soul' refers to an important book first published in 1990 by Nikolas Rose, with a telling sub-title: 'The Shaping of the Private Self'. Rose analyses the evolution of psychological disciplines over more than 80 years and how they have become increasingly powerful means of governing both individuals and social institutions. Rose and Foucault use the term 'soul' to refer to 'aspects of humanity that were previously sacrosanct but that have recently been constructed as objects of psychological and regulatory apparatuses' (Fendler, 2001, p. 123), such as desire, fear and pleasure.

Chapter 6

Gilles Deleuze

Thought, movement and (more) experimentation

Gilles Deleuze (1925–1995) was a French philosopher who wrote on phi-losophy, literature, film and fine art. He and Foucault became friends in the 1960s and had a long and complicated relationship, having a significant influence on each other over the years. Deleuze wrote a book about Fou-cault and his work shortly after his friend's death; while Foucault famously, and perhaps only half-jokingly, said that the 20th century would become known as 'Deleuzian'. But Deleuze's closest working relationship was with Felix Guattari (1930–1992), a French philosopher and psychotherapist, with whom he co-authored a number of important books.

As with Foucault, the immediate question is why include Deleuze in a book on early childhood education, and the immediate answer is because increasing numbers of people in what I have called the resistance movement contesting early childhood are turning to his concepts and ideas – the new perspectives he provides us with – to seek inspiration for alternative narratives. As well as 'doing Foucault', people are 'doing Deleuze' in early childhood education. Like Foucault, Deleuze is preoccupied with how to think and see differently and the potential for becoming something different; both seek to work with a principle of constant and inventive creativity. Like Foucault, Deleuze is also interested in power, though, as we shall see, he argues that with evolving technologies, power is now exercised in new and more effective ways. But Deleuze is perhaps most important for early childhood education because of his invention of new concepts about thought and knowledge, new ways of envisioning them, and of new ideas about how they might be created and how this creative experience affects us.

While Foucault may leave us, sometimes, feeling a little daunted at the forces of power confronting us and their capacity to discipline and govern, Deleuze is more likely to arouse feelings of excitement and joy at the prospect of 'access to universes we did not know anything about'. These are the words of Liselott Mariett Olsson, from her book in the *Contesting Early Childhood* series, *Movement and Experimentation in Young Children's Learning: Deleuze and Guattari in Early Childhood Education* (Olsson, 2009), one of several books in the series that work with Deleuze (and Guattari). We shall hear more from Liselott, and about her work in Swedish preschools, later in the chapter – not least about how working with Deleuze can bring you out in goose bumps!

Thinking differently and thinking new

As Deleuze sees it, we mostly don't really think at all. Instead, we just take into our heads stuff that has been around for a long time. Gerd Biesta, the philosopher of education we have already met, and Deborah Osberg, an educationalist, have described how this passive process works in education, with the transmission of a supposedly true and already known set of ideas from the adult who knows to the child (or it could be to another adult) who needs to know: this is thought as reproduction, what Deleuze terms 'orthodox thought'. Biesta and Osberg argue for a very different concept of education, what they call 'emergentist' because it involves the emergence or creation of something new, of new properties 'that have never existed before and, more importantly, are inconceivable from what has come before' (Osberg and Biesta, 2007, p. 33): this is thought as creativity, as something radically new, as thinking the world differently.

Such is Deleuze's concept of ***thought***, for 'he knows the problem is not to direct or methodically apply a thought which pre-exists in principle and in nature, but to bring into being that which does not yet exist' (Marks, 1998, p. 84). His view of thought is closely related to his view of knowledge and therefore of learning. Like other poststructural thinkers, Deleuze contests the idea that knowledge is about getting a true and objective representation of the world, usually assumed to happen through a simple process of transmission from the teacher to the taught of contents that are already known and defined. Rather, 'learning must be treated as impossible to predict, plan, supervise or evaluate according to predefined standards' (Olsson, 2009, p. 117) but takes place through processes of social construction that may well lead into unexpected and surprising places. Knowledge and learning, therefore, are the products of new and creative thinking.

How does this new, creative thinking come about? Something in the world forces us to think, and for Deleuze that something is the provocation arising from an encounter with difference. Thought, in short, is the product of relations and encounters with the unknown or unfamiliar; learning, therefore, is always a relational practice – but that raises the question: what sort of relationship, what kind of encounter? Returning to our earlier discussion about Levinas and the ethics of an encounter, we could say that with an encounter in which we try only to 'grasp' the Other, making the Other into the Same, applying our existing understandings and classifications in an attempt to recognise in the Other something known and familiar, in such an encounter all we do is apply existing ideas to confirm our existing thinking; the end result is 'orthodox thought'. But if we are open to the otherness of the Other, if we allow ourselves to be surprised and provoked by difference, then thinking differently and thinking new may happen, and we may find ourselves moving to new places from where the world looks very different and we have become different. Moreover, there are no border controls on this movement, for as Marg Sellers puts it in *Young Children Becoming Curriculum: Deleuze, Te Whāriki and Curricular Understandings*, another book in the series strongly influenced by Deleuze,

> [t]here is no limit to what can be thought, at least for those willing "to put their imaginations to work" (Gough, 2006: xiv) as thoughts roam freely, wander, flow outside familiarity towards generating ever-expanding territories of difference and passages of thinking, opening (to) sites of emergence.
>
> (Sellers, 2013, p. 16)

Heady stuff! The consequences of such new and limitless thinking can be physically and emotionally affecting, as Liselott Mariett Olsson explains.

> These encounters [with difference] are particularly violent affairs since they open up thinking to the forces of chaos. When we really think it is like being struck to the ground only to find that you are falling through it, since it does not exist any more. It concerns a kind of vertiginous feeling of losing one's references. But at the same time it is a very joyful and affirmative affair, since it can give us access to universes we did not know anything about.
>
> (Olsson, 2009, p. 26)

The title of Olsson's book – *Movement and Experimentation in Early Childhood Education* – reflects the importance Deleuze attaches not only to thought moving us away from stable and static positions to 'universes we do not know anything about' but also to invention and **experimentation**. For him, 'to think is to experiment', a concept that Olsson develops:

> Thought, in this way [always and continuously created, through relations and encounters], has also got the features of being experimentation, but an idea of experimentation that is something totally different from the idea of experimentation as the lifeless controlling of all parameters as well as working with an expected outcome (Deleuze, 1994). Experimentation here concerns that which is not yet known, it concerns that which comes about, that which is new and that demands more than recognizing or representing truth. Thought as experimentation concerns the new, the interesting and the remarkable.
>
> (ibid.)

Such ideas are very challenging, contesting as they do the dominant discourse in today's early childhood education, that story of quality and high returns I have introduced earlier. For that discourse, that story, seeks to govern and tame children through predicting, monitoring and assessing performance against predetermined standards. It is about the transmission of orthodox thought and the 'lifeless controlling of all parameters as well as working with an expected outcome'.

Working with Deleuze takes us light years away from this. It takes us to an education of *potentiality*, where 'we never know in advance what a body can do' (those words, again, of Baruch Spinoza that resonate today), an education of the unexpected, the unpredicted and the not yet known, an education where new thought has the power to generate new ways of being – an education, indeed, where surprise and wonder are important values. And it is because we don't know what might be possible for a child to learn, to know or become that Hillevi Lenz Taguchi concludes in her book in the series *Going beyond the Theory/Practice Divide in Early Childhood Education* that 'this unknown potentiality and change becomes the most important subject for investigation in pedagogical theory and practice' (Lenz Taguchi, 2009, p. 16).

New concepts and new language

We can go further into the thinking of Deleuze by looking at some of his most important concepts and the language he uses to talk about them – and as ever it is through getting a new language that we can also get a new way of thinking. You can find examples of these concepts being put to work in early childhood education in an excerpt from Liselott Mariett Olsson's book at the end of this chapter.

Let us start with *lines of flight*, a vivid term that conjures up for me the idea of new thought shooting off after an encounter with difference, heading into the unknown, those moments that most of us will have had when suddenly we see things in a totally new light and feel a surge of excitement and energy – we may say we have had a brainwave or a lightbulb moment or an inspiration or been hit by a bolt from the blue. For me, it also conjures up images of lightning, a sudden and unpredictable burst of energy and intense brightness; or of an idea that has escaped, taken flight, from the restraint of orthodox thought. These lines of flight are very different to Deleuze's concept of *rigid lines,* which faithfully follow existing lines of thought, orthodox thinking, such as those created by theories of children's predetermined development, and lead to 'organizing and planning content and method a long time beforehand' (Olsson, 2009, p. 71), as in what Malaguzzi describes as 'prophetic pedagogy'. Very different also to *supple lines*, which might offer more choice to each child or adult, 'but still only to the extent that it serves the goal set; time, space and furniture must still serve a fixed and predetermined goal'. In both cases, the ends are known and fixed. By contrast, a line of flight can lead anywhere; it runs like a 'zig-zag crack in between the other [rigid and supple] lines – and it is only these lines [of flight] that, from the perspective of Deleuze and Guattari, are capable of creating something new' (Olsson, 2009, p. 58).

With lines of flight, we are freed from being tied to a fixed point, whether a predefined problem or solution, enabling the movement of a new line of thought and the beginning of a process of becoming something other, something new. There is a possibility of transformative change, which is 'about opening up to a continuous state of movement, not just a short burst of movement whilst traversing from one static position to another . . . [this is] the world in a constant state of flux and process of emergence' (Moss, 2013, p. 9). Developing this theme, Bronwyn Davies, in her book in the series *Listening to Children: Being and Becoming*, talks about a line of flight as 'a transformative shift into the not-yet-known. . . . It involves invention as well as letting go of what went before' (Davies, 2014, pp. 41, 55), while, in her book, Liselott Mariett Olsson puts it like this:

> From time to time though, there are moments where something new and different may happen, something that increases all participants' capacity to act and create interesting connections and features in between teachers and children as well as between the form and content of the practice. These are the moments of the lines of flight. For Deleuze and Guattari, the lines of flight create a zig-zag crack going in a new direction. . . . When something new and different is coming about, when the lines of flight are created and activated in the practices, it is never taking place as a rationally planned and implemented change by specific individuals. Rather, there are from time to time magic moments where there seems to be something entirely new and different coming about. This is recognized only by the tremendous intensity and, very often, the physical expression of goose bumps that take possession of participants.
>
> (Olsson, 2009, pp. 62–63)

An example of such an experience drawn from Liselott's book comes at the end of this chapter.

Note the thrill and the physicality of the experience: lines of flight come about in 'magic moments' recognised by 'the physical expression of goose bumps that take possession of participants'. This is one physical expression of a 'tremendous intensity' of ***affect***, best described as a surge of vitality, a feeling of being more alive, something that cannot be equated with or described in terms of categories of emotion (happiness, sadness, excitement etc). This feeling precedes recognition, cognition and language; indeed, to try to analyse, measure or say what is going on is to risk disrupting what is happening.

Note, too, the timing of lines of flight. Lines of flight do not occur all the time nor at fixed times; they cannot be 'rationally planned' or predicted. They happen, 'from time to time', as if by magic. Such moments, when 'something entirely new and different [comes] about', are **events,** which Deleuze thought of as moments when a bundle of intensities and forces come together and open up for movement and becoming, for affect and potential – such as lines of flight. The concept of the event was also important for Foucault, who thought we had become preoccupied by the general and the abstract; driven by our need to achieve the predetermined goal, to follow the prescribed programme, to apply the system of categories. In so doing, we ignore the potential of the here and now, of the present moment, of the unexpected encounter with difference, of the emergence of something new, that 'magic moment' of 'tremendous intensity' which can bring participants out in 'goose bumps'. When such events materialise or 'eventualise', the group and the environment are suddenly infused with intense vitality, which holds out the possibility of movement, the creation of lines of flight with their opening up of new thought and knowledge and the release of potentiality. Guattari (1995) stresses the importance of responding to the event, as it holds the possibility for creativity of thought, without which, he argues, we will not be able to solve any of the huge environmental, social and mental problems that face us today.

The issue here is whether early childhood educators are open to and welcoming of such intense and unpredictable experiences, or if they are so focused on predetermined outcomes and abstract standards that these special moments, what is happening here and now, pass them by. As Gunilla Dahlberg puts it,

> [i]f we do not pay notice to the present moment, what we here would like to call *the directly immediate presence*, then we will miss *the dynamic forms of vitality* as they are not readily describable in words. If they are put into words they will lose most of their ability to evoke intensity, affect and vitality. And, hence, we will miss "the feel of the emergence of the thought" (Stern, 2010, p. 10), and its ability to lay the base for social interaction and learning.

The challenge to educators, therefore, is to be 'attuned', that is the capacity for sharing, and indeed matching, the children's affect, intensity and vitality, to be on the same wavelength, we might say, to be part of the event, and not to be just outside observers trying to monitor if children achieve a set of predetermined behaviours.

An example of such an instantaneous event is described by Ingela Elfström and Karin Furnes (2010), where some children in a Swedish preschool are doing 'drawings' in clay of exotic worms. In the midst of the careful and intense work of modelling their ideas and images, they start to play and shoot each other with clay guns produced at the moment. Then they suddenly stop, saying 'We are friends instead', and on the table they make links between the worms, and name this as the 'string of words', a way in which the worms can communicate with each other, warn each other of dangers and ask for help if they get sick. When others follow this event from the outside, the authors observe, they say that they have never seen anything like that before, and many add that they get goose bumps over their whole body.

Encounter and relations are vital to Deleuze's thinking about thinking, and this leads us to his concept of **assemblages**. The idea that new thought emerges from an encounter with difference should not lead us to a simple causal model of A meets B and then C happens. Rather encounters take place within and among multiple and complex bodies or entities, 'multiplicities' of the animate and inanimate, of different forces and ideas, of different perspectives and discourses: these multiplicities form assemblages. Deleuze described an assemblage as

> a multiplicity which is made up of many heterogeneous terms and which establishes liaisons, relations between them across ages, sexes and reigns – different natures. Thus, the assemblage's only unity is that of co-functioning: it is a symbiosis, a 'sympathy'. It is never filiations [the relationship of one thing to another] which are important but alliances, alloys; these are not successions, lines of descent, but contagions, epidemics, the wind.
>
> (Deleuze and Parnet, 1987, p. 69)

The subject's encounters with difference and the new thinking that these may generate, the lines of flight that may emerge, should thus be seen as occurring within such assemblages or bundles of heterogeneous entities, fluid and ephemeral in composition, a rich milieu for the emergence of complex and unanticipated connections and encounters. I have earlier suggested that an important task for the teacher 'is creating rich opportunities and environments', and this work could be reframed as helping to create assemblages with a rich potential for the emergence of new thought.

Assemblages also include **desires**, and desires are important forces for creativity, invention and possibility. It depends, though, what is meant by desire. Desire, says Deleuze, is often thought of as expressing a lack, a need, something missing; for example, in psychoanalysis, you desire something you don't have. This can lead to the imposition of schemas of development stages on children, schemas that construct and define what children are lacking and must strive to fulfil. When thought of in such contexts, desire can lead to taming and control.

> When desire is defined as lack and need, the teacher takes the role of an authority and a judge, supervising the children and judging them against

predefined categories of normal development. Teachers will then arrange and perform activities for the children starting out from these judgements and with the ambition to help them to develop 'normally'. In this situation, children have very few opportunities to influence their lives in preschool.

(Olsson, 2009, p. 99)

But desire can be understood and defined very differently, as a positive, productive force rather than a lacking – in which case, rather than imposing the desires of others onto children, repressing and taming their actual desires, the teacher has a very different relationship to children.

> [T]he teacher first and foremost listens to and detects what kind of desires are at stake in the classroom. These desires are then not seen as children's needs, but rather, they are looked at as very intense forces that are the starting out point for all learning. . . . Instead of judging children from predefined schemas, the logic is now turned around and questions are asked about what the children are after; what they are interested in, that is, what they desire. This is an important reversal for a preschool institution, or for any institution. . . . The preschools enter a new logic of desire where they actually seem to ask children the questions; 'Now, where are your desires, what kind of assemblages are you for the moment experimenting with?'
>
> (ibid.)

I would like to digress for a moment, away from early childhood education and into the world of cocktails, because it provides a perfect illustration of concepts such as events, assemblages and desires and how, out of these, something new can emerge; this example is also a reminder that the phenomena I am discussing are about life itself, in all its diversity, and not just confined to one small part of it. Arnd Henning Heissen is one of the world's finest creators of cocktails and, driven by desire, is constantly experimenting to invent new drinks from new combinations – assemblages – of ingredients (these can also include the qualities of the glass from which the drink will be drunk). Every so often he succeeds, and an event takes place from which a line of flight – a perfect new drink – occurs. In a radio programme about his work, the interviewer asks him how he knows he's made a perfect drink, to which he answers there are two elements:

> One, my goose bumps and I feel the skin on my skull is about to leave. That's the moment I feel something is quite exciting, something is completely new, especially when I use some very ordinary ingredients and I would have never thought they'd mash together so well. Another way

of feeling its magic is when my knees start jiggling. I get happy and feel like dancing.

(Heissen, 2017)

The world of luxury hotels and bars is very different to the world of early childhood education, yet the same magic moments can occur when something new is brought into existence.

Events, assemblages, desires – all require new ways of thinking about learning and knowledge. A common image in early childhood education, embodied in notions about developmental stages, learning goals and school readiness, is the stairway, where children proceed, step by step, in a linear and predefined progression from bottom to top, from a state of unknowing to a state of knowing. Another, related image or metaphor for education and learning is the tree, with its ordered hierarchy of root, trunk and branches, again implying a fixed and predicted order. But Deleuze brings another image of education and learning to mind: the **rhizome**, the tangled mass of roots of a plant, mostly underground, which goes off in all directions and in which there are constant interconnections.

Unlike the staircase or the tree, which have clear starting points, with a well-defined sequence of steps or stages leading to the attainment of predefined finishing points, the rhizome has no beginning and no end: it is a '*multiplicity* functioning by means of connections and heterogeneity, a multiplicity which is not given but constructed'. Marg Sellers, in her book in the series, explains how the 'rhizo approach' of Deleuze and Guattari

> perturbs conventional ordering, sequencing, categorizing and linearity including that represented in/by the (metaphorical) tree of knowledge . . . [which] supports binary logic, representing linearly ordered systems of thinking, which are fixed and rooted . . . [with] 'a logic of tracing and reproduction'. Tracing involves continuous repetitions of structural patterns already present (roots and branches), and reproduction is the continuous reconstitution of the closed structure or fixed entity (as the tree grows). Both tracing and reproduction produce more of the same by following a sequentially ordered process through specific points and positions that are restricted to a particular place and reach conventionally logical and coherent conclusions.
>
> In contrast, heterogeneous connectivity characterizes the complexity of rhizome. . . . A rhizome is comprised of ceaseless interrelational movements – flows of connectivity – among numerous possible assemblies of the disparate and the similar. . . . In thought and thinking, a rhizome maps processes that are 'networked, relational and transversal' (Colman, 2005a: 231). A rhizome familiar in abstract or virtual terms, but also actual in the real world is the Internet, characterized by infinite connectivity.

(Sellers, 2013, p. 11)

The tree and rhizome offer two very different types of logic: the tree with a fixed, determining and linear logic; the rhizome with a dynamic, flexible and 'lateral' logic that encompasses change, complexity and heterogeneity and implies a world that is dynamic, ever-changing and always 'becoming'. More of the same or something new. Adopting the rhizome, Deleuze seeks to move beyond a (linear, universal) logic that produces stable and universal truths of the world towards a (lateral, local) logic that produces shifting and multiple truths, lines of flight to new thinking and knowledge.

With a rhizome, without beginning or end, we are always in the middle, with no fixed beginning or end – so distinctions between 'process' and 'outcome' no longer make sense, just as they make no sense in our personal lives (unless, of course, we perversely treat the whole of life as a process, with death the outcome!). By the same token, we are ever-changing, always becoming, with unknowable potentiality and never arriving at a fixed point of knowledge. Similarly, the rhizome, with its endless possibilities for making new connections provoking new lines of flight going in new directions, moves us away from closed or binary thinking, the either/or approach, and towards an open-ended thinking, where we can always find new possibilities, new directions to take – a case of and . . . and . . . and . . ., always keeping open the prospect of further ideas, new lines of flight. No outcome or closure, as we always leave the door open.

Running through every facet of Deleuze's work, as I hope is apparent by now, is the importance of **movement** and a strong desire to avoid constraint on movement, for example through the taming and braking effects of 'orthodox thought', with its transmission and reproduction of the already known and the importance it attaches to stability, linearity, predictability and closure, qualities that are all intended to fix, determine and represent in predetermined ways. Contesting such thinking, Deleuze's commitment to movement is encapsulated in his concept of the **nomad** and the **nomadic**; indeed for Deleuze, '[t]o think is to seize that which is nomadic, which escapes conventional categories' (Marks, 1998, p. 7).

The nomad is not a traveller starting and finishing a journey at fixed points, where the journey is a pre-planned process of getting from Point A to Point B; rather the nomad is in a constant state of movement, always in the middle, always in-between, with no fixed points or limiting borders. The nomadic conception 'points the way to another idea of what thought and education is about. . . . It directs us towards the processes, the becomings – and these becomings are not to be judged by their results, but rather by how they proceed and continue' while the nomadic subject 'enters into the domain of potentialities . . . unpredictable becomings' (Dahlberg and Moss, 2009, p. xx).

The nomad and the nomadic exist within space, and the nature of that space may enable or restrict their ability to roam free and escape the conventional and orthodox. To enter 'the domain of potentialities', full of 'unpredictable becomings', the nomad needs ***smooth space***; while what the nomad wants to avoid, because it hems her in, is ***striated space***, highly regulated spaces where life's rich diversity and potentiality are forced into moulds, for example by rigid and detailed rules, procedures and classifications. As an example, Deleuze suggested that striated space is to smooth space

> as fabric is to felt. Fabric is closely governed, has verticals and horizon-tals, and is closed by the warp of the loom. It serves as a good example of regulated or administered spaces that are vertically ordered, that is, have a top and a bottom. Felt, on the other hand, is nomadic or smooth; it is produced by the entanglement of millions of microfibers oriented in every direction – it is an accumulation of proximities all at the same level, making it nonhierarchical.
>
> (Roy, 2003, p. 59)

Thus, learning that seeks the certainty of linear progression and predeter-mined goals, perhaps governed by a detailed and prescriptive curriculum, contributes to a striated space that stifles connectedness (entanglement), bor-der crossing and lines of flight; while learning that allows for, indeed values, uncertainty, inter-connectedness and the unexpected helps create smooth space within which the nomad may freely roam. Or, as Marg Sellers expresses the distinction in her book on *Young Children Becoming Curriculum*:

> Smooth spaces are open space throughout which 'things-flows are distrib-uted' whereas striated spaces are closed; they are spaces plotted by points and positions and are concerned with enclosing things linear and solid (Deleuze and Guattari, 1987: 361). The nomad operates within smooth spaces and is oriented to an understanding of speed and movement rather than being confined in coded (striated) spaces. Smooth spaces are char-acterized by passages and passaging in-between, with points becoming relays to be passed through in mo(ve)ments of speed and slowness; the nomad is always already in the middle, in-between, with points passed through constituting a relay or trajectory (p. 380) – a line of flight.
>
> (Sellers, 2013, p. 18)

Marg Sellers, in a further passage, does a nice job of drawing connections between several of the Deleuzian concepts in this section and provides a good note on which to end this brief introduction to some of Deleuze's concepts.

> Flowing nomadically with rhizome involves a complex interplay of fol-lowing lines of flight and passaging through various territories, such as [the] physical and imaginative space of the games children play and the relationships among players. Ceaselessly, more and more connections are generated through the rhizome, assembling as an a-centered milieu

of perpetual and dynamic change without specific end or entry points, beginnings or endings. In this smooth space of nomad-rhizome, there are no points or positions, only lines, and working with these lines, as de-territorializing [fluid, not tied down] lines of flight, opens (to) possibilities for connecting what otherwise may be regarded as disparate thoughts, ideas and activity. In this way a network of interconnections forms – an amassing of middles amidst an array of multidirectional movement among open systems. Generating this nomad-rhizome assemblage, 'open and connectable in all of its dimensions' (Deleuze and Guattari, 1987: 12), disturbs the arborescently [tree-like] informed, linear, sequential progression of modernist thought and action that is always retraced through the same series of points of structuration and always comes back 'to the same'.

(Sellers, 2013, p. 130)

Power and micro-politics

The other side to Deleuze's delight in the prospect of new thought, nomadic roaming through smooth space and the unpredictability of experimentation is a desire to contest and undermine power relations in modern societies. He saw these as driven by a logic of taming and governing through predicting, controlling, supervising or evaluating according to predetermined standards, a logic that 'always begins with formulating preset goals and universal values for our educational practices, [so that we] start with the end – what is to be achieved and assessed' (Lenz Taguchi, 2010, p. 16). Deleuze's philosophy of life resists and challenges that restrictive and controlling logic at every point, which is the logic of today's dominant discourse in early childhood education. To enter the world of Deleuze is to find yourself questioning everything held dear and taken for granted by many early childhood policymakers, researchers and practitioners – and not only questioning these beliefs and assumptions but being offered a totally different way of thinking and living. He is, I think, truly revolutionary.

But in a short article written not long before his death – *Postscript on the Societies of Control* (Deleuze, 1992) – Deleuze undertook a more focused analysis of contemporary power relations. In the course of this analysis, he argued that these relations were undergoing a fundamental transformation, from what he describes as a disciplinary society into a control society. He associates the idea of the disciplinary society with the historical work of Foucault, this model evolving in the 18th and 19th centuries and reaching its height in the early 20th century. In such societies, individuals move over the course of their lives from enclosure to enclosure – family, school, barracks (military service), factory or office, with occasional periods perhaps in hospital or prison. In each enclosure, individuals are governed through the kind of disciplinary powers that Foucault documented and that I outlined in the previous chapter.

But especially since 1945, a new form of society has emerged where controls act on people continuously, without needing them to move from place to place or be subjected to effective but comparatively cumbersome disciplines. Examples of this continuous control given by Deleuze include lifelong learning ('perpetual training'), but 25 years on we can add other examples, not least the capacity of governments and corporations to follow our every move and action via an array of new technologies such as credit and debit card transactions, mobile phone signals and social media. In education, the child and young person's performance can be continually monitored and tracked through child observation, regular assessments and the technology of 'dataveillance', creating a continuous collection of data on the performance of children that is processed, analysed and then fed back into the education system. If Foucault's disciplinary societies are analogue, Deleuze's control societies are digital. Under this system, through constant monitoring and feedback on our performance and the embodying by each of us of the standards expected of us, control increasingly works through internal mechanisms, the subject constantly seeking to achieve the desired outcomes, be it at home, in school or university or in the workplace – hyper-governmentality, we might say.

As with Foucault, we should treat Deleuze's analysis of evolving power relations very seriously, seeking to understand the nature and implications of the changes taking place. Indeed, Foucault's 'governmentality' and Deleuze's 'society of control' make a formidable and frightening pairing. Yet, one of the most concerning features of today's dominant discourse in early childhood education is its total disregard of power and control. The storytellers are silent on these issues.

We should not, however, despair; for like Foucault, Deleuze believes that power can be evaded and suborned, at least to a degree. There are always 'leakages' in any system or structure. As Liselott Mariett Olsson explains, 'a first condition of any structure is that it is leaking; there is always something that deviates from and escapes a structure or a system. . . . [Deleuze's] is a philosophy that focuses upon the ongoing creation of leakages' (Olsson, 2009, pp. 24, 179).

More specifically, Deleuze writes of the potentiality of what he terms 'micro politics', which we might see as the way leakages can be exploited and used to best effect. One way that state or corporate power operates is through macro-politics, the policies, procedures and goals formulated from the top to be applied, for example, in the early childhood centre or school. But then there is what actually goes on in the centre or school, in the 'arena of implementation', where the results of macro-politics need to be activated by adults and children in everyday practice. And here is where micro-politics come in, giving some scope for contestation, resistance and local action through the exercise and interplay of individual beliefs and desires. Liselott Mariett Olsson again:

> [A] curriculum for instance is to be seen as a macro-political decision; but when it encounters preschool practices, an enormous creativity is released that completely and continuously transforms and defines the curriculum and its accompanying practices in a reciprocal relationship. But not only macro-political decisions of an administrative character are involved; everything is involved in the micro-political. . . . [M]icro-political movements can be described as flow or quanta of belief and desire. Flow, or quanta, is all about belief and desire, they are quantities constructing the very beginning of all change. Accordingly, all change in society and in individuals start in flow or quanta of belief and desire. . . . Movements of belief and desire are impossible to predict, control, supervise or evaluate according to preset standards. . . .
>
> Micro-politics was often used as a way to inscribe in one's practice the possibility of a different role as a teacher, questioning the governing of children through judgements and assumed authority. But also, as a consequence of discovering how repressing desire functions, the concept was used as a way to avoid intimidation by the power normally ascribed to the teacher.
>
> (ibid., pp. 74–75, 76, 101)

Micro-politics, or what others have called 'minor politics', is then about contesting power, those dominant discourses that insist they are the only true way – but not doing so head on, not through the structures and processes of conventional politics, but rather in one's everyday life, in one's everyday practice, in the here and now, in what Nikolas Rose calls the 'small concerns, petty details, the everyday and not the transcendental' (Rose, 1999, p. 280). It is about making what others define as technical, and therefore uncontestable, political, by recognising there are in fact alternatives and choosing to think for oneself about which alternative to work with in a given situation, however small and petty; it is, in short, taking opportunities as they arise to refuse the dominant discourse. And as Deleuze makes clear, such micro-politics are fuelled by affect, by 'quanta of belief and desire', for example by the belief and desire of preschool teachers and the children they work with.

We should never under-estimate the potential of top-down power, including its dominant discourses and its human technologies, especially in our contemporary societies of control. It is very potent. But nor should we under-estimate the possibilities of bottom-up transgression, especially when driven by belief and desire.

Does this ring bells?

I have already drawn links between Deleuze and two theorists who have appeared earlier, Levinas and Foucault. I will also shortly look at examples of consciously putting Deleuze to work in early childhood education. But here I would like to ask whether this discussion of the concepts and ideas of Deleuze rings any bells with you, putting you in mind of an example of early childhood education that has already been discussed – the early childhood education in Reggio Emilia? It is true that, as far as I know, Loris Malaguzzi and his educator colleagues in that Italian city have not referred explicitly to Deleuze (though that does not mean they are unaware of his work, being very well and widely read). But it seems to me that there are connections between much of that city's pedagogical thinking and ways of working and Deleuzian concepts and ideas (Dahlberg and Bloch, 2006, also make these connections).

Take the rhizome. In the introduction to a book in the *Contesting Early Childhood* series, *In Dialogue with Reggio Emilia: Listening, Research and Learning*, Gunilla Dahlberg and myself wrote:

> In Reggio they have questioned and rethought. In one of his speeches Loris Malaguzzi talked about their idea of knowledge as a 'tangle of spaghetti'. Carlina [Rinaldi] takes a similar view when she says that 'learning does not proceed in a linear way, determined and deterministic, by progressive and predictable stages, but rather is constructed through contemporaneous advances, standstills, and "retreats" that take many directions'. Equipped with this concept of knowledge, we can understand why project work in Reggio Emilia grows in many directions without an overall ordering principle, challenging the mainstream idea of knowledge acquisition as a form of linear progression, where the metaphor is the tree – very different to the metaphor of the tangle of spaghetti! Project work in Reggio can be seen as a series of small narratives, narratives that are difficult to combine in an additive and cumulative way. This, we think, is similar to an image of knowledge as *a rhizome*.
>
> (Rinaldi, 2006, p. 7)

There are many other similarities. Recall the value attached in Reggio Emilia to experimentation, creativity, the unpredicted and the surprising, interconnectedness and border crossing, all resonating with what Deleuze desires and values. Gunilla Dahlberg and I have argued that for Reggio Emilia

> thought and concepts can be seen as a consequence of the provocation of an encounter with difference. They view the *rhizome* as something which shoots in all directions with no beginning and no end, but always *in between*, and with openings towards other directions and places. It is a *multiplicity* functioning by means of connections and heterogeneity,

a multiplicity which is not given but constructed. Thought, then, is a matter of experimentation and problematization – *a line of flight* and an exploration of *becoming*, echoed in Carlina [Rinaldi's] observation that 'the process of "becoming" is the basis of true education'.

(ibid., p. 8; original emphases)

While Bronwyn Davies in *Listening to Children*, a book strongly influenced by Deleuze, writes of Reggio Emilia's desire to 'escape the stifling tendency of the will-to-know and to predictability', and doing so by making 'the valuing of difference a primary value, along with being open to the emergence of the not-yet-thought in oneself and another' (Davies, 2014, p. 11). For both Deleuze and Reggio Emilia, learning cannot be reduced to something that can be predicted, to the reproduction of predefined standards by means of prophetic pedagogy. It is, instead, about being open to and welcoming the emergence of the not-yet-thought, in oneself and others. As such, when it happens, it will be surprising, unpredicted and a cause of wonder.

Putting Deleuze to work

We might say, therefore, that the educators of Reggio Emilia have been putting many of Deleuze's concepts and ideas to work, even if they may not be doing so knowingly. But a growing number of early childhood workers are deliberately putting Deleuze to work, consciously taking inspiration from his thinking. We have already mentioned books in the *Contesting Early Childhood* series by Bronwyn Davies and Marg Sellers, both of whom use Deleuzian concepts and ideas to help their research into early childhood education. Indeed, for Marg Sellers, Deleuze (and Guattari) not only shape her study of what curriculum means for young children and how it works but also the writing of her book, with its non-linear structure (so the chapters can be read in any order).

Glenda MacNaughton, in her book *Doing Foucault in Early Childhood Studies*, uses Deleuze's work to develop what she terms 'rhizoanalysis', which she describes as

> a way to explore the politics of a text . . . [it both] deconstructs and reconstructs a text. It deconstructs a text (e.g. a research moment or a child observation) by exploring how it means; how it connects with things 'outside' of it, such as its author, its reader and its literary and non-literary contexts . . . and by exploring how it organises meanings and power through off-shoots, overlaps, conquests and expansions.
>
> Rhizoanalysis reconstructs a text by creating new and different understandings of it; and it does so by linking it with texts other than those we

would normally use. For example, we can use rhizoanalysis to replot the links between an observation of a child, and a child development text, a feminist text and a popular culture text.

(MacNaughton, 2005, p. 120)

Glenda includes an example, written by one of her students, Kylie Smith (whom we have already met). Kylie creates a particular 'reading' of an observation of a child by linking it with popular culture texts such as *Buffy the Vampire Slayer*, *Harry Potter* and the *Paper Bag Princess*, deliberately choosing texts that question dominant discourses of the child, gender, race and class and that assist her in reconstructing her understanding of these constructs in that observation: 'as she constructs a rhizome of gender meanings in the observation, she rethinks what it means to "do" gender at four years of age and how she might see and work with children's gendering in early childhood services'. The encounter between the observation and these diverse texts opens up for Kylie new perspectives about the child, new thinking about gender and new possibilities for work on social justice (cf. MacNaughton, 2005, pp. 134–145).

But I want to devote the remainder of this section and chapter to Liselott Mariett Olsson. I include part of a recent conversation with Liselott, discussing her relationship with Deleuze and why she finds his work so important and relevant to early childhood education. But first, here is an excerpt from her book *Movement and Experimentation in Young Children's Learning*. Notice here, also, the important role played by pedagogical documentation, another connection with Reggio Emilia.

'Magic moments' in the preschool

Liselott says that 'every day magical moments' take place in many of the preschools in the city of Stockholm and its suburbs and at the Stockholm Institute of Education (where Liselott was then working), 'magic moments where there seems to be something entirely new and different coming about . . . recognized only by the tremendous intensity and, very often, the physical expression of goose bumps that take possession of participants'. On such occasions, she continues,

Children, preschool teachers, teacher students, teacher educators and researchers come together and are literally caught up in the desire to experiment with subjectivity and learning. In these practices experimentations and intense, unpredictable events are taking place, concerning the idea of what a child is, what a teacher should do, the purpose of a preschool and its organisation, contents and forms.

(Olsson, 2009, p. 11)

Herself a former preschool teacher and working with preschools and preschool teachers, Liselott provides a number of cases of such magic moments in her book, providing concrete examples of how Deleuze's concepts and ideas can be used to see and understand what is happening in early childhood education, in particular how lines of flight, leading to new thought, may occur. Here is one of these examples.

From *Movement and Experimentation in Young Children's Learning*, pp. 63–67

This small project started up after a 'Heart exposition' for St Valentine's Day on the public square in the commune of Trångsund, south of Stockholm, where all preschools in the commune participated. The children in one preschool group, all aged four or five years, had talked a lot about the heart and its rhythm, during the work of preparing for the exposition, and when they were talking and describing the rhythm of their heart to each other, they very often used drawings as a way to show each other their ideas. So shortly after the exposition the teachers ask the children if they can illustrate with paper and pen how they conceive of the rhythm of the heart. The teachers have provided the children with stethoscopes, papers and pens.

The children are sitting around a table and soon they decide to get up and run around the table, they then sit down and listen to each other's heart beats and they then discover that their hearts beat faster.

Then the children decide that they want to try to run around the preschool to see if the hearts will beat even faster. They get up and run and hurry inside to measure the rhythm of the heart with the stethoscope and they then try to illustrate in various ways how they conceive of this changed rhythm of the heart. After the activity the teachers sit down with their own documentations of the children's process and they try to analyze and understand how the children have used their illustrations.

Two girls, Grace and Emma started off by sitting down measuring the rhythm of the heart with the stethoscope. They then wrote numbers like 1, 3, 5 etc. After doing this they run around the table and illustrate the faster rhythm through writing 50. Thereafter they run around the preschool and then change the numbers to 5,000, 1, 5, and 1,000. Then they sit down to have a rest and then go back and write 12; they take off again for another run around the preschool, come back, measure and write 2,000, 2,001 etc.

Two other girls, Kimberley and Erica work together. They immediately start off by illustrating the different rhythms of the heart through dots.

The teachers analyze and discuss several different possible directions to continue working with the children's illustrations and doings. What seems to fascinate the children is the sound of the heart through the stethoscope, but also the mathematical logic of the rhythm and the possibility to illustrate this in different ways – for example, with numbers or dots. They also register that the children seem to agree upon how to proceed when they choose their different activities and strategies, although they do not speak with each other. It seems to the teachers that these agreements and the giving and taking of different strategies take place beyond the spoken word. All this – the sound of the heart, the mathematical logic of rhythm, the different illustrations, the silent agreements and giving and taking of strategies – would be possible directions for the children and the teachers to continue working with. But the teachers, before defining a specific track with which to continue, decide to go back to the children with their documentations and discuss with them, to explore if they can get closer to a possible and interesting problem to work upon together with the children.

The next day the teachers gather the children together again and they have brought the children's illustrations and their own observations and documentations. But to make these more visible they have cut down the children's images and scanned them onto one sheet so that the illustrations should be easier for the children to handle. They have also brought only the parts of the observations that they, as teachers, found most interesting and so they re-read for the children only some of what the children talked about the day before. When doing this, the children react in a very surprising way; they get very upset by the fact that their images have been cut down in size and that the teachers read only parts of what they said the day before.

> Grace says: 'But hello! That is actually not my whole picture!'
> Erika says: 'But why haven't you written down everything we said?'

The teachers try to save the situation by explaining how they were thinking and they try to invite the children to continue the discussion. But the children are not interested; they turn away from the teachers, start to giggle together and show with all possible signs that they are not intending to continue this discussion. The teachers understand that they have to back away for the moment and leave the children for some time. They discuss in between themselves what happened and understand that the children felt that things that they saw as important were not acknowledged by the teachers.

The teachers start discussing that to hook on to children's desires, questions and problems in such a way that the children want to continue the process is the most difficult part of their job. Very often they feel that they miss what children are actually doing; it is hard to identify what kind of desires, questions and problems are actually important in children's thinking, talking and doings and it is difficult to arrange situations where they can meet with the children in collective experimentation and construction of problems. However, they decide to arrange for a new discussion to take place a few days later. They then sit down with the children, this time with the children's original illustrations and all observations present and they explain once again to the children how they were thinking and discuss with them what in the material interests the children the most. This time the children are joining the teachers in the discussion and they quickly decide that they want to look for more sounds, but they want to do this outside in the garden of the preschool.

The next day the teachers provide the children with material and tools needed for exploring sounds outside. The children are intensively engaged in the activity and they find many different sounds that they start illustrating by drawing.

Grace, who on the first occasion used numbers to illustrate the heart beats, now changes strategy and uses Kimberley's technique for illustration through dots. She also borrows the technique of zig-zag lines of another friend in the group.

Kimberley puts away her strategy of illustrating through dots and starts illustrating the sounds with symbols of different kinds. The teachers now register that there is an established and intense interest in between the children around sounds and that they are eager to illustrate these sounds in different ways. They are fascinated and curious about the flow of ideas, strategies and activities that are exchanged in between the children, but they have a hard time observing how and when this happens. They decide to investigate this closer together with the children by making it clear to the children that they have observed all the different ways the children have been using to detect and illustrate sounds and how they have cooperated in doing this.

So they gather the children together and they tell them how they have seen all their different ways of detecting and illustrating sounds and how they have noticed that the children exchange their ideas and strategies. They ask the children if they would like to continue investigating all this through working in pairs where each pair invents three sounds with their mouths that they then illustrate and play for the rest of the group as a charade.

This time the children immediately latch on to the teachers' proposition and they start working straight away. What kind of sounds to create? How to illustrate them? How to show them for the rest of the group? Grace and Adam work together and they immediately start illustrating the sound of talking. Other examples are the sound of laughing and whispering.

The sounds are then silently played out for the rest of the group. This creates an intense atmosphere in the room with a lot of activity and laughter, followed by many other related activities over a period of time.

Lines of flight created in the preschools

This delicate negotiating, this wandering back and forward and this continuous exchanging in between everybody, can occur in preschools that sometimes have taken off on and created their lines of flights. Such examples raise a number of important issues, illustrating which conditions favour the creation of lines of light:

1   A line of flight seems to have been created through the way that children no longer are looked upon as identified and already represented individuals with a predetermined development or as flexible, autonomous learners. In the project described above the idea of subjectivity and learning as a relational field is put to work. Not only are the different strategies for illustrating born through cooperative work; the strategies are being picked up, stolen, and exchanged. Also children and teachers join in their negotiations somewhat outside themselves; on a field, a playground, where they all meet around a problem. This field and the relation itself find themselves in movement; the problem to be worked upon is not clear from the beginning, children and teachers work on its construction. Through the definition of subjectivity and learning as a relational field, interests or desires and beliefs are treated as a flow that takes place in between everybody. This differs both from supple and rigid lines in that it creates a deviation, a zig-zag crack in the construction of the individual and in learning processes. Teachers are no longer able to solely define children as individuals according to rigid lines created by theories of children's predetermined development and children's interests or desires and beliefs are in these moments no longer tamed and controlled. Teachers rather look for what took place in between children, their interests are treated like contagious trends and they do not reside in each individual. This

is exactly where lines of flights are born. This gives an image of the child and of learning as a relational field which is something totally different than both rigid and supple binary segmentarity.[1]

2   A line of flight seems to have been created by the way the teachers now start to prepare themselves even more than when they were planning work that was predefined for the entire semester or the year. They prepare carefully only to find that something always escapes in the actual encounter with the children. This way of acting as teachers in relation to planning the activity can be seen as a line of flight because it differs from the rigid line of organizing and planning content and method a long time beforehand, thereafter to control and supervise to ensure that the planning is being implemented in the right way, and then finally evaluating what took place against predetermined outcomes. But it also differs from the supple line where children are asked to become responsible and flexible in relation to content and method and to take care of the planning themselves. Rather, what happens, in for instance the meeting with the curtailed images, is that not only the children but also the teachers and the content and method are set in motion, demanding a delicate but intense act of collective negotiation and experimentation.

3   A line of flight seems to have been created through the preschool being defined as a place for the collective construction of knowledge and values. This differs from rigid lines that see learning as a question of simple transmission of an already set and defined content of knowledge and values. It also differs from the supple line of governing through autonomy and flexibility. In both these modes of segmentarity the content of knowledge and values are still treated in an essentialist way. The difference with the preschool as a place for collective construction of knowledge and values lies in the actual content of knowledge and values being questioned, assuming the status of a continuously transforming feature in a relational field. In the above example nobody fully knows the problem under construction; is it going to be about rhythm, mathematics, illustrations of sounds, exchanging of strategies? The problem is formulated collectively as the process goes on. Teachers and children struggle with the ethical features of the situation to reach a way of acting in singular and unique ways, while still being united. This can only happen when knowledge and values are treated from the point of view of continuous production and creation.

4   A line of flight seems to have been created in relation to the pedagogical environment. The event above takes place in an environment

where children participate in the organisation of time and space. In morning meetings the day's content and structure is negotiated in between teachers and children. Children can choose to work in groups of different sizes with different contents during a day. The furniture and the material are accessible to children and possible for them to influence and change according to their demands. Within rigid lines of pedagogical environment, the furniture is arranged once and for all, the day's content structured in the same way for everybody. Within supple lines of pedagogical environment, the day might offer more choice to each child, but still only to the extent that it serves the goal set; time, space and furniture must still serve a fixed and predetermined goal.

The architecture and the furniture have been challenged and sometimes replaced in the preschools in Stockholm and its suburbs. In some cases, collaborative work with designers and architects has led to new pieces of furniture and new materials for investigations. By so doing, there has also been created the possibility of new kinds of subjectivities and learning processes for children and teachers. The furniture created by teachers and architects together presents a divergence, a zig-zag crack in the interior of a preschool. Through these new pieces of furniture the pedagogical environment is taken over by children and teachers, they influence the room and the furniture in new and unexpected ways. The furniture was built in such a way that it made possible transformation and new connections in unpredictable patterns. It is when this unpredictability and connectivity inscribed in the furniture is activated that a line of flight is born that differs both from supple and rigid lines of architecture and design.

5 A line of flight seems to have been created when projects focus on the construction of problems and when this process is considered more important than the outcome. This differs from rigid lines of thinking and acting in learning processes in that it does not work with transmission of a predetermined form and content of knowledge. But it also differs from the supple appeal to children to reflect upon and solve problems, but still within the logic of the problem as well as the solution being predetermined. When projects function with the construction of problems they can be considered as lines of flight, since they have given up the idea of pre-existing solutions and answers. Instead they focus on the process of constructing a problem and adapt the methods as the process goes on.[2] This is precisely what is happening in the project on the rhythm of the heart, where there is a circulating around what is maybe going to

become a fully constructed problem, but answers or solutions are not what are focused on or highlighted. This differs from both rigid and supple lines that still consider problems, solutions and methods as a predefined set of relations.

6   A line of flight seems to have been created through pedagogical documentation used as a visualization of the problem under construction. Above we can see how children and teachers meet around the pedagogical documentation and how it functions as a place where the problem worked upon can be visualized. Through the documentation new ideas and actions may take form. This differs from the rigid line of observing children through the lens of normality or spying on them with the ambition to check that they are following a normal trajectory. It also differs from the supple line that would use documentation to domesticate children's desire and learning processes and make of them flexible and autonomous learners. When pedagogical documentation is used as a meeting point in the relational field where the visualization of the problem worked upon can take place, it does not rely on any conscious or taming logic; it is a line of flight in that it is unpredictably experimenting.

These are a few of the line of flights created in these preschools. They do not exist alone. Rather they find themselves on a field of combat where together with rigid lines and supple lines they fight for space to survive. This makes the preschools quite a messy place to be in. Everything takes place at the same time and there is a constant struggle with creating favourable conditions for lines of flight to be created.

Please note that original figures have been removed from this excerpt.

Working with Deleuze in early childhood education: a conversation between Liselott Mariett Olsson (LMO) and Peter Moss (PM)

PM: Tell me about your own background in early childhood work.

LMO: I have a sort of double background. I took my preschool teacher exam [in Sweden], but as soon as I started to work as a teacher I felt I needed to continue studying and took courses at university at the same time as I was working as a preschool teacher. I studied pedagogy and especially pedagogical philosophy or educational philosophy. So my background is this combination of the profession, being a teacher, but also this passion for pedagogy, a knowledge tradition dating back to the very earliest philosophers who thought about education.

And then as I continued working I had the opportunity to become a head of some preschools and I also led a project undertaken in cooperation with the Reggio Emilia Institute [an organisation in Sweden that supports preschools and preschool workers who want to go deeper into the pedagogy of Reggio Emilia] and a research group at the Stockholm Institute of Education led by Gunilla Dahlberg.

PM: And then?

LMO: Through my studies in pedagogy and educational philosophy I had a fantastic opportunity to spend two years in a research group run by Professor Kenneth Hultqvist. He was the Foucault expert, and he and Gunilla Dahlberg also held seminars together. I spent this time studying all of Foucault's original work; a fantastic opportunity because I had not gone into research yet. Kenneth's research group was mostly doctoral students, but he also invited very interesting scholars to talk, such as Thomas Popkewitz and Nikolas Rose. I was a very young student and still working in preschool.

Afterwards I applied to Stockholm Institute of Education and I was lucky enough to get an award to study for a doctorate. This was about 2002. By that time, I had discovered that Foucault went only so far toward what I wanted to do; I had always kept one foot in practice, and I wanted to find something that offered a different relationship between theory and practice and Foucault could not really do that for me at that point. I was on the look-out for some theoretical perspective that could help me with that theory/practice issue and Gunilla Dahlberg told me about Deleuze. So I started reading.

PM: This was your first introduction to Deleuze?

LO: Right. I didn't understand anything! But I knew there was something there I needed to understand.

PM: You understood enough to understand there was something important to understand. How did you go about trying to understand?

LO: A lot of study. It was very hard work and that is important to remember. But it was also very joyful. I read Deleuze as part of a strict academic discipline, but at the same time out of joy because I looked for all the moments in these texts where I felt rather than understood, which I felt I could work with in practice.

Take one concept that I worked with in my thesis and that has followed me in my later research, the idea of desire and desire as a pure productive force, as a production of something real. This is very different to the way that developmental psychology, the theoretical paradigm in early childhood work, or that psychodynamic theories treat the child as lacking. A lot of early childhood practices are based on the child following certain developmental stages and therefore of being in a continuous state of lacking, of not achieving yet the next stage.

But inspired by a different image of the child from the schools in Reggio Emilia and from all the innovations and experimentations we were trying in our preschool practices in Sweden, I encountered this Deleuzian concept of desire in a very fruitful way. I started to read more carefully all the books and most particularly *Anti-Oedipus* [written with Felix Guattari, published in 1972], the main text on desire. Guattari said at one point that the patient in psychotherapy needs to be listened to without applying pre-existing interpretive frameworks; and that was the same as I saw teachers trying to do in early childhood practice with children, to listen to children's desires without a predetermined scheme or constantly looking for something that was lacking to be repaired.

PM: You say you read a lot and that some of that would affect you. Do you mean that Deleuze would write something and you would know something had happened?

LMO: Yes. But I want to emphasise that that required a lot of academic study. And I had support, especially Gunilla Dahlberg, my doctoral supervisor and we had continuous discussions on this in a very passionate way. But I also shared my understandings of Deleuze's concepts with the [preschool] teachers I was working with for my PhD research; I did my fieldwork together with these teachers, with whom I'd been working for a long time beforehand, so we just continued, but this time I had a different role as a researcher. We continued contributing to each other. And later when I started teaching at the university, with preschool teacher students, we were constantly experimenting with these concepts, bringing in material from their preschools.

PM: How did practitioners respond to these ideas?

LO: They were extremely generous, I didn't have a perfect understanding of Deleuze, I still don't. I think we were all a bit confused; we clearly could see something different; it was a different way of reasoning, of thinking about young children and education. There was something in these theories that connected to the daily work in preschool.

PM: You worked as a preschool teacher, part time, until you started your doctoral studies?

LMO: Exactly. But I kept going back and working with the teachers. During my doctoral student period, I taught on in-service courses. Now, I am an associate professor at Södertörn University, near Stockholm, and I'm responsible for one of our preschool teacher education programmes, though at this point I don't use any Deleuzian theories for the programme.

PM: You said earlier you did not find Foucault very satisfying when it came to the relationship between theory and practice.

LMO: That's not entirely true, because Foucault in his preface to Deleuze and Guattari's *Anti-Oedipus* draws a beautiful relation between theory and practice. Also Foucault was absolutely necessary to avoid falling into the trap of describing desire as yet another romantic idea of the child or, worse, falling into the trap set by neoliberalism, with its idea of the autonomous, flexible, problem-solving subject. Because this is also something I am trying to be very careful about, avoiding this ideological notion of the subject. This has been a very hard struggle.

I think we continuously and inevitably fall into these traps. There is a risk that these concepts seduce us – 'creativity', 'affirmation', 'innovation', in the worst-case scenario they become 'flower [empty] language'.

I wanted to talk to you about the 'line of flight'. Since you chose this example to be illustrated in the book, it is important that we 'contest' it a little bit. That is one concept I misunderstood a bit and I'm much more careful about that now. Because lines of flight can include fascism, in any form, which can also be read as a line of flight, and it can be dangerous if we describe lines of flight without applying critical thought to it. That is one trap. Deleuze can be used in ways not intended.

I am sometimes worried about what has happened with Deleuze and Guattari in terms of the political situation; it has become a tremendously popular perspective in Sweden and internationally. You asked me before who I could talk to when I was studying, but I need to add one very essential person, Liane Mozère [a French sociologist who worked with Deleuze], because I was living in France when I was a doctoral student and I was part of Liane's research group in Metz [north-east France]. I discussed everything with Liane and her doctoral students and what I got from that and reading Deleuze in French was that I understood the political dimensions of these theories, and now I am afraid they are losing that dimension.

PM: Can you say more about your understanding of the political dimension?

LMO: These theories and concepts cannot be used as decoration or flower language because they need to be connected to the political situation of the society you are working within. If you think about the 'competent child', this concept might relate to a line of creativity, but also to fascism, you can go down that line as well, and to neoliberalism and new governmentality. Sometimes when concepts are used too, let's say, 'enthusiastically', that political dimension gets lost and that is dangerous. So these concepts may seem very revolutionary and you can even get ecstatic about them, but bear in mind there is always a political and an ethical responsibility.

PM: You say there is a need to bring a certain critical perspective to working with Deleuzian ideas and concepts. For example, you don't just say anything is fine as long as it emerges from an event?

LMO: I remember having this discussion with students during my doctoral period, in in-service courses, and they would say 'what about paedophilia?' So it's really very complicated, a tricky business. We can never leave Foucault and his critical approach.

PM: You were talking earlier about experimentation and Reggio Emilia. How did Reggio Emilia create an opening for working with Deleuze?

LMO: Quite early I had the opportunity to visit the schools in Reggio Emilia, and what I felt there was such a strong and vital pedagogical tradition, I was studying this at the same time, but also a fantastic connection between theoretical issues and practice – it was so well thought through. It was also obvious they gave children a different position in society and that was very important. Deleuze and Guattari's writing and concepts seemed to fit very well with that practice and experimentation that was only found then in Reggio Emilia as far as I could see.

PM: Are they aware of Deleuze and Guattari?

LMO: I think so. It seems to me that theory has always been such an important part of their practice. I admire their eclectic approach, in the best sense of the term, and that they make theories their own, they talk for example of 'Our Piaget'. For me its fantastic practice because it joins these two lines that I've always been passionate about – with one foot in the practice and one in really complicated theories.

Also, and most importantly, they work politically, they approach education as a political subject, focusing attention on public education. Citizenship and educational questions are the driving force of the society – and that was really my inspiration.

PM: When working in Sweden you are in a place where there is a lot of interest in Reggio Emilia and experimentation. If you go into preschools in Sweden can you talk about experimentation to teachers, are they open to this?

LMO: Yes. But they are also under great pressure now. The very logic I was trying to challenge in my book, the logic of taming, supervising and controlling, is going strong in Sweden, way beyond my expectation. The preschool inspectorate has come out with a report stating the need for enhancing the notion and practice of teaching in Swedish preschools. The definition of teaching in the report, however, is quite reductive and does not take account of the many and various teaching practices that already exist in our early childhood education. Teachers today are caught between these developments and the wish to experiment.

PM: But many teachers are open to experimentation, to working in new ways?

LO: I think there is a revolutionary spirit among preschool teachers because this [early childhood education] was – at least in Sweden – a story of female pioneers, this was a project from the very beginning, about children's place in society. It is a beautiful and fantastic field to be engaged in. I can feel it when I visit the preschools and talk to teachers, and it's something I try to bring into the education of preschool teachers today.

PM: You've done further research since your doctoral work in which Deleuze has been important?

LMO: When I finished my PhD and the book [Olsson, 2009], Gunilla Dahlberg and I got research funding for a research project called the 'Magic of Language'. Our aim was to better understand young children's relation to language – reading and writing – but also to experiment with new didactic strategies [ways for teachers to work with children]. Deleuze and Guattari's writing on language became really important. One concept was particularly important, and that was the event, and within the event, Deleuze's theory of sense.

In a simplified way, we can say 'sense' is connected to the question of problems and solutions. Normally we think solutions come before problems and the teacher's task is to present the children with the problem they need to solve and for which the teacher already has the solution. Deleuze, with the help of Henri Bergson [a French philosopher] contests this idea by saying that the real issue is how we construct a problem and how the construction of a problem stands in a totally proportional relation to the sense that is produced in this construction. So solutions are only an effect of how the problem is constructed in relation to the sense produced. The most important point about 'sense' for Deleuze is that it's not a given and is produced through the construction of problems rather than answering already defined problems with already defined solutions, which makes it possible to value children's sense-production and problem-constructing differently.

When we approach language, this concept of sense is a fantastic resource with young children. Because what do they do? They reinvent language over and over again. They invent new letters, new alphabets, new words, they do not just inherit the sense that we think is right, is inherent in language – what we, as adults, say is the problem. A theory that is capable of acknowledging the way children give sense to or construct the problem of language is very helpful here.

PM: Teachers tend to say I know what the problem is, the children have to learn how to read and write, and I need to focus on how to do that. You find it productive working with Deleuze in this context?

LMO: Yes, because we were capable of seeing, even with 1½- to 2-year-olds, how they constructed linguistic problems, and when we could come to such a detailed level of analysis we were much better equipped to arrange a pedagogical approach that was responsive to the children. For instance, children are making sounds connected to the signs they produce; this is one of the most basic linguistic problems, concerning the representational relation between 'phoneme' and 'grapheme'. If we are open for not only linguistic representations that we already know but also how children invent these, we can create environments for children that give them more opportunities to continue to explore the problem they have constructed, starting out from their sense-production of the relationship between signs and sounds. This leads to different practices.

PM. So working with Deleuze and Guattari is not abstract, but very concrete.

LMO: It's very difficult but very practical, yes.

PM: Could they be worked with more widely in early childhood education, and that extends to other philosophers? Could more preschools find them useful? What contribution do you think Deleuze can best make to early childhood education?

LMO: There is the possibility of using some of his philosophical reasoning and concepts in relation to classical educational problems, such as the relationship between the individual and society, and knowledge reproduction versus knowledge production. Deleuze's theories and concepts can be very useful tools.

But there is still that risk, I talked about earlier, that these theories and concepts could be used to do the work of contemporary governmentality, to use Foucault's concept, to better control and govern. Or they could be put in the service of neoliberalism, to produce the flexible, problem-solving subject that neoliberalism wants. These are the risks if these theories are put to use in a non-political way.

On the other hand, Deleuze and Guattari can help us to resist and to create new thinking, for example to revalue children's contribution to the world. There are many authors, very different to Deleuze and Guattari, who share this endeavour, like Hannah Arendt [a German-born American political scientist], who continuously talks about new generations' inevitable transformation of society, of culture, of values, of knowledge.

PM: You are saying Deleuze and Guattari offer a way to revalue children's contribution to the world.

LMO: That is complex because we have an image of the competent child, and we need to distinguish what that means. A competent child can become an essentialist description fitting perfectly into the neoliberal version of the flexible subject. Working with Deleuze, you couldn't talk about the competent child, not in that sense. You would have to talk about the necessity of offering time and space to new generations to open up for a transformation of society. With Deleuze and Guattari we can ask, what can children bring to this world, how can they transform this world?

Deleuze defines the philosopher's task as to create concepts, and he attaches very particular importance to a creative thought. What many of us have been trying to say is that there is something about Deleuze's thinking that fits well with the educational task of giving time and space to a new generation for the renewal of society. His theories help us to highlight how very, very young children do contribute to the world. So the new generation must always be allowed to transform society, to create it anew. But we must also pass on those things we consider too valuable to lose, that we want to give to the new generation.

It's a reminder of the very origins of the school, the Greek concept of the school, as giving time and place for new generations *simultaneously* to study and renew society.

PM: Are there other points you'd want to add about the potential of Deleuze to early childhood education?

LMO: I really think that the most important contribution can come from connecting his theories and concepts to some classical educational problems. They can particularly throw light on how young children can contribute to the world, how they transform culture, values, knowledge. That is the absolute main contribution of Deleuze.

Questions – yours and mine

Don't forget to share and discuss the questions you have after reading this chapter, including the ones I suggested at the end of Chapter 1.

Here though are some of my questions to you:

- Think of an example of an event and/or a line of flight that you have experienced, in early childhood education or anywhere else. Talk about what happened and why it happened. What were some of the components of the assemblage from which the line of flight emerged?
- What conditions do you think might be favourable to lines of flight in early childhood education?
- Have you ever been physically affected, for example with goose bumps, by something unexpected or new you have experienced?
- What are the challenges for early childhood education of starting from problems that children construct rather than solving adult-defined problems?
- Can you think of some examples of micro-politics in action, practiced by yourself or someone you've worked with? What happened, and with what effect?

Notes

1 Deleuze and Guattari argue that

> The human being is a segmentary animal. Segmentarity is inherent to all the strata composing us. Dwelling, getting around, working, playing: life is spatially and socially segmented. The house is segmented according to its rooms' assigned purposes; streets, according to the order of the city; the factory, according to the nature of the work and operations performed in it. We are segmented in a *binary* fashion, following the great

major dualist oppositions: social classes, but also men-women, adults-children, and so on. . . . We are segmented in a *linear* fashion, along a straight line or a number of straight lines, of which each segment represents an episode or 'proceeding': as soon as we finish one proceeding we begin with another, forever proceduring or procedured, in the family, in school, in the army, on the job. School tells us, 'You're not at home anymore'; the army tells us, 'You're not in school anymore'.

(Deleuze and Guattari, 2004, p. 230)

2 For another example of how children and teachers construct a problem, see 'The Crow Project', a chapter written by Swedish preschool teacher Ann Åberg in *Transformation Change and Real Utopias in Early Childhood Education*. Ann narrates how teachers at her preschool replaced their usual project on birds with a project that started from the children's expressed interest in a particular bird, a crow. Reflecting on the experience, in which pedagogical documentation played a key role, Ann writes:

When I think back on other bird-related projects over the years, I recall that we, as pedagogues, focused primarily on teaching the children basic bird facts. We were, for example, teaching the children the names of the most common birds. In retrospect I ask myself: To whom were these names so important? And I wonder how meaningful it was for the children. Did they actually learn something that they thought was exciting to know about birds? I don't recall choosing bird themes because the children actually demonstrated an interest in or curiosity about birds. Birds were simply one of many important 'categories' that we were supposed to look at with the children. In the crow project, however, we wanted to listen to the children more consciously and proceed in a fashion other than our conventional way of thinking about and understanding a science project. Our aim was not to impart to the children any scientific truths about birds. Instead, we wanted to understand how we might shape a meaningful context for the children's keen interest in crows that we had observed.

(Moss, 2013, p. 145)

Chapter 7

Posthumanism, the posthuman child and intra-active pedagogy

I move now to my last example from the multitude of perspectives in early childhood education and that are helping to create alternative narratives. I want to emphasise again that this is not the last of such stimulating ideas, just my final example – there are many more, just as there are many alternative narratives. In this chapter, I will move away from a focus on individual local projects (Reggio Emilia) and individual thinkers (Foucault, Deleuze) to a way of thinking about things, a perspective on the world and relationships, a 'navigational tool' (Braidotti, 2013, p. 5): what has been termed posthumanism. While many people have worked with posthumanist perspectives, including Gilles Deleuze, a name that recurs frequently is that of Karen Barad, an American feminist scholar but also, by background, a physicist who builds on the theories of the Danish physicist Niels Bohr, whose work on quantum physics challenged mainstream physics and Albert Einstein in the 1930s. Her concepts of 'agential realism' and 'intra-action' will be encountered in this chapter, and their relevance, and more broadly posthumanism's, to children and early childhood education will be explored.

For just as the concepts and theories of Foucault and Deleuze are today being put to work in early childhood education, provoking us to think and practice differently, so too is posthumanism and the concepts and theories that it generates. All three, and indeed Reggio Emilia, question today's dominant discourses, in particular contesting the divisions and oppositions so deeply embedded in the positivist paradigm and which enable it to claim the ability to discipline and control (you could say that positivism's tactic for gaining control is to divide and rule or classify and govern). What emerges instead from Reggio Emilia, Foucault and Deleuze is an understanding of the profound, welcome and inescapable inter-connectedness of people, things and ideas. This lies at the heart of posthumanism too, which is fundamentally transdisciplinary, working with diverse perspectives and methodologies, including relatively new fields such as science and technology studies, animal studies, posthuman philosophy and ethics and environmental humanities. Rather than the dominant discourses' reliance on a handful of disciplines, developmental psychology and economics in particular, we are exposed to a multitude of disciplinary riches.

The *Contesting Early Childhood* series has three books that pay particular attention to posthumanism, and I will draw extensively on these valuable resources during the course of this chapter: Hillevi Lenz Taguchi's *Going beyond The Theory/Practice Divide In Early Childhood Education: Introducing an Intra-active Pedagogy* (Lenz Taguchi, 2009); Affrica Taylor's *Reconfiguring the Natures of Childhood* (Taylor, 2013); and Karin Murris's *The Posthuman Child: Educational Transformation through Philosophy with Picturebooks* (Murris, 2016).

Humanism and its problems

For many centuries, humanism has exerted great influence over human thought and actions. At its heart is the privileged and central position given to human beings, lording it over the planet, apart from and above the environment, and alone having the capacity for agency – to act on the world to achieve a particular effect. At its worst, humanism has led to a state of affairs described by the Dark Mountain Project, an ecological group who we met at the beginning of the book, where '[t]he dominant stories of our culture tell us that humanity is separate from all other life and destined to control it'. This is mankind as the autonomous and rational ruler of all he surveys, exercising unrestricted choice and mastery over everything that is not human, whether animate or non-animate, and denying the possibility of agency to all such nonhumans. Humans and nonhumans are divided from each other, in an exclusive binary.

This picture needs to be qualified. For this idea(l) of mankind is rather exclusionary. For a start, there is a strong developmental element, which confines full humanity and exclusive capacity for agency to adults, the child being not fully human but rather an immature and incomplete person, unequal to the developed and knowing adult. Then, humanism has also been inclined to treat a range of other persons as not fully human, including women, people with disabilities, people of colour and dispossessed others.

Humanism of this kind, with its hierarchy of existence topped by the white adult male, has come to be increasingly questioned. One reason is the refusal of the majority any longer to privilege the position of the white adult male. Another is the ecological and nuclear crises confronting us, the dominant discourse of separation and mastery 'falling apart before our eyes' and having brought us to such a dangerous state of affairs that the Doomsday Clock of the Bulletin of Atomic Scientists now stands at just two minutes to midnight (https://thebulletin.org/timeline). We are, it transpires, all in this together, which means urgently forging new relationships between humankind and the rest of the planet, relationships imbued with greater respect, care and sustainability; the jury is out on whether we can achieve this in the requisite time-scale.

But pragmatic reasons for change have been accompanied by philosophical changes, rethinking in a fundamental way the position and relationships of everyone and everything on planet Earth. There has been a 'material turn', leading to a shift in paradigm, from humanism to posthumanism – at least among some humans.

The material turn and posthumanism

I have already referred, in Chapter 2, to the 'linguistic turn', as accompanying a shift (for some, at least) from a positivist to a postfoundational paradigm. More recently, there has been a 'material turn' also. The 'material turn' builds on the 'linguistic turn', as Hillevi Lenz Taguchi describes in her book in the series, going further

> to include the material as an active agent in the construction of discourse and reality. Physical matters become dynamic materials or trans-materials with a capacity of changing to its form in various ways, as well as intra-acting with other matter and organisms in processes of transformation. Hence, unlike the 'old' materialism, which was either connected to positive science (positivism) or to Marxism in the social sciences, the 'new' material turn is about an increased interest in the active role of the material world, material culture, material agency and 'artifactuality'.
> (Lenz Taguchi, 2009, pp. 18–19)

Put crudely, these turns attach new importance not only to language and its role in how we make meaning (the 'discursive') but also to all aspects of the nonhuman, both animate and non-animate, and their active role in shaping the world (the 'material').

With the material turn, and its different thinking about the nonhuman, human beings are brought into a new relationship with the other occupants of planet Earth, and humanism gives way to posthumanism. The central, privileged and autonomous position of human (adult) beings, lording it over all else from on high, along with the belief in their superiority and separateness from all else, is superseded: the world is no longer centred on human beings and their affairs (Prout, 2004). Instead, the place of human beings in the world is de-centred, with the focus moving to inter-dependence within what has been termed 'more than human worlds', a term that encompasses a wide range of constituents: 'things, objects, other animals, living beings, organisms, physical forces, spiritual entities, and humans'. The term 'entanglements' is often used to convey a sense of the multiplicity, complexity and inescapability of the relationships involved.

From this new, posthuman perspective, old boundaries, especially those that sustain a distinct and privileged position for human beings, have begun to break down and blur, to be replaced by an attention to inter-dependencies, interconnections and (shades of the rhizome) entanglements. Hillevi Lenz Taguchi again:

> [W]e also need to go beyond the human/nonhuman divide, as we understand our existence as a co-existence with the rest of the world. There is no hierarchical relationship between different organisms (human and non-human) and the material world around us. . . . We are all in a state and relationship of inter-dependence and inter-connection with each other as human or non-human performative agents. 'Existence is not an individual affair', writes Barad; 'both human individuals and non-human organisms and matter emerge through and as a part of entangled intra-relations' (2007: ix). Everything around us affects everything else, which makes everything change and be in a continuous process of becoming – *becoming different in itself* – rather than being different in relation to another (Deleuze, 1994). In these processes there is a central element of unpredictability, creative and inventive change in the interconnections between different matters and organisms with different potentialities. All matter and organisms have agency and affect each other in a continuous flow of force and intensities that work in both predictable and sometimes in totally unpredictable ways (Grosz, 2005, 2008). What happens here and now in the actual present is a result, just as much of the repeated habitual self-organising behaviours of all organisms and matter, as it is of chances, mistakes or an act of creativity and invention that occurs in the intra-activities between all things and organisms at work. The limits of change, and the potentialities of all organisms and matter to develop and change, are unknown to us.
>
> (Lenz Taguchi, 2009, p. 15; original emphasis)

'Everything around us affects everything else, which makes everything change and be in a continuous process of becoming' – this is the nub of the posthumanist perspective, and it changes everything. Instead of a hierarchical world, topped by humans, there are now **common worlds** that human beings 'share with all manner of others – living and inert, human and more-than-human' (Taylor, 2013, p. 62), forming dynamic collectives and unexpected partnerships.

In this reconceptualised world, mankind is not alone in having agency. There is no longer a divide between humans as active and intentional, the powers that be exercising agency, with everything else providing a passive background to be acted upon. Instead, everything is dynamic, not passive, so that

> [h]ow chairs, dots and floors feel and sound *matters* in our intra-actions with them. They have force and power to transform our thinking and

being in a particular space or in the world at large. In*tra*-activity is different from in*ter*-activity, which refers to inter-personal relationships between at least two persons. In*tra*-activity here relates to physicist terminology and to relationships between any organism and matter (human or non-human). Hence, what Barad and other material feminists (Alaimo and Hekman, 2008) are suggesting is that it is not only humans that have agency – the possibility of intervening and acting upon others and the world. Rather, *all matter can be understood as having agency in a relationship in which they mutually will change and alter in their on-going intra-actions.* Consider for instance the simple example of how hot tea or coffee intra-acts with our bodies to heat them from within and perhaps somewhat relaxing them when they tense. Or the more complicated interconnections between that which we conceptualise as our body and mind, when somatic illnesses can emerge from emotional events that will profoundly affect the body in different ways. Or, consider how birds and crickets sing and sound more loudly and develop better 'sound-instruments' as an evolutionary process living in the noise of the big cities.

(Lenz Taguchi, 2009, p. 4; emphasis added)

In this reconceptualised world, the nonhuman as well as the human thus become 'performative agents'; indeed, Spinoza's view that 'we never know in advance what a body can do' applies as much to the nonhuman as to human bodies. But this extended understanding of agency is not about some simple, interactive process, of one acting on the other, a straightforward relationship of cause and effect. Rather, this happens through 'a dynamic process of intra-action'; this is Barad's theory of 'agential realism'. This is both an epistemological and an ontological theory; that is, it reconceptualises how knowledge is created and also how reality is actually shaped.

To understand this thinking, we must leave behind the idea of separate, individualised existences, whether humans or nonhumans, that exert agency on each other. Rather we have to imagine a world in which subjects – human or nonhuman, animate or inanimate – 'are' because they are in relationship to and influencing each other, all entangled with each other to the extent that it is impossible to say where the boundaries are of, say, each child, teacher, furnishing or drawing. In such relationships of mutuality, all matter alters and changes in ongoing intra-actions.

As Karen Barad emphasises, agency is 'not something that someone or something *has* to varying degrees, since I am trying to displace the very notion of independently existing individuals'; rather it is an 'enactment, a matter of possibilities for reconfiguring entanglements. So agency is not about choice in any liberal humanist sense; rather . . . it is about response-ability, about the possibilities of mutual response' (Barad, 2009). Karin Murris, in her book *The Posthuman Child*, has illustrated this mutual intra-agency of entanglement by drawing on an analysis by Karin Hultman and Hillevi Lenz Taguchi of a photo of a young girl playing in a sand pit.

> They [Hultman and Lenz Taguchi] first describe how the photo could be analysed (somewhat simplified as they declare) through a humanist lens as follows:
>
>> What we see with a habitual anthropocentric [human-centred] style of seeing is a girl in a sandbox who is playing with sand. The girl as the subject of the photograph is separated and detached from the sandbox, which merely becomes the backdrop. In this way of looking, our reading of the image relies on a subject/object binary divide. This also applies to the researcher as the subject of seeing who understands herself or himself as separated and detached from the photograph as the object to be analysed. Moreover, this constitutes a foundational division between subjects understood as humans (subjects-humans) and objects understood as part of nature (objects-nature) (Mol, 2002, 33). This division is asymmetrical in terms of value, that is, the girl playing with sand is given a far greater value and is seen as superior to the sand, the bucket and the sandbox. She is active and the sand is passive. As a subject she acts out her intentions and competences.
>>
>> (Hultman and Lenz Taguchi, 2010, p. 527)
>
> From a humanist perspective, the material in the photo is merely the backdrop to what really matters. Physical objects are discrete, clearly separated, in a causal relationship with other objects and 'acting only when acted upon by an external agent' (Jackson and Mazzei, 2012, p. 111). Hultman and Lenz Taguchi (2010, p. 529) suggest an alternative to this 'vertical', hierarchical reading of the photo above. Their reading is 'horizontal' or 'flattened'. . . .
>
> A posthuman methodology resists starting out by focusing on the human in the picture. . . . Hultman and Lenz Taguchi (2010, p. 530) offer us the following unusual – therefore again worthy of quoting at length – *horizontal* reading of the photo:
>
>> the sand and the girl are doing something to each other simultaneously. They transform as an effect of the intra-actions that emerge in between them. Thus, all bodies in the event are to be understood as *causes* in relation to each other (Deleuze, 1990, 4). In another way of understanding this, the sand offers certain possibilities in its relations with the girl. In the intra-action between the girl and the sand, new problems to be solved *emerge* as an effect of their mutual engagement. . . .

The girl and the sand have no agency of their own. Rather, what is understood as 'agency' in a relational materialist approach is a quality that emerges *in-between* different bodies involved in mutual engagements and relations: muscles lifting the arm and hand which slowly opens up and lets go of the sand, which by the force of gravity falls with specific speed into the bucket, where it lands – one grain upon the other with force causing it to roll over and down and simultaneously constructing a hill of sand in the middle of the bucket. The uneven foundation of the sandbox forces the body of the girl to adjust to find the perfect balance to be able to perform her task. She directs her whole body around the sand. . . . The force of gravity, the uneven foundation, the bucket and the quality of the grains of sand are all active forces that intra-act with her body and mind and that she has to work with and against.

From the perspective of a relational materialist methodology the sand is active and has agency. There are no absolute boundaries between the two bodies: sand and girl. They are overlapping forces. The girl plays with the sand and the sand plays with the girl. Both child and sand are continually *becoming* (Hultman and Lenz Taguchi, 2010, p. 530). The girl certainly has agency, but [not as] an intentional superior autonomous humanist subject (Hultman and Lenz Taguchi, 2010, p. 530).

(Murris, 2016, pp. 94–96)

One of the important points made in this example, which may get lost, is how intra-action is about something happening 'in-between different bodies'. The concept of 'in between' is important for rethinking agency, moving from a simple idea of A acting upon B to a more complex idea of entanglements out of which intra-action emerges something new. (The reader may have noticed that turning away from simple causal relations has been a theme running through this book.)

A final point of clarification should be added about the relationship between humanism and posthumanism. Humanism has also been associated with an emancipatory agenda that includes solidarity, social justice and equality, and posthumanism does not reject this agenda for human betterment. What posthumanism objects to is the 'epistemic violence' (Braidotti, 2013, p. 30) done to all occupants of the planet by humanism: 'The acknowledgment of epistemic violence goes hand in hand with the recognition of the real-life violence which was and still is practised against non-human animals and the dehumanized social and political "others" of the humanist norm' (Braidotti, 2013, p. 30)' (Murris, 2016, p. 56). The issue is to hold on to the solidarity, social justice and equality whilst rejecting the violence, exploitation and mastery.

A note on agency and choice

I have talked earlier about the possibility of choice: to choose, for example, a personal identity, a narrative, a perspective, the image of the child and other political choices. I should, perhaps, have made it clearer that I don't see this as a straightforward exercise of personal agency, akin to the autonomous consumer deciding in a supposedly rational and calculative way which product constitutes a best buy. I would accept that choice and agency are, in fact, always constrained, be it by inadequate information, the workings of power relations or other structural forces; we are never totally free agents.

But posthumanists would go further, to question the very possibility of agency and choice. You have just read Barad's view that agency is 'not something that someone or something *has* to varying degrees, since I am trying to displace the very notion of independently existing individuals'. Karin Murris develops this theme in her book in the *Contesting Early Childhood* series:

> Posthumanism does not offer just another 'conceptual' framework for teaching and research that educators can *choose* from out of a range of other options (like the choice of clothes to wear when waking up in the morning). It would presuppose a notion of intentionality that assumes a humanist subjectivity – theories as mere *discursive* tools freely chosen by human animals. But human animals are neither in charge of nature, nor of culture. As a matter of *fact*, they are *part* of natureculture and cannot take a transcendental, detached point of view (from 'nowhere' in particular). It simply is not an option (Haraway, 1988). We cannot simply change our *stories* about child.
>
> (Murris, 2016, p. 121; original emphasis)

In other words, the way I have framed the book – in terms of alternatives and choices – is evidence of the position I have taken, which might be described as broadly social constructionist, a position not shared by a posthumanist. Indeed, as we shall see now, posthumanists are critical of the very idea of social construction.

The posthuman child

Posthumanism questions what it regards as humanist conceptions of the child, including: the 'developmental child' of developmental psychology, developing innately, according to general universal natural laws, through clearly identifiable stages of intellectual growth, chronologically ordered, hierarchically arranged; the 'child with rights', active, capable, visible, powerful, but still in the process of *becoming adult*, requiring protection and special provision, individualistic, decontextualised and universal; and the 'social child', contextualised in particular socio-economic, linguistic, cultural, and historical environments, and socially constructed.

In these conceptions, posthumanists see a recurring divide or binary, either/or, between nature (the developmental child) and culture (the 'child with rights' or the 'social child'). This has been described by Affrica Taylor as

> the polarised camps of nature or culture [that have] been most popularly expressed within the long-standing 'nature/nurture' debates. . . . [These] deep-seated epistemological differences have been manifest in the disciplinary demarcations between the nature realists on the one hand and the social constructionists on the other. The nature realists are predominantly physical or behavioural scientists, seeking the biological/chemical/neurological determinants and 'hard facts' of childhood. The social constructionists are those social scientists who argue that we can only ever know childhood through our culturally produced discourses about it – including scientific discourses about the 'facts' of childhood.
>
> (Taylor, 2013, p. xvii)

But having queried and broken down established divides between humans and nonhumans, in favour of the entanglements of common worlds, posthumanist thinking further queries the divide, or binary, between nature and culture, 'nature realists' and 'social constructionists'. This is exemplified by Alan Prout, a leading figure in the 'new' sociology of childhood and childhood studies, though not a posthumanist, who in his book *The Future of Childhood* (Prout, 2004) offers a challenge to the social constructionist position that he himself spent decades promoting. The future of childhood studies, he suggests, lies in doing something different, rejecting the nature/culture or biological/social divide, in which over time first one side becomes ascendant in understandings of the child then the other, in favour of an open interrelationship in which they are 'mutually constitutive' (ibid., p. 84) of the child. Prout, Affrica Taylor explains,

> is not calling for scholars to discard insights about the discursive [social] construction of childhood and default to accepting its realist definitions, but rather to pursue ways of studying childhood that do not require mutually exclusive choices between the assumed-to-be-purely-natural [i.e. the biological] or the assumed-to-be-purely-cultural [i.e. the social constructionist]. . . . Prout proposes that ' . . . the future of childhood studies rests on ways of treating childhood as a "nature-culture'. . . . [O]nly by understanding the ways in which childhood is constructed by the heterogeneous elements of culture and nature, which in any case cannot be easily separated, will it be possible to take the field forward' (Latour, 1993, p. 44).
>
> (Taylor, 2013, pp. xvii, xix).

By treating childhood as *nature-culture*, Prout and others (he refers for example to the work of biologist and philosopher Donna Haraway) want to get beyond the either/or debate of whether childhood is either a biological entity or a socio-cultural construction; and indeed, beyond any attempt to see childhood as a certain proportion of biology and a certain proportion of culture – a bit of material and a bit of discursive. Instead, 'nature-culture' implies that the biological and the socio-cultural are interconnected, in fact completely entangled. There is no way we can draw a border between the biological and the cultural or socially constructed, since childhood is an inextricable mixture of both. In the words of Karen Barad:

> The relationship between the material and the discursive is one of mutual entailment. Neither discursive practices nor material phenomena are ontologically or epistemologically prior. Neither can be explained in terms of the other. Neither is reducible to the other. Neither has privileged status in determining the other. Neither is articulated or articulable in the absence of the other; matter and meaning are mutually articulated.
>
> (Barad, 2007, p. 152)

The posthuman child is, therefore, 'an entanglement, constituted by concepts *and* material forces, where the social, the political, the biological, *and their observing, measuring and controlling machines are interwoven and entwined –* all elements intra-act' (Murris, personal communication).

Intra-active pedagogy

Posthumanist perspectives have been put to work in early childhood education through Hillevi Lenz Taguchi's concept of 'intra-active pedagogy', which explores the implications for education of the entanglement of the human and nonhuman and of the discursive and the material. She starts with a number of important questions:

> Is it possible to think in another way that does not separate matter as "dead" or passive in relation to the discursive? Is it possible to think of the material in early childhood practices as having agency of its own? Can we think of the material as being active in producing our meaning making of the child and learning and of ourselves as teachers? Would it be possible to think of the material as being active in producing our discursive meaning-making?
>
> (Lenz Taguchi, 2009, p. 29)

If we answer yes to these questions, pedagogical practices emerge not just discursively but also by 'materials actively and discursively materialising practice into existence through their agentic engagement in an intra-active production of our discursive understandings' (ibid.).

Following this thinking through, all kinds of organisms and matter are understood as performative agents. For example,

> even dots on the floor that children are supposed to sit on in a circle at assembly actively act upon the bodies of children. These dots actively make themselves intelligible to the child by keeping it in place on the floor and signalling when a child is out of place by becoming visible to us (Hultman, 2009). Provided it is acknowledged to be the source of any kind of action, a performative agent can be both non-human and human (organic and inorganic).
>
> (ibid.)

An intra-active pedagogy requires recognition of and working with material beings that are just as agentic as humans and with the interdependent and entangled nature of the relationship between things, matter and organisms, always in relationships of intra-action. As such, they not only depend on each other, but are also affecting each other mutually all the time: 'The material affects our discursive understandings just as much as our discursive understandings affect the material reality around us' (Lenz Taguchi, 2010, p. 30).

An intra-active pedagogy, or indeed any pedagogy influenced by post-human perspectives, de-centres humans, and that includes children. This means, for example, that with its emphasis on entanglement, intra-active pedagogy contests the idea and language of child-centredness, so common in today's early childhood education. As Affrica Taylor sets out in her book in the series:

> the orthodox child-centred focus upon the child's individuality and their developing autonomous agency . . . runs completely counter to the task of appreciating that no-one stands or acts alone, that all human lives are inextricably enmeshed with others (human and more-than-humans) and that all human actions are implicated with and have implications for others (including nonhuman others).
>
> My point is that *twenty-first century children need relational and collective dispositions*, not individualistic ones, to equip them to live well within the kind of world they have inherited . . . they will need a firm sense of shared belonging and shared responsibility within the natureculture collective of their immediate common worlds . . . they will need to be able to build upon a foundational sense of connectivity to this natureculture collective. Such dispositions and capacities will never be fostered through the application of a child-centred and hyper-individualistic developmental framework.
>
> (Taylor, 2013, p. 117; original emphasis)

The child in an intra-active pedagogy is not the centre of things but rather part of an entangled web or network of relationships, connecting the human and the nonhuman, culture and nature, the material and the discursive. Relations, not the child, are central to everything.

Doing posthumanism in early childhood education: two examples

Sticks, guns and dolls

I conclude this chapter with two examples of posthuman perspectives being put to work in early childhood education. My first example is from Hillevi Lenz Taguchi's book in the series. It starts with Kristine Rende, an undergraduate student in the second semester of her preschool teacher education in Sweden, presenting a sequence of documentation from a small project she had done with 2- to 3-year-old children in a preschool. For Lenz Taguchi, this is an example of intra-active pedagogy, illustrating that learning is not something the individual child achieves in isolation but is produced in the intra-actions that emerge when different organisms, matters and discourses intra-act with each other. This understanding of pedagogy calls for everyone involved to become aware of how everything is connected and affects everything as part of an interdependent whole. Note, by the way, the appearance of 'lines of flight' in this account, reflecting how Lenz Taguchi is working with and weaving together the ideas of Gilles Deleuze and the perspectives of posthumanism – as well as taking inspiration from Reggio Emilia, reflected here in the reference to pedagogical documentation and a pedagogy of listening.

> **From *Going beyond the Theory/Practice Divide in Early Childhood Education: Introducing an Interactive Pedagogy*, pp. 30–38; original emphasis**
>
> One of the aims of this vocational training was to learn how to use pedagogical documentation as a tool for learning and reflection on behalf of both the children and staff, i.e. making the learning visible to challenge the children further as well as critically challenging teachers' preconceptions about learning, taken-for-granted ways of thinking and organizing practice. The students had been told to pick something that was 'going on' among the children; a question or issue that kept on reappearing in their play or everyday life at the preschool, document it and use the documentation to inform further play and learning.

For her presentation later at the [Stockholm] Institute of Education, this student had made a short power-point presentation. She immediately startled us as she started to describe how she had come to document [the] boys using wooden sticks picked up from the ground as guns or pistols when playing outside in the afternoons. They were shooting and shouting, and hunting each other around the yard. So, when the student said that 'this is a project on ethics and gender', I could feel my heart beating faster and harder with a mixture of doubt and anticipation.

She told us how she had observed the boys and seen embarrassed staff members trying to calmly restrain the little bodies of the boys without succeeding in getting them to take an interest in something else than this aggressive play, which often ended up in tears. On other occasions staff became angry, forcing the boys inside and assembling them to talk about the norms and values of the preschool, stating that playing violent games was not allowed. This, however, did not seem to prevent the boys from picking up this game again. Rather it almost seemed as if it became even more desirable. The adults started to plan an extra parental meeting to discuss values and norms, and ask parents to please throw away toy guns and swords and forbid war games at home.

One day this student heard one boy shout out loudly: 'My gun is alive and it wants to kill you!' pointing his stick, taken from an old pine tree, at his friend. The student called to this boy and, using what she described as an equally forceful but also very curious and interested voice, she asked him: 'If your gun is alive, it must have a name? What's the name of your gun?' The boy seemed startled and stood there quiet. 'Does it live with you?' she continued 'Or does it live here in the preschool yard?' The boy gave her a long silent look and then answered: 'His name is Erik and he lives with his mum under that tree', pointing at the tree under which he had found his stick. Then he ran off again. The student documented the short conversation in her process diary, which was a part of the pedagogical documentation she collected during her vocational training.

The next morning she asked the group of boys playing with sticks if she could talk to them for a minute. They agreed and she assembled them sitting down on the floor. She said that the previous day she had had a small talk with X that she had found so interesting that she wrote it down. She then asked X if it was alright for her to read out the short conversation they had had to the whole group, which he agreed to. The boys immediately started to talk out loud in unison, eagerly claiming their stick too had names and lived at home, or under the bench in the hall, etc. The student said: 'Ok, let's listen to each of you one at the time', and as they each told their stories, they became increasingly full of fantasy and humour, assigning the stick a certain look, specific traits and social contexts of families and friends. 'Go get your sticks and we can paint and decorate them so we can see which one is which', the student suggested.

Without getting into further details about the processes of this small project, I think you can imagine from these images how the boys' interest shifted from using the stick as a gun or pistol to making it into a friend – a doll – to play with, to make a family for, and to decorate in ways that made shooting with it impossible. Moreover, this shift of interest also invited girls to take part in the process. They too wanted to make dolls out of sticks. The play and aesthetic work with the sticks expanded to include more or less the whole group. Moreover, for some of the children the interest in sticks as being part of a tree evolved in the participatory discussions about the stick dolls and their lives. The children wondered about how the stick had been a part of the tree, which is a part of nature, dependent on rain, sun, soil etc. Discussions about the life and death of sticks, after falling off trees, became interesting to some of the children. The sticks had been adopted into the community of the preschool as dolls instead of being a part of the tree or used as a weapon.

I am telling this story to frame some of the aspects of an intra-active pedagogy. . . . How can I, for instance, say that the theory/practice and the discourse/material divides were transgressed in this example? Were any other binary divides transgressed as well? Where were the inventive turning points in this process? How did matter – the material – come to matter in this example, both for children's learning and in the construction of children's subjectivities as learners?

In relation to this student's project it is easy to see the importance of taking into account and being inclusive of the children's world and their play, and negotiate with them from within their own language and life experiences. This is the basis for a listening pedagogy developed so successfully in Reggio Emilia, which has inspired Swedish preschools and schools. . . . By being inclusive and actively making use of the children's ways of understanding their play and the way they spent their time in the preschool yard, maybe another way of theorising and doing practice would be the result? Maybe we would understand that the boys were simply bored and not seriously challenged to play in any other way than simply picking up sticks and running around? Maybe we would find that they imitated a television show that they frequently looked at, that we perhaps should know more about, and make use of, to challenge and expand their play? Or maybe these boys had just got the strong message in our culture about what a boy should be doing to perform masculinity in expected ways? Being inclusive of this knowledge, how are we to use it to challenge new ways of playing, thinking and doing that might expand their playfulness and/or deepen their learning of any aspect we chose to pick out as important or interesting?

There are many possible ways to go here, but either way, what is important in an intra-active approach is for us as teachers to try to make visible and do justice to what the learning child brings into the play or learning situation, without imposing our own moral values and aims of learning on them. Rather, we want to be in a listening dialogue, where we negotiate our different understandings, and learn about the diversities and differences in meaning-making and strategies of doing things. It is what the children already do and bring with them that we can make use of and further investigate or challenge to produce a deeper learning. . . .

In this example the student decided to challenge the boys' play by offering them to intra-act with the sticks in a different way. In the dominance of our taken-for-granted worldview, the understanding that seems to lie most easily at hand is to think that the children "humanise" their sticks by giving them names and human traits expressed in their usage of various aesthetic materials [such as paints, ribbons, shiny paper and glue] to transform the sticks from guns to dolls. Reading it this way the agency is still with the child who uses the passive materials to transform the stick. If we change our gaze to the perspective of the materials, it becomes possible to see how the material realities can be understood to have agency in relation to what happens in the discursive-material intra-active processes taking place between the materials, the children and the student. It becomes possible to see the agentic forces of the shiny papers evoking desires in the child to transform the stick in a way s/he first did not think was possible. It becomes possible to listen to the agentic rustle or swish of the thin coloured papers as they swirl around in the air from the top of the stick. This rustle connects to the discursive thinking of the child and the stick transforms again and again in the play taking place with other sticks and children.

The discursive meaning of the sticks agentially shifts in the different aspects of the play, depending what the children are doing with the sticks. They come to know them differently as they play with them in different fashions and keep on adding materials to them. In a simple understanding, the stick shifts from being a weapon to a friend or doll to care for and interact with in the process of using and connecting to materials, such as paints, ribbons, shiny paper and glue. The materials thus *materialise* the looks and traits of the friend-stick-dolls, making them alive and 'humanised'. In the way Barad thinks about materialisation it is not just a matter of how discourse and meaning-making come to matter, but how matter comes to matter in its agency (1998: 108). In a more complex way of understanding it, from the viewpoint of the material, the material *matters* and intra-acts with the boys in their play and their continuously displaced understandings of the sticks. The gaze shifts from the inter-action between the boys and the teacher in how they speak about the sticks and move them around, etc., to the wider and expanded gaze from the point of view of the swirl and rustle of the paper and its intra-action with the discursive understandings.

For the teachers, the focus shifts from being exclusively preoccupied with the individual children's cognitive knowledge constructions or the dialogue between the children, to the learning event taking place *in-between* the child and the material in the space and event of learning. How can pieces of shiny paper act upon a boy and his wooden stick with the help of a little glue in the atelier [arts workshop] of the pre-school? What will the transformation of the stick do to the boy's thinking and conceptualising of the stick as he now continues to play with it? Are new inter-connections made possible with other materials, ideas or children? We are of course as interested in the learning processes of the individual child in an intra-active pedagogy as in any other pedagogical approach to learning and play. However, to be able to know anything about what the individual child might have learnt or experienced, an intra-active pedagogy does not simply focus on and analyse the child and what the child says and does as separate from the environment and the materials it handles. We need to be just as attentive of the questions posed by the teachers that linger in the space of the learning event, as we must be of the material possibilities in the room and the codes that regulate how children will use the materials and/or continue playing in this room. *It is the material-discursive forces and intensities that emerge in the intra-actions in-between the child and the materials in the room that together constitute the learning that can take place.* Hence, learning does not simply take place inside the child but is the phenomena that are produced in the intra-activity taking place in-between the child, its body, its discursive inscriptions, the discursive conditions in the space of learning, the materials available, the time-space relations in a specific room of situated organisms, where people are only one such material organism among others.

In this perspective all of these organisms and matter in the event of learning must be understood as having agency of their own, being performative agents. They are intra-acting with each other differently, with different intensities and force, depending on the different potentialities of each organism or matter. Some matters cannot engage as easily or smoothly as others in change or transformation. For instance, the walls of the room cannot be moved, but the interior of the room can easily be altered in intra-action with furniture, things and materials. Water and clay can transform with great intensities and speed, but so can construction blocks when, for example, a construction of blocks is knocked down. The intensity and speed of the forces between materials vary depending on innumerable material-discursive conditions in the pedagogical space. This also goes for the discursive production of words and meaning-making that the child is engaged in, in the intra-active processes. An older child with more available concepts might speed up the discursive-material intra-action when handling material and simultaneously conceptualising what is going on. The phenomena that we call knowledge, experience or learning, is totally dependent on all of these material-discursive conditions in intense intra-action with each other. The consequences of this thinking is that the teacher needs to make herself aware of how the room, space, time and things are organised and structured, and what kinds of intra-action between the different organisms might be possible.

Knowledge as phenomena can be viewed as material-discursive materialisations; that is, meanings negotiated in the material world within a material and discursively embodied being, for example the child or the student-teacher. . . . In relation to the example with the stick, intra-activity dissolves the divide between our discursive meaning-making (of a doll) and the material objects (of the stick, paint and papers), and between contents of learning (friendship, social relations and what a tree is and how it lives) and the learner's subjectivity (how the boys understand themselves as good or bad friends, or being curious about social life, or life of trees and wanting to learn more about these things). Understanding the processes of learning in this way means going beyond the theory/practice divide, but also the discourse/material and subject/object divides – the inseparability of the learner from what is learnt. Moreover, how the events of this example developed also entailed going beyond the masculine/feminine divide, as the boys transformed their play and started to investigate friendship and trees instead, in ways that should be labelled as neither feminine nor masculine. However, this displacement in content of their play made girls interested to participate and made the larger group of children take part in the different learning and play situations that emerged.

Moreover, we might think of what happened in this process in terms of a series of very specific events, where there were some very important turning points that would change the learning and becoming of the children. The first turning point emerged in the event when the student teacher asked the boy about the name of his stick. The second turning point took place as the children started to talk about the stick as part of the living tree in terms of life and death. In these specific events something entirely new was made possible. The questions posed and put out into the pedagogical space can, with inspiration from Deleuze, be understood in terms of evoking an inventive 'line of flight' (Deleuze and Guattari, 1987) into new becomings for the boys' understanding of their play with sticks, and the group of children's collective thinking on trees as living beings.

As you can see, it is very important how we as teachers choose to discursively understand – code, de-code or re-code – what the children do or say, or how we allow the children to code, de-code or re-code, what they do: that is, how we give and read meaning, and then re-construct such meaning-making in the intra-active processes taking place. This will determine what kinds of play and learning we will give the children the preconditions to enact, and thus what learning phenomena will emerge from this play. Or in other words, that which will eventually materialise as learning is dependent on what we say to children, how we encourage them or limit their possibilities to further investigation, how we organise the schedule for play or investigating processes, what materials we offer them, during what time span and in what environments, etc. . . .

Furthermore the words of the boys in their play and investigations took on a material reality in the form of documentation when they were written down and their play photographed. When the words were *made material* as written text, the documented words were given strong agency as the student decided to read them aloud to the boys from her process diary. This immediately made possible new intra-action taking place: that is, the documentation enabled new processes of meaning-making and investigative actions involving the offered materials. This student chose to use her photographed, taped and written documentation of the processes taking place as a way to enable adults and children to read, listen and look at what had been done and said, and collaboratively negotiate what to do, and challenge learning into new events of learning and questions to investigate. What was in the written notes and photographs constituted material limits to what could be understood, and intra-acted with the discourses available to the teacher-student. The meanings constructed in the discussion based on the documentation made the teacher-student direct her further investigations with the children to trees that the sticks once had been a part of, and the life of the living tree, needing to drink and breathe just like the children themselves.

Childhoods in natureculture common worlds

My second example is not of a specific instance of putting posthuman perspectives to work in a particular preschool but rather a wide-ranging reflection by Affrica Taylor in her book in the *Contesting Early Childhood* series of what it might mean to resituate childhood in a 'natureculture common worlds' perspective, not centred on or privileging human beings, who are, instead, viewed as having a shared belonging and shared responsibility to a 'natureculture collective'. Her reflections, closely related to the converging environmental crises of our times, include discussion of a pedagogical shift, some examples of pedagogical initiatives that 'draw upon human/more-than-human relations', and end by suggesting a number of pedagogical principles that flow from a shift in perspective, the first of which is 'an understanding that relations are central to everything'. We meet here some concepts from earlier chapters, including power relations, relational ethics and assemblages.

From *Reconfiguring the Natures of Childhood*, pp. 116–124; original emphasis

By shifting our relationship to nature through resituating childhoods within down-to-earth natureculture common worlds, we are not just making our lives hard and condemning children to live with their lot. Instead, we are making a shift that is congruent with and has direct relevance to the rapidly globalizing 21st century landscape that children inherit and inhabit, and is therefore ultimately useful to them. There are arguably two central ethical challenges facing 21st century children.

The first is the challenge of living peacefully within an increasingly complex, interconnected, mixed-up, boundary-blurring, hybrid and radically uneven world characterized by difference (human and more-than-human). The second is the challenge of ensuring the sustainability of this ecologically interdependent and yet human-dominated and damaged planetary environment. A common worlds approach is directly relevant to both of these present-future scenarios. It centrally addresses the questions of cohabiting with entangled 'throwntogether' differences (Massey, 2005), and of grappling with the ethical and political 'sticky knots' thrown up by these differences (Haraway, 2008a). It also underscores the inter-determining effects of entwined human and more-than-human relations within the wider natureculture world. In terms of sustainability, these inter-determinations are perhaps most profoundly and disturbingly played out within the macro natureculture event of human-induced global warming. This is the world that we bequeath to children. I am arguing that we have some responsibility to equip them, as well as we can, to deal with it.

In Chapter Three I noted that contemporary nature-based education emphasizes the correlation between young children's embodied experience of and connections with the natural world and their dispositions to become future environmental stewards. . . . These relationships of responsibility are premised upon the child learning 'in' and 'from' nature, not just 'about' it (Sobel, 1996 & 2008; Pyle, 2002) and upon the developmentalist belief that childhood is the critical life stage for bonding with nature. The notion of the timely immersion of the child in nature is framed by a double dualism, with spatial as well as temporal dimensions. Not only is the child taken from the cultural domain (where Rousseau's 'education of Man' takes place) and handed over to the uncontaminated space of nature (where Nature is teacher), but this hand-over must take place when the child is still in the pre-rational and primarily sensory stage of life, in order to prepare her/him for the ultimate heroic (and cultural) task of championing nature as a fully rational and agentic adult. As well as being framed by the nature/culture and child/adult divides, these calls for nature education as the precursor for environmental stewardship are also construed within the overarching paradigm of humanism. Humanism invests the (rational adult) human with the exclusive capacity for intentional agency and identifies the autonomous individual as the fundamental unit for exercising this agency (for being self-determining and for saving the world).

Within humanist developmental discourses, the concomitant emphases upon the developing (and thereby becoming rational, autonomous and agentic) individual child, upon child-centredness, and upon the primacy of their individual needs, might be good for growing consumers and capitalist entrepreneurs, but it does little to prepare children to deal with the already entangled and increasingly interconnected, boundary blurring and hybridizing global world, that carries the challenges that I have identified above. Humanist developmental discourses, even those that dovetail with environmental educational discourses and enlist nature to nurture and teach budding young environmental stewards, inevitably reinforce human exceptionalism and individual acts of heroicism. Whether or not we are speaking about Nature's child, the orthodox child-centred focus upon the child's individuality and their developing autonomous agency (even their agency to protect nature) runs completely counter to the task of appreciating that no-one stands or acts alone – that all human lives are inextricably enmeshed with others (human and more-than-human), and that all human actions are implicated with and have implications for others (including nonhuman natureculture others).

My point is that *twenty-first century children need relational and collective dispositions*, not individualistic ones, to equip them to live well within the kind of world that they have inherited. If they are to peacefully co-exist in this heterogeneous world, with differences that often pose ethical dilemmas, and if they are to do so without seeking to dominate, assimilate or appropriate these differences, they will need a firm sense of shared belonging and shared responsibility within the natureculture collective of their immediate common worlds. If they are to effectively respond to the big picture challenges of co-existing sustainably in an already disturbed planetary ecology, they will need to be able to build upon a foundational sense of connectivity to this same natureculture collective. Such dispositions and capacities will never be fostered through the application of a child-centred and hyper-individualistic developmental framework, nature-loving or not.

An Inclusive Shift

It is my interest in inclusivity and justice that also drives my efforts to shift our relationship to nature. A desire to practice inclusion in new ways and upon expanded grounds not only motivates me to shift far beyond individual conceptualizations of Nature's Child, but also beyond the notion of children as embedded in their socio-cultural contexts (Vygotsky, 1978). It has been my intention, in writing this book, to stretch the bounds of inclusivity to encompass the common worldly vision of 'a collective of humans and non humans' (Latour, 2009). . . . [C]hildren's common worlds are human and more-than-human collectives or 'whole-lot' worlds. They are not selective and depoliticized worlds that only admit nature's good, beautiful, innocent, pure and enriching qualities. They require us to relinquish protectionism and separatism and to open up to the whole lot – including reconfigured technoculture kin and interspecies relations (Haraway, 2004d), often discomforting geo-historical legacies, proliferating natureculture hybrids (Latour, 2004), new technologies, uneven power relations and challenging knotty dilemmas. To make this shift, we must firstly resist the urge to sequester childhood in a natural enclave (as Rousseau would have us do) and then step out into the less-than-perfect but worldly world to actively collect, encounter, acknowledge and include all of the significant other players (or actants) in children's entangled lives.

Early childhood education is a field that prides itself on being inclusive. It works hard at respecting diversity and making all children feel that they belong – through welcoming their families; being attuned to the significance of their gendered, classed, religious and cultural backgrounds and their special needs; and building their relationships with key people in the local communities (Bernard van Leer Foundation, 2007; Friendly & Lero, 2002). This is all very important, but rarely does the understanding of diversity and inclusion extend beyond the exclusively human or social domain (see Elliott & Davis, 2008). At the same time, it is also significant that in a field that has from its inception invested heavily in the ideal of natural education, early childhood educators rarely frame nature-related or environmental concerns within an ethos of inclusion and justice. This is because the nature/culture divide, or what Latour (1993) calls the 'Great Divide', ensures that we approach the social world and the natural environment as separate projects conducted in separate domains. It is always an either/or scenario. By resituating childhood within the common worlds of blended naturecultures we dispense with these separations, blend the projects and widen the scope of possibilities for inclusion and for justice.

A common worlds' approach includes the whole lot because it recognizes the entanglement of human and more-than-human relations. . . . [It] recognizes that children often inherit messy, mixed up and inseparable relations that they must ultimately respond to. Beyond the stock-in-trade human-centric understandings of social inclusion and early childhood communities, a common worlds framework includes all of children's significant and worldly relations – chosen and inherited, human and more-than-human – as worthy of our careful and considered attention.

The more-than-human others in the worldly collective include (but are not restricted to) nonhuman living and nonhuman-made inert entities and elements that are typically separated out into the valorized and exteriorized 'nature' camp – such as other animals, plants, weather, water and 'natural' materials . . . However, instead of restoring and/or enhancing childhood by extending the amount of time that children spend in valorized external nature (for instance by taking children 'outdoors' to play in all weathers, or taking them into the forest), bringing in natural materials (for instance clay instead of play dough, wood instead of plastic), and constructing opportunities for children to interact with plants and domesticated animals (for instance gardening, keeping chicks or guinea pigs in cages) – the inclusive scope of a common worlds perspective attends to the members of the natureculture collective that are *already integral to and constitutive of* children's lives. These are not carefully chosen or selected for their value-adding qualities or educational benefits to children – they are included because they are already matted into the geo-historical trajectories of children's situated discursive and material natureculture collective worlds. They are the already-entangled cohabitants and unlikely partners, including the 'queer kin' (Haraway, 2004d, 2004e, 2008a, 2008b & 2011) that have already shaped particular children's lives and been shaped by them . . . [included because they are] the already-there and already-significant players and kin within these particular natureculture entanglements.

A Pedagogical Shift

A common worlds framework not only offers a new relationship to nature and childhood, it also portends a shift in understandings about the 'nature' of learning and gestures towards some new pedagogical possibilities. The prospect of new pedagogical possibilities should appeal to those early childhood educators who are interested in being inclusive of the more-than-human world (including 'nature', 'technology' and hybrid formations of both) and tackling the real world challenges facing 21st century children (such as cohabiting peacefully with difference and ecological sustainability). . . .

[M]any nature-based pedagogies rehearse the human-centric traps that Haraway implies in the opening quotation,[1] and which flow from the Great Divide (Latour, 1993). These include: reifying nature (treating nature as Nature – as a fixed, singular and often personified entity); possessing it (claiming Nature as the providence of science and/or the state of childhood); appropriating it (using Nature to authorize essentialist or universalist 'truths' – including 'truths' about childhood and learning); and investing it with wistful, sentimental and nostalgic adult projections (positioning Nature as desirable exotic otherness).

As an alternative to this entrapment, an understanding of common worlds as entangled naturecultures affords an embedded, emplaced and above all *relational* understanding of diverse childhoods and natures. This, in turn, fashions new sets of pedagogical possibilities. For if we can firstly recognize our common worlds and then utilize them as the collective 'new ground for meaning making together' that Haraway (2004:158) talks about, we will inadvertently make a pedagogical shift – away from knowing about nature and towards learning *with* those others with whom we are already entangled (see also Giugni, nd). We will be tapping into the pedagogical opportunities inherent in the imbroglio of common worlds relations and on our way to inventing all kinds of emergent collective and collaborative (human and more-than-human) pedagogical ventures.

Although pedagogies that draw upon human/more-than-human relations are far from the norm, I would like to acknowledge a few initiatives that have already tapped into the possibilities of 'changing our relations to nature' and 'making meaning together' (Haraway, 2004:158). For instance, Miriam Giugni (in Taylor, Blaise & Giugni, 2012) writes about a 'companion species curriculum' (following Haraway, 2003 & 2008) that unfolded in an urban Australian early childhood education centre. This curriculum emerged from educators and children grappling with some of the dilemmas, or 'sticky knots' thrown up by cohabiting in the centre, first with caged rented chooks [chickens] and then with the chooks once they were released from their cage and allowed to roam free. Her 'companion species curriculum' taps into the possibilities of learning with others that is enabled by such grapplings.

Margaret Somerville (2011) reports on a place pedagogy in which primary school children living in a highly industrial mining area in Australia engaged with frogs in nearby constructed wetlands . . . the children [forming] relationships with frogs that operate on a number of different levels. Not only did they establish scientific relationship with frogs, by learning how to be junior frog scientists – counting, observing, recording and classifying frogs, but they also constructed an emplaced and embodied relationship with frogs based upon their actual encounters with frogs in frog worlds. Drawing upon Deleuze's and Guattari's (1987) writings on 'becoming' and Grosz's (1994) dynamic conceptualization of human and nonhuman body connectivities as central to these becomings, Somerville identifies the most interesting aspects of this place pedagogy as the children's embodied process of 'becoming frog'. She describes the multi-sensorial ways in which the children were corporeally engaged with nonhuman wetland bodies and elements during regular 'Community Frog Watch' evenings – engaged with the moonlight, the wind, the frog call noises. . . . Drawing upon these embodied and emplaced experiences of frog worlds, children enacted what it is like to be frogs by emulating frog movements and performing frog dances to the frog-call music that they recorded during the wetland visits.

A large research project in ten Aotearoa/New Zealand early childhood centres, conducted by Jenny Ritchie, Iris Duhn, Cheryl Rau and Janita Craw (2010), set out to establish a 'culture of ecological sustainability' in everyday early childhood pedagogical practice based upon the enactment of an 'ethics of care for self, others and the environment' and an 'ethics of place'. Although the project unfolded quite differently in the different centres, it was built upon some common principles that challenged the standard separations between the human and more-than-human world. Most significantly, it incorporated kau-papa Māori onto-epistemologies about the productive interrelation-ships between people and place and related Māori ecological tenants, including kaitiakitanga, or guardianship and manaakitanga, or care. The indigenous perspectives underpinning this project, together with its focus upon the pedagogical affordances of place, ensured a distinc-tively local and ethical pedagogical approach.

As this small selection of 'making meaning together' pedagogical projects indicate, there are no prescribed road maps or blueprints for making the shift from learning about nature to learning with others in the human and nonhuman collective. What unfolds is always new and often surprising. It is always the product of the specific constella-tions of thrown together relations that exist within specific common worlds. Like all learnings-with, the unfolding children's learnings with neighbourhood wetlands and frogs; with indigenous ecological onto-epistemologies and ethical practices; and with rented chooks in the examples above were determined by the composition of their particular natureculture collectives. Even though it is not possible to predict or pin down the ways in which learning-with will unfold in different com-mon world contexts, there are a number of key concepts and principles that I assembled in Chapter Four and enacted in my child-animal com-mon worlds stories in Chapter Five that might provide some useful scaffolding to support such pedagogical unfoldings.

Pedagogical Principles

Attending to children's relations in common worlds

An understanding that relations are central to everything would be the first guiding principle. Flowing from this, an attendance to children's enmeshed relations with others in their worlds would be the focus of any common worlds pedagogy. This is in-line with what Karen Martin (2007) refers to as the centrality of 'relatedness' in Aboriginal Austral-ian onto-epistemology [Karen Martin is an early childhood education scholar and a Quandamoopah Aboriginal woman from Queensland, Australia]. Martin urges early childhood educators to take account of the mutually constituting relationships between children and the world around them when thinking about teaching and learning. She explains that in her Quandamoopah people's cultural traditions, children's grow-ing up is seen as a process of building 'ever-increasing sets of related-ness . . . to people, plants, animals, waterways, climate, land and skies' (2007:18). This is a very different from the modern western teleological view of childhood as the first stage in the process of becoming (rational) adult. While I am not suggesting that educators everywhere should simply adopt Martin's Aboriginal world-views, I do want to stress that the location of individual children within registers of human development is neither a universal practice, nor the only way to structure pedagogy. It is relations that constitute common worlds, not sets of individual developmental trajectories. By relocating children within common worlds, the relations themselves become the locus of pedagogical attention (see also Lenz Taguchi, 2010).

Relations of difference would be of particular interest within common worlds pedagogies – including the queer kin relations that children form with more-than-human others. The focus on relations of difference would support children to directly engage with the heterogeneity of their common worlds, and to face the challenges of co-existing peacefully with others who are not necessarily like them. Along with this focus comes the acknowledgement that relations of difference are often asymmetrical and infused with power. The asymmetry of power relations, based upon difference, requires an ethical response. Children would be supported to reflect upon the uneven valuing of differences in their common worlds – between humans and between humans and other species – and upon the responsibilities that come with being implicated within such asymmetrical relations. This would be an important aspect of a common worlds pedagogical process. It would require fostering a reflective and questioning disposition and a sense of collective, not just individual, responsibility. In other words, children would not only be encouraged to recognize and celebrate human difference (as they often already are), but to respond to the dilemmas that are thrown up by co-existing with a whole host of different co-inhabitants, not all of whom are equally valued. By encouraging children to question the relations they have inherited as well as chosen, and to reflect upon the best ways of co-existing with relations of differences, early childhood educators would be supporting children to practise what Sarah Whatmore (2002), along with others, refers to as a 'relational ethics'.

Attending to children's emplacement in common worlds

Children's relations take place on the grounds of common worlds. Like all relations, they are produced and enacted in particular times and places. They are situated and emplaced relations. The generative or productive nature of place, as well as time, is another key principle for common worlds pedagogies. Most people view place as fixed and static (a back drop or stage on which human actions take place) and see history as the active and dynamic determinant. However, as Foucault (1980) observed, not enough attention is paid to the spatialities of power in history, or to the ways in which geography (space and place) disperses history. The seemingly banal fact that things turn out differently in different places (Philo, 1992) helps us to recognize the productive significance of place, and by association, of common worlds. An appreciation of the ways in which geometries of power are constelled in local places (Massey, 1993) alerts us to the political and uneven grounds of common worlds. The concept of places as 'spatio-temporal events' (Massey, 2005: 130) replete with power relations is key to understanding the significance of children's common worlds and to designing learning-with pedagogies. As we attend to the pedagogical significance of children's emplacement in their common worlds we need to appreciate that places are productive and also non-innocent grounds.

A number of educational scholars have promoted the pedagogical affordances [potential uses] of place (Greunewald & Smith, 2008; Sobel, 2004; Somerville, 2010 & 2011), but Iris Duhn (2012) offers a concept of place-as-assemblage that is synonymous with common worlds and that elucidates its principles. Duhn urges early childhood educators to view place as a 'lively' assemblage of human and more-than-human others, in which agency is exercised by all matter (not just humans) and as a kind of routine maintenance work. Conceived of this way, agency is no longer restricted to a series of exclusively human (and often heroic) interventions. She argues that a pedagogy of place-as-assemblage, in which agency is distributed beyond the human, has the potential to blur the distinction between knowing (human) subjects and known-about objects that characterizes and limits western pedagogy. In the same way, common worlds pedagogies would endeavor to circumvent children-as-subjects learning about nature-as-object. An early childhood pedagogy that emplaces children in their common worlds, and emphasizes their entangled relations within this world, would follow the principle of learning with or becoming worldly with the others in the collective.

Using collective inquiry

It is not possible to appreciate the pedagogical opportunities of children's common worlds without being curious about their human and more-than-human composition and without undertaking some form of collective inquiry into the connective threads that constitute these natureculture worlds. Collective inquiry would be the method of a common worlds learning-with pedagogy. It would be the way of enacting its guiding principles and impulses.

This collective inquiry would involve educators and children learning with a whole host of others (human and more-than-human) to find out more about the worlds in which they are already located and embroiled. The first task would be to exchange perspectives on where they are, who and what is there with them, how they all got to be there, the different kinds of lives that are lived and stories that are told there, and where they and others fit within these interconnected lives and stories. What they find and where it might lead would depend on the natureculture composition and affordances of their particular common worlds.

To add an ethical dimension to this pedagogical inquiry, early childhood teachers would support children to grapple with the challenges of inheritance and co-existence that are thrown up in their common worlds. They would encourage inquiring questions about the different regard for differences and the asymmetry of relations related to these unequally valued differences. They would ask children to reflect upon the overarching ethical questions of how best to deal with the uneven grounds of their inheritance and how to cohabit in ways that allow all differences (human and more-than-human) to flourish.

In acting upon these principles, the collective inquiry method would foster children's dispositions to include all members of their common worlds natureculture collective, to trace threads of connection between themselves and others in their common worlds, to be curious about the differences of others in these common worlds, and to work on the challenges and opportunities thrown up by these relations of difference. This kind of pedagogy would encourage children to situate themselves within the real worlds in which they live. It would show them ways of acting together with the others with whom they share these worlds, to ensure that they collectively create the best possible enmeshed future.

Questions – yours and mine

Don't forget to share and discuss the questions you have after reading this chapter, including the ones I suggested at the end of Chapter 1.

Here though are some of my questions to you:

- As a human being, how do you respond to the posthuman view of human beings and their relationship to the rest of the world?

- Do you agree with the posthuman questioning of choice and social constructionism?
- Can you think of an instance, like the example by Hillevi Lenz Taguchi, when matter – the material – has come to matter both for children's learning and in the construction of children's subjectivities as learners?
- Does this chapter change your thinking about children and childhood? How do you respond to the posthuman questioning of 'child-centredness'?
- Take one of Affrica Taylor's three pedagogical principles and discuss it. Do you generally agree or disagree? How might the principle be worked with in a setting you know?

Note

1 'We must find another relationship to nature besides reification, possession, appropriation, and nostalgia . . . all the partners in the potent conversations that constitute nature must find a new ground for making meanings together' (Haraway, 2004, p. 158).

Chapter 8

What next?

The story so far . . . but there's much more to tell

I began this book by setting out my intentions.

> I hope this book will leave you with a clearer idea of some of the 'alterna-
> tive narratives' and 'multitude of perspectives' in early childhood educa-
> tion today, of the different ways of thinking, talking and doing early
> childhood education that are out there; 'some' note, not all, as I do not
> claim to know, understand and therefore cover the whole rich diversity of
> narratives and perspectives that are out there. I hope, too, that this book
> will leave you feeling unsettled and uncertain, leaving you questioning
> things you had previously taken for granted; more ready and able to be
> critical; but also excited, optimistic and more ready and able to explore
> new perspectives on early childhood education. Last but not least, I hope
> this book will encourage you to read further into the rich literature of
> books and articles that contest early childhood education and offer alter-
> native narratives.

This hope, and my main motive for writing the book, spring from a strong
belief that many students and practitioners, and also others engaged with
early childhood education, are disenchanted with what I have termed the
dominant discourses in today's early childhood education, those stories about
quality and high returns and about markets with their technical, instrumental and economistic character, and that there is a desire to know more about
alternative stories and the multitude of perspectives and debates that are to be
found in today's early childhood education. But I have also been motivated
by another belief: that the future well-being and vitality of early childhood
education depends on fostering a democratic politics in the field – which
means encouraging and spreading alternatives, that diversity of often conflicting answers to political questions and debates about these alternatives. More
dissensus, less consensus.

This book is about alternatives, but it is only an introduction. I have offered
one alternative narrative and a few alternative paradigmatic and theoretical

perspectives. There are many more. Moreover, I have only offered an introduction to Reggio Emilia, Foucault, Deleuze and posthumanism – there is much more that could be said and has been said about them. Indeed, some may feel that I am guilty of oversimplification in attempting to present these rich and complex subjects in a few pages and in seeking to do so in as accessible form as possible. I may well have run the risk of not doing them justice.

At the same time, I am conscious that despite my best efforts, many readers may still have found much of what I have written rather forbidding and off-putting, even at times impenetrable. Despite my efforts at simplification, some terms and concepts may prove hard to get a purchase on. Doubtless this reflects on my ability to communicate clearly enough. But I think the problem, if such there is, may go further.

Most of us have grown up and been educated in a positivist paradigm, which as I argued earlier has been productive of the current dominant stories in early childhood education. Most of us have embodied the assumptions, beliefs and general world view that define this paradigm; they have become second nature to us. In general, positivism offers a simple and accessible view of the social world, one in which we can split life into distinct and measurable parts, define how one part acts on another and then change things by manipulating the parts based on this simple causal model. The fact this rarely works, consistently and universally, does not seem to undermine a deep belief, at least amongst certain people and organisations, that this mechanistic model, with its promise of certainty, control and closure, is the way forward, the solution to solving the many problems and challenges that beset us.

Abandoning this model, and its positivistic paradigm, can feel exciting and emancipatory, a 'very joyful and affirmative affair' – but it can also feel unsettling and stir anxieties. To listen to new stories, to try out new perspectives, to participate in new debates means entering new territory with unfamiliar landscapes, dominated by inter-connections and complexities, messiness and uncertainties. The traveller here has to rely far more on thinking for herself and taking responsibility for contextualised meaning making, but must also be ready and able to dialogue with others as part of that process. The rule book has less sway here, rigorous subjectivity far more. Unsurprisingly, the prospect of such nomadic movement, with no fixed end point, can create ambivalent feelings, exacerbated because, as I shall discuss further, working with alternative stories and different perspectives raises a number of practical questions, most of which are yet to be fully answered.

Where next for you?

As well as an introduction, I described the book as 'a bridge that leads readers away from more familiar ground to encounter new ways of thinking about and doing early childhood education'. The bridge does not have to be crossed permanently; having taken a look at the other side, the reader could decide to cross back and stay on familiar ground; and that, from my perspective, is fine, as long as that is understood to be a political choice and a position deliberately taken, a decision made while being fully aware there are alternatives. But I hope that having crossed the bridge some readers will decide that the familiar ground no longer appeals and wish to continue instead beyond the bridge to listen to alternative narratives and to engage with some of the multitude of perspectives and debates that are out there.

How to do this? First and foremost, reading. There is a wealth of literature out there, both books and articles. I have drawn heavily on volumes from the *Contesting Early Childhood* series, but as I suggested in Chapter 1, there is much else available for you to read. Personally, and some may disagree, I think it important to read beyond early childhood education, to attempt to understand what is going on in the world today (politically, culturally, scientifically, economically, socially) so as to form a 'diagnosis of our time'. It seems to me important that early childhood education, indeed all education, should engage with that diagnosis, having in mind the words of Loris Malaguzzi, arguing for a 'living pedagogy', which

> is only possible if our conception of pedagogy is dynamic, not mummified. Either pedagogy – like all the human sciences – is remade, reconstructed and updated based on the new conditions of the times, or it loses its nature, its function, its proper capacity to correspond to the times it lives in, and above all to foresee, anticipate and prepare the days of tomorrow.
>
> (Cagliari *et al.*, 2016, p. 143)

I do, however, recognise several problems with reading. First, accessing books and articles is usually fine if you have access to a university library; it's much harder if you do not, not least because of the cost involved. Second, it takes time and sustained concentration, neither of which are in ample supply in today's frenetic and distracted world. Third, though reading is important, indeed I would say essential, it can be much more productive if you can discuss what you are reading with others, indeed if you can talk with others about the new knowledge you are constructing and the uncertainties and complexities that will often attend this process of creative thinking. You might find those others to discuss with via existing groups (such as the networks I mentioned in Chapter 1), or else more informally by, for example, looking for a local reading group or even forming your own.

Some people may choose to focus on a particular perspective and go deeply into that, for example deciding to go much further into the work of Foucault or Deleuze or to study posthumanism much more intensively. That could be the work of a lifetime, and deeply satisfying. Or you might decide to read around, to get a broader, if less detailed, understanding of a range of perspectives and debates, indeed to take what you find interesting and useful from this varied diet to help build your own narrative. I must confess that this magpie approach has been the one I have adopted, but I also recognise that some would find this rather superficial and guilty of ignoring the contradictions that exist between many perspectives.

Whatever your strategy for moving further into the world of alternative narratives and perspectives, it would be naïve to think that this will not bring some problems with it. I have already touched on the problem of understanding what is unfamiliar and unsettling and the importance of working, if at all possible, with others. Then there is the problem of finding yourself isolated in environments where the dominant discourses rule without challenge and conformity is expected, environments where critical thinking is not appreciated and where discussion of alternative narratives and diverse perspectives may be met with blank incomprehension or dismissive disdain. This may be particularly hard for practitioners who find themselves working in centres and other organisations where the story of quality and high returns and the story of markets are treated, in the words of Nikolas Rose, as 'timeless, natural, unquestionable' and are backed up by a daunting array of human technologies and strong pressure to adopt a certain identity and subjectivity, compliant and technical.

Of course, once you become clearer about the alternatives and perspectives that you desire, it may become possible to find a workplace where these are shared or at least respected, for example a nursery or school or college where educators are interested in, indeed inspired by, the pedagogical ideas and practices of Reggio Emilia. But this will not be an option for many. Where not, I can only acknowledge the difficulties you will face and refer you back to the ideas in earlier chapters about conducting a politics of refusal or micro-politics, taking advantage of such opportunities as you will have to work on your own subjectivity and to subvert the intentions of a prescriptive curriculum and a prophetic pedagogy. Here the concept of 'walking on two legs' may be useful, the idea that you have to conform to certain requirements (people have to pay the rent or mortgage) while at the same time taking every opportunity that presents to think and practice differently. In that way, you may manage to evolve 'the art of voluntary inservitude, of reflective indocility'. But far from easy, I readily acknowledge.

Fears, hopes and a lot of work to be done

There is much to be fearful about today; no point in denying it. The Doomsday Clock is close to midnight, as our world teeters on the edge of an environmental abyss; a neoliberal political and economic regime generates inequality, insecurity and endless destructive consumption; while that same regime has helped undermine those very qualities that might enable humankind to address its converging crises – democracy, care, cooperation and solidarity. More specifically, the dominant stories of quality and high returns and of markets can seem like unstoppable juggernauts, fuelled by the neo-liberal *zeitgeist* and proclaimed by a powerful alliance of governments, non-governmental organisations (both international and more local), business interests and some academics. Despite a variety of resistance movements across many fields, it can sometime seem a hopeless prospect, with the world set on an inevitable trajectory of more of the same until we all end up in that abyss that seems to beckon.

I think we must be realistic about the future. It looks and could be really bad, and there is no cause to be Pollyannaish, expecting the best. But this does not mean we must be despairing. There are reasons to be hopeful, not that a better world is inevitable but that it might be possible. There is a growing awareness of our environmental peril and creative action to extract human-kind from the mess it has got into; as the Dark Mountain Project put it (from Chapter 1), the stories that have led us into 'an age of ecological collapse, material contraction and social and political unravelling . . . are losing their power', and new stories that might enable us to weave a new reality are finding their voice. The same, arguably, applies to the story of neoliberalism, which is losing its power, its assumptions proving to be wrong, its values corrosive to social well-being, its consequences dysfunctional and unsustainable: as economist Kate Raworth concludes, 'putting blind faith in markets has taken us to the brink of ecological, social and financial collapse' (Raworth, 2017, p. 70).

In early childhood education, the global and growing resistance movement is a sign of hope, exploring alternatives and, equally important, doing them, showing they can be put to work. I hope the examples in this book will show the rich potentiality of these alternatives – and remember, there are many other examples to be found. One reason for this hopeful state of affairs is, I believe, a growing disenchantment with the dominant discourses, which like neoliberalism seem to assume and promise an impoverished view of life, dominated by calculation, competition and managerial control and reduced to a simplified and simplistic set of cause-and-effect relationships, which accords neither with most people's experience of life nor with most people's hopes for the future.

So, on one admittedly hopeful view of the future, we are approaching or have even entered a period when transformation becomes possible because the existing dominant stories are losing credibility and followers, opening up possibilities for a better world – both generally and, more specifically, in early childhood education. But if those possibilities really do exist (and we cannot be sure on that), then there is a lot of work to be done to realise them. That work involves creating new stories but also thinking through what conditions may be needed to enact – put to work – those stories. In other words, as I wrote in Chapter 4, our 'real utopias' call not only for desirability but also for viability and achievability.

In *Transformative Change and Real Utopias in Early Childhood Education*, I wrote about how the neoliberal storytellers understood this way back in the 1950s and 1960s, when a very different economic regime predominated and the neoliberal story went mostly unheard or, if heard, seemed implausible. But despite these unfavourable circumstances, these storytellers

> retained a sense of history. They did not give up. They did not assume their day had passed never to re-appear. No: they treated neoliberalism as a real utopian project; they developed their stories and sought new listeners; and they worked together behind the scenes on designing what were in their terms desirable and viable alternatives. . . . They expected change to come with the faltering of the dominant post-war Keynesian regime; and when it did, they had to be ready to take the opportunity, to put forward their stories, to achieve their real utopia. Their strategy was outlined back in 1962 by economist Milton Friedman (1912–2006), the arch priest of the neoliberal resurgence:
>
> > Only a crisis – actual or perceived – produces real change. When that crisis occurs the actions that are taken depend on the ideas that are lying around. That, I believe, is our basic function: to develop alternatives to existing policies, to keep them alive and available until the politically impossible becomes politically inevitable (Friedman, 1982, p. ix).
>
> (Moss, 2013, pp. 203–204)

So, in my hopeful moments, I see the strategic role of the resistance movement (in early childhood education, but in other fields too) as to be ready for the crisis, with developed ideas (compelling stories) and 'alternatives to existing policies' (conditions for enacting stories). As we saw in Chapter 4, Reggio Emilia provides an excellent example of combining the two – stories and conditions, the result being an extensive, long-lasting and dynamic system that has wide appeal. There are many aspects of Reggio Emilia that can provoke us to think, not least its political choices and pedagogical ideas and practices. But the ability to combine utopian thinking with intense practicality should not be overlooked.

The story that I find appealing is the story of democracy, experimentation and potentiality, which I have written about in Chapter 4 as well as, at greater length, in *Transformative Change and Real Utopias in Early Childhood Education*. This is a story about diversity and complexity, movement and lines of flight. But, at the same time, it is possible to envisage this story being enacted within a wider municipal, regional or national framework, which defines common *rights* for all children and adults (e.g. an entitlement to a place in an early childhood centre from an early age; the right of educators to good pay and working conditions; the possibility for educators, parents and citizens to be involved in the democratic management of services); sets out common *images, values and goals* (expressed, for example, in a relatively short framework curriculum); and ensures *conditions* are implemented that will enable democracy, experimentation and potentiality (e.g. adequate public funding;[1] a well-educated workforce; *ateliers* and *atelieristas* specialising in various languages; a competent system (see page 86); and well-designed environments, with attention given to the design of all materials as well as buildings). In other words, the story of democracy experimentation and potentiality can be about individual local projects, able to respond to local contexts and produce relevant local experiments, but it can also be about creating networks or systems of such projects, which can work together to share experience and co-construct knowledge as part of a coherent whole.

Two areas where developing 'alternatives to existing policies' is most pressing for the enactment of the story of democracy, experimentation and potentiality are curriculum and evaluation. Both are essential, not least if early childhood education is to be democratically accountable to the societies that have taken responsibility for providing such education and, in doing so, have (or should have) agreed certain images, values and goals for that education. Both are also essential for achieving the 'rigorous subjectivity' that has cropped up several times in these pages, and also rigorous experimentation, and so hopefully quelling concerns that without a positivistic approach and a belief in objective Truth, anything goes.

The issue is how can curriculum and evaluation be commensurate with, indeed promoting of, democracy, experimentation and potentiality. Huge resources have been deployed in curricula and evaluations that are commensurate with the story of quality and high returns. But these are quite unsuited, indeed damaging to, other stories. Just a fraction of those resources deployed to exploring alternative approaches to curriculum and evaluation would make a big difference.

The future of early childhood education is in the balance. But the more people who are prepared to question dominant discourses, the more people who are willing to engage with alternative narratives and the multitude of perspectives and debates, the more people who are prepared to commit to the hard work of building real utopias, the better the prospects will be. I hope this book will increase participation in this important work.

Questions – yours and mine

Don't forget to share and discuss the questions you have after reading this chapter, including the ones I suggested at the end of Chapter 1.

Here though are some of my questions to you:

- What are your next steps? Do you want to follow up on any narratives or perspectives? Which appeal? Why? How might you do this?
- Do you think that universities, colleges and/or employers could do more for students and practitioners who want to question dominant discourses and go deeper into alternatives? What might they do?
- What are your fears for early childhood education? What are your hopes?
- Can you tell a story about early childhood education that you find appealing, even if it's only short?
- What are some of the conditions that you think are needed to enact that story?
- What is your country's public expenditure on early childhood education and care? What do you think it should aim to spend?
- Consider either curriculum or evaluation. Can you sketch out what curriculum/evaluation might look like in the story you find appealing?

Note

1 The OECD, in its Family Database, has a table comparing public expenditure among member states on early childhood education and care, presented as a percentage of gross domestic product. This shows wide differences in public funding, from 0.2% in Turkey and 0.3% in the United States to 1.6% in Sweden and 1.8% in Iceland; the OECD average (for 31 countries) is 0.7% (www.oecd.org/els/soc/PF3_1_Public_spending_on_childcare_and_early_education.pdf).

References

* Indicates a book in the Contesting Early Childhood series

Allen, G. (2011) *Early Intervention: Smart Investment, Massive Savings*. London: Cabinet Office. (www.gov.uk/government/publications/early-intervention-smart-investment-massive-savings).

Alvaredo, F., Chancel, L., Piketty, T., Saez, E. and Zucman, G. (2017) *World Inequality Report 2018: Executive Summary* (http://wir2018.wid.world/files/download/wir2018-summary-english.pdf).

Archer, M. (2008) 'Childcare and early years provision in a diverse market – the government's approach', paper presented at a seminar organised by the *International Centre for the Study of the Mixed Economy of Childcare*, London, 12 May 2008. (www.uel.ac.uk/icmec/seminar/index.htm).

Ball, S. (2013) *Foucault, Power and Education*. London: Routledge.

Ball, S. (2016) 'Subjectivity as a site of struggle: Refusing neoliberalism?', *British Journal of Sociology of Education*, 37 (8), 1129–1146

Ball, S. and Vincent, C. (2006) *Childcare, Choice and Class Practices: Middle-Class Parents and Their Children*. London: Routledge.

Barad, K. (2007) *Meeting the Universe Halfway: Quantum Physics and the Entanglement of Matter and Meaning*. Durham: Duke University Press.

Barad, K. (2009) 'Matter feels, converses, suffers, desires, yearns and remembers', *interview with Karen Barad*, 6 June 2009. (https://quod.lib.umich.edu/o/ohp/11515701.0001.001/1:4.3/--new-materialism-interviews-cartographies?rgn=div2;view=fulltext).

Bauman, Z. (1993) *Postmodern Ethics*. Oxford: Blackwell.

Bauman, Z. (1995) *Life in Fragments: Essays in Postmodern Morality*. Oxford: Blackwell.

Berger, P. and Luckmann, T. (1966) *The Social Construction of Reality*. New York, NY: Doubleday.

Biesta, G. (2007) 'Why "What works" won't work: Evidence-based practice and the democratic deficit in educational research', *Educational Theory*, 57 (1), 1–22.

Bloch, M.N. (1992) 'Critical perspectives on the historical relationships between child development and early childhood education research', in S. Kessler and B.B. Swadener. (eds) *Reconceptualizing the Early Childhood Curriculum: Beginning the Dialogue*. New York: Teachers College Press.

Bloch, M.N., Swadener, B.B. and Cannella, G. (eds) (2018, 2nd edn) *Reconceptualizing Early Childhood Care and Education: Critical Questions, New Imaginaries and Social Activism: A Reader*. New York: Peter Lang.

Bradbury, A. and Roberts-Holmes, G. (2017) *The Datafication of Primary and Early Childhood Education: Playing With Numbers*. London: Routledge.

Braidotti, R. (2013) *The Posthuman*. Cambridge: Polity Press.

Bruner J.S. (1990) *Acts of Meaning*. Cambridge: Harvard University Press.

Bush, J. and Phillips, D. (1996) 'International approaches to defining quality', in S. Kagan and N. Cohen (eds) *Reinventing Early Care and Education: A Vision for a Quality System*. San Francisco: Jossey-Bass.

Butin, D.W. (2001) 'If this is resistance I would hate to see domination: Retrieving Foucault's notion of resistance within educational research', *Educational Studies*, 22 (2), 157–176.

Cagliari, P., Barozzi, A. and Giudici, C. (2004) 'Thoughts, theories and experiences: For an educational project with participation', *Children in Europe*, 6, 28–30.

*Cagliari, P., Castegnetti, M., Giudici, C., Rinaldi, C., Vecchi, V. and Moss, P. (eds) (2016) *Loris Malaguzzi and the Schools of Reggio Emilia: A Selection of His Writings and Speeches 1945–1993*. London: Routledge.

Catarsi, E. (2004) 'Loris Malaguzzi and the municipal school revolution', *Children in Europe*, 6, 8–9.

Colman, F.J. (2005b) 'Rhizome', in A. Parr (ed) *The Deleuze Dictionary*. Edinburgh: Edinburgh University Press.

Cousins, J. (2003) *Listening to Young Children: How They Can Help Us to Plan Their Education and Care*. London: Jessica Kingsley.

Dahlberg, G. (1985) *Context and the Child's Orientation to Meaning: A Study of the Child's Way of Organizing the Surrounding World in Relation to Public Institutionalized Socialization*. Stockholm: Almqvist and Wiksell.

Dahlberg, G. (2000) 'Everything is a beginning and everything is dangerous: Some reflections on the Reggio Emilia experience', in H. Penn (ed) *Early Childhood Services: Theory, Policy and Practice*. Buckingham: Open University Press.

Dahlberg, G. (2003) 'Pedagogy as a loci of an ethics of an encounter', in M. Bloch, K. Holmlund, I. Moqvist and T. Popkewitz (eds) *Governing Children, Families and Education: Restructuring the Welfare State*. New York: Palgrave Macmillan.

Dahlberg, G. and Moss, P. (2005) *Ethics and Politics in Early Childhood Education*. London: Routledge.

Dahlberg, G. and Moss, P. (2009) 'Foreword' to Olsson (2009).

Dahlberg, G. and Bloch, M. (2006) 'Is the power to see and visualize always the power to control?', in T. Popkewitz, K. Pettersson, U. Olsson and J. Kowalczyk (eds) *The Future Is Not What It Appears to Be: Pedagogy, Genealogy and Political Epistemology. In Honour and in Memory of Kenneth Hultqvist*. Stockholm: HLS Förlag.

Dahlberg, G., Moss, P. and Pence, A. (2013, 3rd edn) *Beyond Quality in Early Childhood Education and Care: Languages of Evaluation*. London: Routledge.

Dark Mountain Project (2009a) *Uncivilisation: The Dark Mountain Manifesto*. (http://dark-mountain.net/about/manifesto/).

Dark Mountain Project (2009b) *FAQs*. (http://dark-mountain.net/about/faqs).

*Davies, B. (2014) *Listening to Children: Being and Becoming*. London: Routledge.

Deleuze, G. (1992) 'Postscript on the societies of control', *October*, 59 (Winter), 3–7.

Deleuze, G. (1994) *Difference and Repetition*, trans. Constantin Boundas. New York: Columbia University Press.

Deleuze, G. and Guattari, F. (2004) *A Thousand Plateaus: Capitalism and Schizophrenia*. London: Continuum.

Deleuze, G. and Parnet, C. (1987) *Dialogues*, trans. Hugh Tomlinson and Barbara Habberjam. London: The Athlone Press.

Department for Education (England) (2013) *More Great Childcare: Raising Quality and Giving Parents More Choice*. London: Department for Education. (www.gov.uk/government/uploads/system/uploads/attachment_data/file/170552/More_20Great_20Childcare_20v2.pdf.pdf).

Department for Education (England) (2015) *Review of Childcare Costs: The Analytical Report: An Economic Assessment of the Early Education and Childcare Market and Providers' Costs*. London: Department for Education (www.gov.uk/government/uploads/system/uploads/attachment_data/file/479659/151124_Analytical_review_FINAL_VERSION.pdf).

Dewey, J. (1976) 'Creative democracy: The task before us', in J. Boydston (ed) *John Dewey: The Later Works, 1925–1953, Volume 14*. Carbondale: Southern Illinois University Press.

Diedrich, W.W., Burggraeve, R. and Gastmans, C. (2003) 'Towards a Levinasian care ethic: A dialogue between the thoughts of Joan Tronto and Emmanuel Levinas', *Ethical Perspectives*, 13 (1), 33–61.

Edwards, C., Gandini, L. and Forman, G. (eds) (2012, 3rd edn) *The Hundred Languages of Children: The Reggio Emilia Experience in Transformation*. Santa Barbera: Praeger.

Eisenstadt, N. (2011) *Providing a Sure Start: How Government Discovered Early Childhood*. Bristol: Policy Press.

Elfström, I. and Furnes, K. (2010) 'Solmasken och signaljärnmasken' ['The sun mask and the signal iron mask'], in I. M-C. Colliander, L. Stråhle and C. Whener-Godée (eds) *Om värden och omvärlden: Pedagogik och teori med inspiration från Reggio Emilia*. En vänbok till Gunilla Dahlberg. Stockholm: Stockholms universitets förlag.

Fendler, L. (2001) 'Educating flexible souls: The construction of subjectivity through developmentality and interaction', in K. Hultqvist and G. Dahlberg (eds) *Governing the Child in the New Millennium*. London: RoutledgeFalmer.

Fisher, B. and Tronto, J. (1990) 'Toward a feminist theory of caring', in E. Abel and M. Nelson (eds) *Circles of Care, Work and Identity in Women's Lives*. New York: State University of New York Press.

Flyvbjerg, B. (2006) 'Social science that matters', *Foresight Europe* (October 2005–March 2006), 38–42.

Fortunati, A. (2006) *The Education of Young Children as a Community Project: The Experience of San Miniato*. Azzano San Paolo: Edizioni Junior.

Foucault, M. (1978) *The History of Sexuality, Volume 1: An Introduction*, trans. Robert Hurley. New York: Pantheon Books.

Foucault, M. (1987) 'The ethic of care for the self as a practice of freedom', in J. Bernauer and D. Rasmussen (eds) *The Final Foucault*. Cambridge: MIT Press.

Foucault, M. (1988a) *Politics, Philosophy, Culture: Interviews and Other Writings 1977–1984*, trans. Alan Sheridan and others. London: Routledge.

Foucault, M. (1988b) 'Technologies of the self', in L.H. Martin, H. Gutman and P.H. Hutton (eds) *Technologies of the Self: A Seminar With Michel Foucault*. Amhurst: University of Massachusetts Press.

Foucault, M. (1990) 'Qu'est-ce que la critique?' *Bulletin de la Société Française de Philosophic*, 84, 35–63.

Freire, P. (2004) *Pedagogy of Hope*. London: Continuum.

Friedman, M. (1962, 1982 edn) *Capitalism and Freedom*. Chicago: University of Chicago Press.

Gesell, A. and Ilg, F. (1946) *The Child From Five to Ten*. New York, NY: Harper and Row.

Giamminuti, S. (2013) *Dancing With Reggio Emilia: Metaphors for Quality*. Mt Victoria, NSW: Pademelon Press.

Gillies, D. (2011) 'State education as high-yield investment: Human capital theory in European policy discourse', *Journal of Pedagogy*, 2 (2), 224–245.

Giudici, C. and Krechevsky, M. (eds) (2001) *Making Learning Visible: Children as Individual and Group Learners*. Reggio Emilia: Reggio Children.

Gough, N. (2006) 'Foreword [sous rature]', in I. Semetsky (ed) *Deleuze, Education and Becoming*. Rotterdam: Sense Publishers.

Gray, J. (2009) *Gray's Anatomy: John Gray's Selected Writings*. London: Allen Lane.

Greenhalgh, T. and Russell, J. (2006) 'Reframing evidence synthesis as rhetorical action in the policy making drama', *Healthcare Policy*, 1 (2), 34–42. (www.ncbi.nlm.nih.gov/pmc/articles/PMC2585323/).

Grosz, E. (2005) *Time Travels: Feminism, Nature, Power*. Durham: Duke University Press.

Grosz, E. (2008) 'Darwin and Feminism: Preliminary investigations for a possible alliance', in S. Alaimo and S. Hekman (eds) *Material Feminisms*. Bloomington and Indianapolis: Indiana University Press.

Guattari, F. (1995) *Chaosmosis: An Ethico-Aesthetic Paradigm*, trans. Paul Bains and Julian Pefanis. Bloomington: Indiana University press.

Harari, Y.N. (2016) *Homo Deus: A Brief History of Tomorrow*. London: Harvill Sacker.

Haraway, D. (1988) 'Situated knowledges: The science question in feminism and the privilege of partial perspective', *Feminist Studies*, 14, 575–599.

Haraway, D. (2004) 'Otherworldly conversations: terran topics; local terms', in *The Haraway Reader*. London: Routledge.

Heissen, A.H. (2017) 'The Art of Mixology', *BBC World Service*, 5 December 2017. (www.bbc.co.uk/programmes/w3cswccz)

Hoyuelos, A. (2004) 'A pedagogy of transgression', *Children in Europe*, 6, 6–7.

Hoyuelos, A. (2013) *The Ethics in Loris Malaguzzi's Philosophy*. Reykjavik: Isalda.

Hultman, K. and Lenz Taguchi, H. (2010) 'Challenging anthropocentric analysis of visual data: A relational materialist methodological approach to educational research', *International Journal of Qualitative Studies in Education*, 23 (5), 525–542.

Hyslop-Margison, E.J. and Sears, A.M. (2006) *Neo-Liberalism, Globalization and Human Capital Learning: Reclaiming Education for Democratic Citizenship*. Dordrecht: Springer.

Klenke, K. (2016) *Qualitative Research in the Study of Leadership*. Bingley: Emerald Group Publishing Limited.

LaingBuisson (2014) Online order form for 'Children's Nurseries, UK Market Report, Thirteenth Edition' (www.laingbuisson.com/wp-content/uploads/2016/06/ChildrensNurseries_13_bro.pdf).

Lather, P. (1991) *Getting Smart: Feminist Research and Pedagogy With/In the Postmodern*. London: Routledge.

Lather, P. (2006) 'Paradigm proliferation as a good thing to think with: Teaching research in education as a wild profusion', *International Journal of Qualitative Studies in Education*, 19 (1), 35–57.

Latour, B. (1993) *We Have Never Been Modern*. Cambridge: Harvard University press.

Latour, B. (2009) 'A collective of humans and non-humans: Following Daedelus's labyrinth', in D.M. Kaplan (ed) *Reading in the Philosophy of Technology*. Lanham and Plymouth: Rowman & Littlefield.

*Lenz Taguchi, H. (2009) *Going Beyond the Theory/Practice Divide: In Early Childhood Education: Introducing an Intra-Active Pedagogy*. London: Routledge.

Lenz Taguchi, H. (2010) 'Rethinking pedagogical practices in early childhood education: A multidimensional approach to learning and inclusion', in N. Yelland (ed) *Contemporary Perspectives on Early Childhood Education*. Maidenhead: Open University Press.

Levinas, E. (1987) *Time and the Other*. Pittsburgh: Duquesne University Press.

Luke, A. (2011) 'Generalising across borders: Policy and the limits of educational science', paper presentation to the *American Educational Research Association Annual Meeting*, 8–13 April 2011, New Orleans. (https://eprints.qut.edu.au/41118/1/C41118.pdf).

*MacNaughton, G. (2005) *Doing Foucault in Early Childhood Studies: Applying Poststructural Ideas*. London: Routledge.

Marks, J. (1998) *Gilles Deleuze: Vitalism and Multiplicity*. London: Pluto.

Mirowski, P. (2013) *Never Let a Serious Crisis Go to Waste: How Neoliberalism Survived the Financial Meltdown*. London: Verso.

Monbiot, G. (2017) *Out of the Wreckage: A New Politics for an Age of Crisis*. London: Verso.

Moss, P. (2007) 'Meetings across the paradigmatic divide', *Educational Philosophy and Theory*, 39 (3), 229–240.

*Moss, P. (2013) *Transformative Change and Real Utopias in Early Childhood Education: A Story of Democracy, Experimentation and Potentiality*. London: Routledge.

Moss, P., Dahlberg, G., Grieshaber, S., Mantovani, S., May, H., Pence, A., Rayna, S., Swadenere, B. and Vandenbroeck, M. (2016) 'The Organisation for Economic Co-operation and Development's International Early Learning Study: Opening for debate and contestation', *Contemporary Issues in Early Childhood*, 17 (3), 343–351.

Moss, P. and Urban, M. (2017) 'The Organisation for Economic Co-operation and Development's International Early Learning Study: What happened next?', *Contemporary Issues in Early Childhood*, 18 (2), 250–258.

Mouffe, C. (2007) 'Artistic activism and agonistic spaces', *Art and Research*, 1 (2, Summer).

*Murris, K. (2016) *The Posthuman Child: Educational Transformation Through Philosophy With Picturebooks*. London: Routledge.

OECD (2011a) *Investing in High-Quality Early Childhood Education and Care (ECEC)*. (www.oecd.org/education/preschoolandschool/48980282.pdf).

OECD (2011b) *Divided We Stand: Why Inequality Keeps Rising*. Paris: OECD.

OECD (2012) *Starting Strong III: A Quality Toolbox for Early Childhood Education and Care*. (www.oecd.org/edu/school/49325825.pdf).

OECD (2015) *Call for Tenders: International Early Learning Study*. (www.oecd.org/callsfortenders/CfT%20100001420%20International%20Early%20Learning%20Study.pdf).

OECD (2017) *Early Learning Matters*. (www.oecd.org/edu/school/Early-Learning-Matters-Project-Brochure.pdf).

OECD (2018) *Family Database, Child Poverty*. (www.oecd.org/els/CO_2_2_Child_Poverty.pdf).

*Olsson, L.M. (2009) *Movement and Experimentation in Young Children's Learning: Deleuze and Guattari in Early Childhood Education*. London: Routledge.

Olsson, L.M. (2013) 'Taking children's questions seriously: The need for creative thought', *Global Studies of Childhood*, 3 (3), 230–253.

Osberg, D. and Biesta, G. (2007) 'Beyond presence: Epistemological and pedagogical implications of "strong" emergence', *Interchange*, 38 (1), 31–51.

Otto, D. (1999) 'Everything is dangerous: Some poststructural tools for human rights law', *Australian Journal of Human Rights*, 5 (1), 17–47.

Popkewitz, T. (1997) 'A changing terrain of knowledge and power in educational research: A social epistemology', in T. Popkewitz (ed) *Critical Theory and Educational Discourse*. Johannesburg: Heinemann.

Prout, A. (2004) *The Future of Childhood*. London: Routledge.

Raworth, K. (2017) *Doughnut Economics: Seven Ways to Think Like a 21st-Century Economist.* London: Random House.

Readings, B. (1966) *The University in Ruins.* Cambridge, MA: Harvard University Press.

Rinaldi, C. (2006) *In Dialogue With Reggio Emilia: Listening, Researching and Learning.* London: Routledge.

Roberts, C., Lawrence, M. and King, L. (2017) 'Managing Automation: Employment, Inequality and Ethics in the Digital Age', *IPPR.* (https://www.ippr.org/files/2018-01/cej-man aging-automation-december2017.pdf).

Roberts-Holmes, G. and Bradbury, A. (2016) 'Governance, accountability and the datafication of early years education in England', *British Educational Research Journal*, 42(4), 600–613. DOI: 10.1002/berj.3221.

Rose, N. (1999) *Powers of Freedom: Reframing Political Thought.* Cambridge: Cambridge University Press.

Roy, K. (2003) *Teachers in Nomadic Space: Deleuze and Curriculum.* New York: Peter Lang.

Santos, B. de S. (2004) 'Interview with Boaventura de Sousa Santos', *Globalisation, Societies and Education*, 2 (2), 147–160.

*Sellers, M. (2013) *Young Children Becoming Curriculum: Deleuze, Te Whāriki and Curricular Understandings.* London: Routledge.

Sevenhuijsen, S. (1998) *Citizenship and the Ethics of Care: Feminist Considerations on Justice, Morality and Politics.* London: Routledge.

St. Pierre, E.A. (2000) 'The call for intelligibility in postmodern educational research', *Educational Researcher*, 29 (5), 25–29.

St. Pierre, E.A. (2012) 'Another postmodern report on knowledge: Positivism and its others', *International Journal of Leadership in Education*, 15 (4), 483–503.

St. Pierre, E.A. and Pillow, W. (2000) *Working the Ruins: Feminist Poststructural Theory and Methods in Education.* New York: Routledge.

Steadman Jones, D. (2014) *Masters of the Universe: Hayek, Friedman, and the Birth of Neoliberal Politics.* Princeton: Princeton University Press.

Stiglitz, J. (nd) *Inequality and Economic Growth.* (https://www8.gsb.columbia.edu/faculty/ jstiglitz/sites/jstiglitz/files/Inequality%20and%20Economic%20Growth.pdf)Tan, E. (2014) 'Human capital theory: A holistic critique', *Review of Educational Research*, 84 (3), 411–445.

*Taylor, A. (2013) *Reconfiguring the Natures of Childhood.* London: Routledge.

Tobin, J. (2007) 'Rôle de la théorie dans le movement Reconceptualiser l'éducation de la petite enfance', in G. Brougère and M. Vandenbroeck (eds) *Repenser l'éducation des jeunes enfants.* Brussels: P.I.E. Peter Lang.

Tronto, J. (1993) *Moral Boundaries: A Political Argument for the Ethics of Care.* London: Routledge.

Truss, E. (2013) 'More great childcare', speech to a *Policy Exchange meeting*, London, 29 January 2013.

Unger, R.M. (2005a) *What Should the Left Propose?* London: Verso.

Unger, R.M. (2005b) 'The future of the Left: James Crabtree interviews Roberto Unger', *Renewal*, 13 (2/3), 173–184.

Urban, M., Vandenbroeck, M., Lazzari, A., Van Larer, K. and Peeters, J. (2012) *Competence Requirements in Early Childhood Education and Care: Final Report.* (https://files.eric.ed.gov/ fulltext/ED534599.pdf).

Vadeboncoeur, J. (1997) 'Child development and the purpose of education', in Richardson, V. (ed.) *Constructivist Teacher Education.* London: Falmer Press.

Vecchi, V. (2004) 'The multiple fonts of knowledge', *Children in Europe*, 6, 18–21.

*Vecchi, V. (2010) *Art and Creativity in Reggio Emilia: Exploring the Role and Potentiality of Ateliers in Early Childhood Education.* London: Routledge.

Vygotsky, L.S. (1978) *Mind in Society: The Development of Higher Mental Processes.* Cambridge: Harvard University Press.

Wave Trust (2013) *Conception to Age 2 – the Age of Opportunity.* London: Wave Trust. (www. wavetrust.org/key-publications/reports/conception-to-age-2).

Wilkinson, R. and Pickett, K. (2009) *The Spirit Level: Why More Equal Societies Almost Always Do Better.* London: Allen Lane.

Wootton, D. (2016) *The Invention of Science: A New History of the Scientific Revolution.* London: Penguin Books.

Wright, E.O. (2006) 'Compass points: Towards a Socialist alternative', *New Left Review*, 41 (September–October), 93–124.

Wright, E.O. (2007) 'Guidelines for envisioning real utopias', *Soundings*, 36 (Summer), 26–39.

Young, R. (1990) *White Mythologies: Writing History and the West.* London: Routledge.

Zigler, E. (2003) 'Forty years of believing in magic is enough', *Social Policy Report*, XVII (1), 10–11.

Index

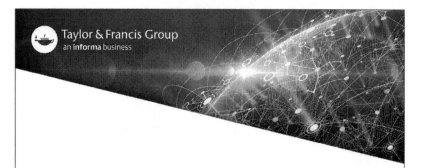